THE
YORKSHIRE
POST
COOK BOOK

JANET · HORSLEY

WILLOW BOOKS
Collins
8 Grafton Street, London
1985

DEDICATION
To my Parents

Willow Books
William Collins & Sons Ltd
London . Glasgow . Sydney
Auckland . Toronto . Johannesburg

© Janet Horsley 1985

Illustrations by Barbara Wardle and
Lynn Chadwick

Horsley, Janet
The Yorkshire Post Cook Book
1. Cookery
I. Title
641.5 TX717
ISBN 0 00 218179 7

Filmset in Meridien
By Wyvern Typesetting Ltd, Bristol
Printed in Great Britain by
Butler & Tanner Ltd, Frome and London

CONTENTS

GLOSSARY

AL DENTE   A term used to describe the texture of cooked pasta, rice and vegetables. The food is cooked until barely tender, with just a little resistance to the bite.

ARAME   A delicately flavoured seaweed originating in the Far East. It is sold as a tangled mass of thin, crisp, blackish strands which weigh next to nothing.

BESAN FLOUR   See chick pea flour.

BLANCHING   The brief cooking of food in boiling water to soften it or to loosen its skin. Used for fruit and vegetables in particular.

BLIND BAKING   The baking of a pastry case before a filling is added.

BROWN RICE   Also known as unpolished rice. It has a stronger flavour, is superior in food value and is easier to digest than white or 'pearled' varieties. It also contains valuable dietary fibre which is absent from white rice. Both long and short grain varieties can be used in savoury dishes.

BUCKWHEAT FLOUR   A speckled khaki-coloured flour, ground from whole buckwheat. It has a distinctive flavour and makes excellent pancakes. Buckwheat flour contains no gluten and if used to make bread should be mixed with a wheat flour.

BUCKWHEAT SPAGHETTI   A whole grain spaghetti made from buckwheat flour. It is also known as soba.

BULGUR or BURGHUL   Cracked wheat which has been hulled, parboiled, dried and then ground. This makes the grain light in flavour and texture and considerably shortens the cooking time.

CHICK PEA FLOUR   Also known as gram or besan flour. It is milled from chick peas and contains no gluten. Chick pea flour is unsuitable for breadmaking unless mixed with a wheat flour, but it does make excellent batters.

COLD PRESSED OILS   See vegetable oils.

CONCENTRATED APPLE JUICE   A thick syrup made by concentrating natural, unsweetened apple juice. Choose a brand free from added sugars, preservatives, colour or flavouring agents.

CORIANDER   Coriander is most commonly thought of as a spice in the form of the ground seeds. It may come as a surprise to learn that fresh coriander is reputed to be the world's most commonly used fresh herb. It is sometimes referred to as Chinese or Japanese parsley. Some cooks suggest using fresh European parsley if coriander is unavailable, but in my opinion they are as different as chalk and cheese.

CORNMEAL   See maize meal.

COUSCOUS   A word used to describe a rich, meaty stew, popular in North Africa, and also a wheat product. When mentioned in this book couscous refers to the small, cream-coloured granules made from semolina which can be eaten instead of rice or another grain with a main course meat or vegetable dish.

CREAMED COCONUT   A solid white block of pulverised coconut flesh. Its smooth texture makes it ideal for flavouring sauces and savoury dishes.

CROÛTONS   Small squares of fried bread used as a garnish.

CUP MUSHROOMS   Sometimes sold as open mushrooms. They are larger than button mushrooms but nowhere near as big as 'flats'. Cup mushrooms are ideal for making mushroom soup as, unlike flats, they do not turn the soup an unpleasant brown colour; they are also cheaper than buttons.

DRY FRYING   Also referred to as dry roasting, this is a term used for the browning of food without the use of fat over a moderate to high heat, under a hot grill, or in a hot oven. It is used mainly in the preparation of nuts, seeds and whole grains to bring out their flavour and to reduce their cooking times. When dry roasting over heat or under a grill, the food should be stirred frequently to prevent uneven browning or burning.

GOMASIO   See sesame salt.

GRAM FLOUR   See chick pea flour.

GROUNDNUT OIL   Also known as peanut oil. It has a high smoking point and is excellent for deep frying. It has a bland flavour.

HERBS   The use of herbs has declined to such an extent that few modern gardens contain anything more than a small patch of mint or parsley. Nonetheless there is no reason why fresh herbs shouldn't be available to any cook all the year round. Most are much better flavoured than dried varieties and can be used both as a seasoning and as a garnish. Herbs grow well in a window box or in pots and are ideal plants for small gardens. If you have difficulty obtaining the herbs needed for my recipes do use dried ones but remember that their flavour is much stronger and one teaspoon of dried herb is the equivalent of one tablespoon of fresh herb.

JULIENNE STRIPS   Delicately cut vegetables in the shape and size of matchsticks.

LEMON THYME and LEMON OREGANO   If these herbs are unavailable use ordinary thyme or oregano plus a little grated zest and juice of lemon.

MILLET   A small round yellow grain. Millet has a delicate flavour and becomes light and fluffy when cooked.

MUGI MISO   A Japanese flavouring made from soya beans and cereal grains, fermented with water and salt. There are three basic types of miso – mugi miso, genmai miso and hatcho miso. I prefer mugi miso, finding it more versatile than genmai miso which is a little sweet for my palate. I find hatcho miso too strong in flavour. The consistency of miso is that of a stiff paste and generally it is thinned down with a little stock or water before being stirred into soups, stews, sauces etc. Whenever possible add it at the very last minute, just before serving, because much of its goodness is destroyed by heat.

ORGANICALLY GROWN FLOURS   Grown according to the recommendations of the Soil Association the wheat used to make organically grown flour is free from chemical fertilisers, pesticides and the like.

PEANUT OIL   See groundnut oil.

PEELING TOMATOES   I rarely peel tomatoes as so much of their flavour and goodness lies just beneath the skin. However, there are some exceptions, notably when preparing dishes where the appearance would be spoiled if the skins were left on. One method of peeling tomatoes is to spear each one with a fork and hold it over a gas ring, rotating the fork so that all sides of the tomato come into contact with the flame. When the skin begins to blister and split open, remove from the heat and peel. If you cannot use an open flame or you have lots of tomatoes to skin, place them in a large bowl and cover with boiling water. Leave to stand for a minute or two until the skins split open. Remove from the bowl with a slotted spoon and peel when cool enough to handle.

PINE KERNELS   Small cream-coloured oval nuts, popular in the Mediterranean. Their texture is smooth and their flavour subtle but distinctive.

ROASTING NUTS   See dry frying.

RYE FLOUR   A dark-coloured flour ground from whole rye.

SAUTÉ   To cook or lightly fry food rapidly in a small quantity of fat, stirring or turning all the time.

SESAME SALT   Also known as gomasio, sesame salt is sold in many delicatessen and wholefood shops. It is made from roasted sesame seeds ground to a fine powder with a little sea salt. It is an excellent condiment to serve with brown rice.

SOYA FLOUR   A yellow flour made from soya beans. Unlike most flours it is high in protein and low in carbohydrates.

SOYA SAUCE   Soya sauce is a common seasoning agent in the Far East and is becoming increasingly popular in the West too. It is made from fermented soya beans, wheat flour, water and salt and is similar in flavour to miso. It is very easy to become totally reliant on soya sauce with the result that everything from nut cutlets to shepherd's pie tastes exactly the same. Continual heavy use of soya sauce is said to be bad for the liver to say nothing of the effect the high salt content has upon one's blood pressure. Discounting those made artificially from monosodium glutamate, caramel, sugar and water, there are two grades of natural soya sauce, tamari and shoyu. Tamari is richer and thicker than shoyu and is consequently more expensive. However, it is used in much smaller quantities, one teaspoon of tamari being equivalent in strength to two teaspoons of shoyu.

STEAMING   An excellent way of cooking food, particularly vegetables. Fewer nutrients are destroyed and both flavour and texture of the vegetables are better than when boiled in water. Steamers come in a variety of shapes and sizes, the most common type consisting of a container with a perforated bottom which is placed over a pan of boiling water. It is covered with a tight-fitting lid during the cooking period so that the steam cannot escape. Another type, known as a collapsible or rose steamer, opens out and sits in the bottom of an ordinary pan, holding the food just above water level. It is possible to improvise with a colander or a metal sieve provided that it sits snugly into the top of the pan and very little steam is allowed to escape from around the sides or from the top. The food must always be covered.

TAHINI   A smooth paste made from sesame seeds. It is also known as 'sesame cream', 'sesame butter' or 'creamed sesame'.

TOFU (SILKEN)   Also known as soya bean curd it is low in fat and high in protein and can be used instead of yoghurt, soft cheese and cream in many recipes. Silken tofu is smoother and creamier than other varieties.

UNBLEACHED WHITE FLOUR   100 per cent wholewheat flour should normally be used in the kitchen. Occasionally, however, it is useful to have a lighter, refined flour for making some types of sauces and pastries. Choose an 'unbleached' variety that contains no additives or bleaching agents. Don't be surprised if it looks 'grubby' in comparison to its 'whiter than white' counterparts.

VEGETABLE OILS   The best oils are labelled cold pressed, unrefined or virgin oils. They retain the flavour and nutritional value of the seed or fruit from which they have been extracted. They are free from all chemical additives.

WALNUT OIL   A dark-coloured oil with a deliciously nutty flavour. It is excellent in salad dressings.

WHOLEWHEAT SELF RAISING FLOUR   Ideal for cakes and puddings. If unavailable use wholewheat flour (plain) and baking powder; 100 g (4 oz) wholewheat flour plus 1 tsp baking powder is equal to 100 g (4 oz) wholewheat self raising flour.

WHOLEWHEAT SEMOLINA   A semolina containing fine bran flakes and wheatgerm. It has a sweeter, nuttier flavour than mass-produced varieties.

NOTE
Unless otherwise stated all the recipes included in this book will serve 4–6 people.

INTRODUCTION

As soon as anyone discovers that I am a cook they usually ask 'what sort?'. The question invariably finds me unprepared and fumbling for an answer. They are not satisfied with a few details about my work but want to know the foods I prepare and write about. I often think life would be easier if I specialised in haute cuisine, cordon bleu or cuisine minceur or perhaps wholefoods or vegetarian foods but I don't. I am what could loosely be termed a modern cook, taking ideas from all branches of cookery and adapting them to my own particular style. I love food and everything about it, the colours, shapes, textures, tastes and smells; but I also appreciate the need for a healthy diet. My style of cooking attempts to satisfy the tastebuds and our physiological and nutritional requirements. It is not a faddy 'health food' diet with rules and regulations but a natural approach to eating in which flavour, freshness and simplicity are encouraged.

I believe that the time has come to re-appraise the term 'good food' which traditionally stands for lavish dishes enriched with butter, cream and eggs. Haute cuisine and cordon bleu are both far too time consuming, rich and fattening for today's busy, health-conscious gourmet and the emphasis should now be on food which is sophisticated, original, interesting and beneficial to our health. I am not alone in my ideas for Drew Smith of the *Good Food Guide* has, in the past year, been critical of restaurants which continue to ignore current trends. He challenges them to recognise that good food ought to be synonymous with healthy food. Such developments are to be welcomed, not only from the point of view of restaurant-goers but also because they will help to shake off the 'cranky' image that many healthy and natural

foods have had in the past.

Although dietary recommendations seem to change with alarming frequency the basic message remains the same: we should be eating more fresh fruit and vegetables; more unrefined carbohydrates (wholewheat bread, pasta and flour, brown rice and potatoes); more fibre; and less fat, sugar, salt and processed foods. The relationship between diet and health has been recognised for years and back in the mid-nineteenth century George Meredith wrote, 'if medicine be ranked amongst those arts which dignify their professors . . . cookery may also lay claim to an equal if not superior distinction; to prevent diseases is surely a more advantageous art to Mankind than to cure them.'

It is important, however, not to be obsessive or paranoid about the food we eat. I would hate to think of the pleasures of the table being regulated by a set of rigid rules or worse still being replaced by a thrice daily quota of nutritious pills. Eating should, whenever possible, be a relaxed and leisurely affair, conducive to conversation and *bonhomie*, and an occasion when good food can be enjoyed without worrying unduly about one's waistline or heart.

The key to preparing good healthy food lies in the choice of ingredients, for no matter how good the recipe is or how well you prepare the dish it will not taste as it should if the vegetables used are wilted, the cheese stale and dry and the meat tough and tasteless. However, freshness is not the only criterion by which we must judge our purchases. Today we must also try and think about their food value, by asking ourselves whether each product has been refined and processed and if so what has been removed and what has been added. This is not as difficult as it sounds and if you simply substitute brown rice for white rice, unrefined or cold pressed oils for chemically-treated ones, yoghurt for cream, butter for margarine, fresh fruit and vegetables for tinned ones and herbs and other natural seasonings for synthetic flavourings and try to reduce the amount of fat and sugar in your cooking, there is no reason why you should not prepare dishes which are attractive, appetising and healthy.

The recipes included in this book, whether they be traditional favourites or brand new, meat based or vegetarian, reflect this modern approach to food. Some have already appeared in my food column but inevitably pressure for space has meant the omission on more than one occasion of some of my favourite dishes. Writing this book has given me the opportunity to make amends on this score and to include many more recipes, and also to put my thoughts in some sort of order, which I hope will be useful to those new to both my ideas and style of cooking.

JANET HORSLEY, JULY, 1985

EGGS, MILK, YOGHURT AND CHEESE

MILK PRODUCTS

Milk has been valued as a source of nourishment ever since the first herdsmen domesticated milk-producing animals. In spite of the fact that these early dairy men had no idea that milk was a good source of protein, digestible fat, calcium and vitamins A, B, C and D they realised that it had a value greater than that of simply quenching their thirst. All over the world milk from asses, goats, camels, sheep, horses and even buffalo has, at one time or another, been drunk and made into butter, yoghurt and cheese.

In Britain there is a strong tradition of dairy farming, with the docile, homely cow being the most important milk-producing animal. Until the middle of the last century, most households, from the grand manor and large farm down to the small cottage, kept a cow. Cows could also be found in Central London until the turn of the century and were milked on the streets so that prospective customers could see that the milk was fresh and pure, as it was a common practice in those days to adulterate or water-down the milk.

Our apparent strong liking for milk (due perhaps to its affinity with tea) has resulted in Britain being one of the few countries to have a door-to-door delivery service. Since the establishment of the Milk Marketing Board in 1933 home production of milk and dairy products has all but disappeared. One of the principal reasons for the board being set up was to control the quality of milk, and now all milk distributed through its outlets has to be pasteurised.

Pasteurisation is a food preservation technique which is particularly suited to milk. It kills about 99 per cent of the micro-organisms found in milk, including those responsible for foot and mouth disease, typhoid, tuberculosis, scarlet fever, diphtheria, polio, septic sore throat, dysentery and summer diarrhoea without seriously affecting the flavour. Unpasteurised milk is now the exception rather than the rule and is sold as 'raw', 'untreated' or 'green top' milk. It is nonetheless stringently tested at the farm to ensure that it contains no harmful bacteria.

Unfortunately pasteurisation not only kills undesirable bacteria but also beneficial enzymes which are needed to sour and ripen milk. Although this hasn't seriously affected the commercial production of cheese, yoghurt, cream etc (they simply replace the enzymes with a culture) it has made a difference to the DIY dairyman.

The small old-fashioned farmhouse dairy tucked away at the back of the house, filled with bright shiny pails, butter churns, scoops and ladles and with long cool stone shelves laden with eggs, milk, butter and cream is far removed from the kitchens and pantries of my childhood but that didn't stop my mother from making an occasional pot of soft cheese. I am not sure which came first, her enjoyment of making good food or the pressing need to use up several pints of milk which had 'gone off'.

Although there has been a move away from butter in recent years I still prefer to use it both at the table and in the kitchen. Bearing in mind that I eat very little meat and only moderate amounts of cheese and milk I am far happier using butter, a natural product free from chemical additives, than 'artificial' margarine. In many of my recipes I substitute a good quality vegetable oil for some of the butter and hope that I am getting the best of both worlds – the creamy taste and texture of butter and a relatively healthy heart. It is worth remembering that the saturated fat content of some of the hard cooking margarines and those made with coconut or palm oil is not very different from that of butter.

Butter-making is the oldest method of preserving milk. It entails stirring the milk until the fatty cream globules become solid. The liquid residue (buttermilk) is then drained away. It is perhaps the most difficult of all the dairyman's jobs to emulate at home. I have never got further than reading a book on the subject. Simply reading the instructions about shaking the milk in a large screwtop jar for what seemed like hours was enough to make my arms ache.

However, I do make good use of buttermilk – not the frothy fresh buttermilk but the slightly thicker and sharper cultured variety. Even this purpose-made product is not always readily available. Sometimes I buy half a dozen cartons at a time and pop them in the freezer. I had been doing this for several years before I noticed that each tub bore the words 'DO NOT FREEZE'. Needless to say I still freeze them, the only difficulty being that once thawed the buttermilk takes on a curdled appearance. I get round this by giving it a quick whisk in the blender before using it and find it ideal for making scones and soda bread. In the summer when I use it regularly in soups and chilled drinks I sometimes make my own.

HOME-MADE BUTTERMILK

Stir 30 ml (2 tbsp) of cultured buttermilk into 575 ml (1 pint) of pasteurised skimmed milk. Cover and leave in a warm place for 10–12 hours.

CHILLED LEEK AND POTATO SOUP WITH BUTTERMILK

4 leeks, trimmed and sliced
275 g (10 oz) potatoes, peeled and chopped
575 ml (1 pint) water
575 ml (1 pint) buttermilk
seasoning
fresh parsley, chopped

Put the leeks, potatoes and water in a large pan. Bring to the boil. Cover and simmer until the vegetables are soft. Purée the mixture by passing it through a sieve or vegetable mouli or by processing it briefly in a food processor or blender. Add sufficient buttermilk to give a smooth creamy consistency. Stir well and season to taste. Chill. Sprinkle with parsley before serving.

Curd cheeses
I like the tart, soft, moist curds which we used to spread on bread or eat with salady things, so much so that it was one of the first things I tried to make when I had a kitchen of my own. Unfortunately I had not appreciated the subtleties of the art and was ignorant then of the difference between pasteurised and unpasteurised milk. My milk did not turn sour or thicken as I had expected, it simply went bad. I have even tried adding lemon juice to aid the souring but without much success. Although I have read that it is possible to make soft cheese from pasteurised milk I obviously haven't got the knack.

HOME-MADE SOFT CHEESE

Leave the unpasteurised milk in a warm place to sour and curdle. Pour into a sieve lined with butter muslin and stand over a bowl. Drain. Anything from three to five days later the whey will have dripped into the bowl leaving behind the soft curd cheese. Lightly season before serving.

In France such cheese is known as fromage blanc and is a basic ingredient in the sauces of cuisine minceur. If you do not want to make your own try blending equal parts of cottage cheese and yoghurt with a dash of lemon juice. Natural yoghurt itself can be drained through muslin and makes a tangy soft cheese. Cottage cheese, cream cheese and quark are all variations on the same theme.

In bygone days the curds were also eaten with a little sweetened whey. They are perhaps at their best made into curd tarts, mixed with currants, eggs, spices and sweetenings and then baked in a pastry case.

SWEET CURD TART

FOR THE PASTRY:
225 g (8 oz) wholewheat flour
75 g (3 oz) butter, diced
2 tbsp sunflower oil
8 tsp cold water

FOR THE FILLING:
50 g (2 oz) butter
100 g (4 oz) currants
1–2 tbsp concentrated apple juice
225 g (8 oz) curd
2 large eggs, beaten

To make the pastry put the flour in a bowl and rub in the butter and oil, using your fingertips, until the mixture resembles breadcrumbs. Add the water and knead to form a dough. Turn onto a lightly-floured board, roll out and line a 20 cm (8 in) flan ring. Prick the pastry base lightly with a fork and blind bake in a preheated oven, gas mark 6 (200° C/400° F) for 10 minutes.

Put the remaining butter, currants and apple concentrate in a pan and heat until the butter has melted. Remove from the heat and stir in the curd and eggs. Pour the filling into the pastry case and return to the oven. Bake for a further 25 minutes until golden brown and firm to the touch. Serve hot or cold.

Home-made cream
Happily, for my figure at least, cream is my least favourite dairy food. In the case of cow's milk the cream separates out after the milk has been left to stand and can easily be skimmed from the top. Before the days of mechanical separators a pail of milk would be left for 8–10 hours if the dairyman wanted single cream and 24 hours for double.

Some aficionados claim that cream made from unpasteurised milk tastes better than that made from pasteurised varieties but I am in no position to judge. Clotted cream and sour cream on the other hand can be made from raw, untreated milk only (although commercial sour cream is now made with a culture).

HOME-MADE CLOTTED CREAM

Leave the raw milk to stand for 6–8 hours in a warm place. Put in a pan and heat gently until small bubbles appear on the surface. Do not boil. Stand in a cool place for 10–12 hours. Then spoon out the thick clotted cream.

HOME-MADE SOUR CREAM

Simply add a squirt of lemon juice to double cream.

BAKED TROUT WITH SOUR CREAM AND CUCUMBER

4 trout
25 g (1 oz) butter
juice of 1 lemon
2 tbsp fresh parsley, finely chopped
$\frac{1}{2}$ cucumber
275 ml ($\frac{1}{2}$ pint) sour cream

Clean and trim the fish, leaving their heads and tails in place. Remove the gills.

Melt the butter in a small pan and brush a little over a shallow ovenproof dish. Lay the fish in the bottom, pour over the lemon juice and sprinkle with parsley. Cover with a piece of buttered foil. Bake in a preheated oven, gas mark 5 (190° C/375° F) for 15 minutes. Meanwhile peel the cucumber and cut into julienne strips (shaped like matchsticks). Heat what remains of the melted butter and toss in the cucumber. Sauté for 3–4 minutes and then pour in the sour cream. Heat through gently.

Remove the foil and pour the sour cream and cucumber mixture over the fish. Replace the foil and bake for a further 5–10 minutes until the trout are tender. Serve with new potatoes and a salad.

PASTA WITH VEGETABLES AND SAFFRON SAUCE

This serves 2 as a main meal or 4 as a starter.

50 ml (2 fl oz) milk
a good pinch of saffron strands
100 g (4 oz) French beans
$\frac{1}{4}$ cauliflower
2 carrots
$\frac{1}{4}$ cucumber
olive oil
225 g (8 oz) wholewheat spaghetti
a knob of butter
275 ml (10 fl oz) sour cream

Put the milk and saffron in a small pan and bring to the boil. Remove from the heat and leave to stand for 10–15 minutes.

Wash and trim the vegetables. Slice the French beans, break the cauliflower into sprigs and cut the carrots and cucumber into julienne strips (shaped like matchsticks).

Bring a large pan of water to the boil and add 1 tablespoon of olive oil and the pasta. Boil briskly, uncovered, until the pasta is al dente. Meanwhile, steam the beans, cauliflower and carrots in a colander or steamer over a pan of simmering water until barely tender. Melt the butter in a pan, add the cucumber and sauté for 3–4 minutes.

Sieve the saffron milk and return the milk to a clean pan. Stir in the sour cream and heat through but do not boil. Place the cooked pasta and vegetables in a serving dish. Pour the sauce over the top and serve immediately.

EGGS

Opinion varies as to how many eggs we should be eating. Some people regard an egg as the perfect food, rich in protein, fat, iron, calcium and vitamins A and B$_{12}$ and say that it should be eaten daily while others consider it to be detrimental to our health and even go as far as to advocate an egg-free diet. No one disputes the fact that eggs are highly nutritious but what worries many people is that they also contain high levels of cholesterol.

Cholesterol is suspected of promoting atherosclerosis, a narrowing or hardening of the arteries leading to the heart. High blood cholesterol levels are thought to be a contributory factor in the aetiology of coronary heart disease. It is, however, important to realise that some cholesterol is manufactured in the body and, within certain limits, it is essential for good health. Only when it is eaten in excess is it associated with atherosclerosis and related disorders.

As a result of research linking high levels of blood cholesterol to coronary heart disease many authorities are promoting low cholesterol diets. Recent evidence has shown, however, that while dietary cholesterol itself affects the blood cholesterol level in many people, the effect is small. In fact it is thought that most cholesterol rich foods such as eggs, kidneys, brains and liver are not eaten in sufficient quantities to justify any severe restrictions in their consumption. Rather than struggling to eat a low cholesterol diet it is now considered more valuable to eat a cholesterol lowering diet. Just as there are foodstuffs which increase the amount of cholesterol in the body so there are foods which help to break down deposits of cholesterol. For example, saturated fats are reputed to build up levels of cholesterol in the body whereas polyunsaturates have the reverse effect.

This idea is significant as far as eggs are concerned for although they are rich in cholesterol they also contain lecithin and choline, both of which help to protect the arteries against a build up of cholesterol. No doubt the controversy surrounding the dietary value of the egg will continue to swing back and forth, and perhaps one day the truth will be known. In the meantime, I suggest that we hedge our bets and continue to savour the delights of fresh eggs, but in moderation.

The controversy surrounding the egg doesn't rest with discussions of its dietary value. Some people believe brown eggs to be better than white and free range eggs to be far superior to battery eggs. Fortunately this debate is easier to resolve, for generally speaking all eggs have the same nutritional value and flavour provided that the hens are fed properly. Nor does the colour of the shells reflect the quality of the egg but simply the breed of fowl.

From a gastronomic point of view the most important consideration is that of freshness for without doubt an egg is at its best when fresh. A simple but often depressing way of testing for freshness is to place the egg in water. If it lies flat on its side on the bottom of the dish it is fresh. If it begins to float it is between two and four weeks old and if it floats to the surface it is probably several months old and may even be bad.

Unfortunately most of the eggs on sale in our shops and supermarkets fall into the middle category. Should you be lucky enough to obtain a newly-laid egg do not be surprised if the white does not thicken when poached or beaten. Here is a word of advice on the subject from Mrs Beeton:

'eggs for poaching should be perfectly fresh, but not quite new-laid; those that are about 36 hours old are the best for the purpose.'

I have encountered the problem of runny, stringy egg whites only once, and in this case I suspect the problem was one of old age rather than extreme freshness. Eggs will stay fresh for 12 days at room temperature and up to three weeks in a domestic refrigerator. They should be stored away from strong smelling foods with their rounded ends uppermost. Always bring them up to room temperature before boiling or their shells may crack.

EGG AND LETTUCE AU GRATIN

This makes a delicious light meal or starter for 4 people.

SERVES 4
1 large lettuce
a knob of butter
4 hard-boiled eggs, shelled

FOR THE SAUCE:
25 g (1 oz) butter
1 rounded tbsp unbleached white flour
275 ml (10 fl oz) milk
1 tbsp Dijon mustard

FOR THE TOPPING:
2 tbsp soft wholewheat breadcrumbs

Wash, drain and shred the lettuce. Melt the butter in the bottom of a large pan and add the lettuce. Cook over a low heat for 10–15 minutes, stirring frequently. When soft, spoon into a shallow ovenproof dish. Cut the hard-boiled eggs into quarters and arrange on top of the lettuce.

Make a Béchamel sauce by melting the remaining butter in a saucepan. Stir in the flour and cook for 2–3 minutes, stirring often. Remove from the heat and gradually add the milk. Return to the heat and stir constantly as you bring the sauce to the boil. Cook until it begins to thicken and then add the mustard.

Pour the sauce over the eggs and sprinkle with breadcrumbs. Bake in a preheated oven, gas mark 6 (200° C/400° F) for 10–15 minutes until lightly browned and bubbling.

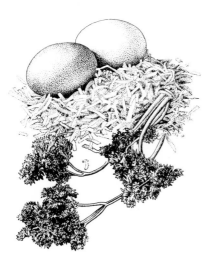

LETTUCE WITH EGGS AND YOGHURT

Another excellent way of making full use of a surfeit of lettuce from the garden. The flavour of lettuce and eggs goes together very well and I much prefer them cooked than in the usual array of salad dishes.

SERVES 4
a knob of butter
1 large lettuce, trimmed and shredded
4 eggs
5–6 tbsp natural yoghurt
1 rounded tsp unbleached white flour
75 g (3 oz) Gruyère cheese, grated

Melt the butter in a metal au gratin dish or frying pan, add the lettuce and sauté until it softens. Remove from the heat, make four small hollows in the cooked lettuce and break an egg into each. Beat the yoghurt and flour together in a bowl and stir in most of the cheese. Pour the mixture over the lettuce; try to avoid covering the egg yolks. Sprinkle the remaining cheese over the top.

Return to the heat and cook on a moderate flame until the yoghurt begins to bubble and the egg whites firm up. Serve immediately while the egg yolks are still runny.

EGGS EN COCOTTE WITH HAM

SERVES 4
25g (1 oz) butter
50 g (2 oz) ham, finely chopped
1–2 tsp fresh parsley, finely chopped
4 eggs
seasoning

Grease 4 small cocotte pots with butter. Sprinkle a little of the ham and parsley in the bottom of each. Break an egg into each and season with black pepper. Dot with the butter. Stand the pots in a large dish of hot water and cover with greaseproof paper or a lid (the lid must allow the steam to escape). Bake in a preheated oven, gas mark 7 (220° C/425° F) for 10 minutes until the egg whites begin to set.

LEEK QUICHE WITH HERBED PASTRY

The green-flecked pastry complements the leek and cheese filling in colour and flavour.

FOR THE PASTRY:
225 g (8 oz) wholewheat flour
75 g (3 oz) butter, diced
2 tbsp sunflower oil
1 level tsp mixed dried herbs
1 level tsp dried oregano
2 tbsp fresh parsley, chopped
2 tsp Dijon mustard
8 tsp cold water

FOR THE FILLING:
2 leeks, sliced and lightly steamed
2 eggs
150 ml (5 fl oz) milk
2 tbsp natural yoghurt
seasoning
50 g (2 oz) Gruyère cheese
a little Parmesan cheese

Put the flour in a mixing bowl and rub in the butter and oil, using your fingertips, until the mixture resembles breadcrumbs. Add the herbs and Dijon mustard and mix together well. Pour in the water and knead to form a pastry dough. Turn onto a lightly-floured board, roll out and line a 25 cm (10 in) flan ring. Prick the pastry base with a fork and blind bake for 8–10 minutes in a preheated oven, gas mark 6 (200° C/400° F).

Meanwhile, prepare the filling. Lightly steam the leeks. Arrange the cooked leeks on top of the pastry case. Beat the eggs, milk and yoghurt together and pour over the pastry. Season with black pepper. Grate the cheese on top and sprinkle lightly with Parmesan. Return to the oven and bake for 25 minutes until firm to the touch and golden brown. Serve hot or cold.

VEGETABLE LAYER BAKE

Couscous is the name given to a rich, spiced stew made from vegetables, chick peas and mutton, popular in North Africa, where it is served with a veritable mountain of a light fluffy grain. This grain is also known as couscous in Europe and North America where it can be bought, ready to cook, in many food stores. It is becoming increasingly popular because of the speed and ease with which it can be prepared. Simply place one part couscous in a bowl and pour over two parts boiling water. Leave to stand for 10–15 minutes during which time it will absorb all the water, soften and double in volume. The bowl can be placed in a warm oven or in a pan of warm water to keep the grain hot and ready to take to the table as soon as it has absorbed all the water.

1 teacup of couscous (approx. 175 g/6 oz)
2 teacups of boiling water
3 carrots, sliced
1–2 tbsp olive oil
1 clove garlic, peeled and crushed
3 courgettes, sliced
1 green pepper, deseeded and sliced
4–5 tomatoes, chopped
1 tbsp fresh lemon thyme, chopped
1 tbsp fresh marjoram, chopped
seasoning
1 large egg
275 ml (10 fl oz) natural yoghurt
1 tbsp unbleached white flour

Put the couscous in a small bowl and pour over the water. Leave to stand for 10–15 minutes. Put the carrots in a pan of boiling water and cook for 15–20 minutes until they become tender.

Meanwhile heat the oil in a pan, add the garlic and the remaining vegetables and soften. Add the cooked carrots and herbs. Season to taste. Put the couscous into the bottom of a deep ovenproof dish and spoon over the vegetables. Beat the egg, yoghurt and flour together and pour over the top. Place, uncovered, in a preheated oven, gas mark 6 (200° C/400° F) for 25–30 minutes until lightly browned and firm to the touch.

CARROT AND COTTAGE CHEESE BAKE

Quiches and flans are popular and versatile. They can be made in advance, eaten hot or cold and served at almost any meal. There are occasions, however, when one simply doesn't want to make pastry. Time is often the critical factor but in recent years adverse publicity about the effects of saturated fats on our health has made many people think twice about the type of foods they eat. Unfortunately pastry is moderately high in saturated fats and calories.

This recipe scores low on both counts and is ideal for everyday meals and when catering for friends and relatives on special diets.

> sunflower oil
> 25 g (1 oz) wheatgerm
> 350 g (12 oz) carrots
> 225 g (8 oz) cottage cheese
> 2 eggs
> 150 ml (5 fl oz) milk
> 1 tbsp fresh thyme, finely chopped
> freshly ground black pepper

Brush a 20-cm (8-in) flan tin with sunflower oil and sprinkle liberally with wheatgerm. Scrub, trim and grate the carrots and steam until tender. Mix them with the cottage cheese and spoon into the bottom of the tin. Beat the eggs and milk together and season with thyme and black pepper. Pour over the carrots and bake in a preheated oven, gas mark 6 (200° C/ 400° F) for 25 minutes.

MILLET SOUFFLÉ

This soufflé recipe is easy to prepare and foolproof. It has never failed to rise beautifully and once, after I had taken it from the oven too soon, it actually rose a second time.

Millet is a pleasant, highly nutritious grain which has a nutty flavour and a light fluffy texture. When cooked it resembles couscous but the method of preparing the grain is slightly different. To bring out the full flavour of the millet and to reduce the cooking time I dry fry the grains before simmering them in water. Put the millet in an old pan over a high flame. Shake the pan frequently to ensure even roasting and continue to cook until the millet becomes a little darker in colour. Tip the millet from the pan as soon as it is ready to prevent it burning. Simmer in $2\frac{1}{2}$ times its volume of water for 15 minutes until light and fluffy.

> 100 g (4 oz) cooked millet
> seasoning
> 3 large eggs, separated
> 150 ml (5 fl oz) milk
> 100 g (4 oz) mature Cheddar cheese, grated
> 1 tsp Dijon mustard
> pinch of paprika

Mix all the ingredients together in a bowl EXCEPT FOR the egg whites and 25 g (1 oz) of the cheese. Beat the egg whites until stiff and peaked and fold into the mixture. Spoon into an oiled soufflé dish and top with the remaining grated cheese. Bake in a preheated oven, gas mark 5 (190° C/375° F) for 25 minutes until firm.

PIPÉRADE

A dish consisting of eggs and peppers that originated in the Basque region. There are many versions but this one is my favourite.

SERVES 4
2 tbsp olive oil
2 onions, sliced
2 cloves garlic, peeled and crushed
1 red pepper, deseeded and sliced
1 green pepper, deseeded and sliced
4 tomatoes
seasoning
4 eggs

Heat the oil in a pan, add the onions and fry lightly until soft. Add the garlic and peppers to the pan. Roughly chop the tomatoes and stir into the other vegetables. Season well. Cook slowly, stirring occasionally, until the mixture is reduced to a thick stew.

Break the eggs into a small bowl and beat lightly with a fork. Pour over the cooked vegetables and stir well as if you were making scrambled eggs. As they begin to thicken and set turn out onto a hot serving dish. Eat straightaway.

CRUSTY PIPÉRADE

For a supper or picnic dish take a small French loaf and cut off the top. Remove the soft crumbs from the inside and brush the hollowed out loaf with garlic butter. Place the bread in a preheated oven, gas mark 4 (180° C/350° F) for 15 minutes or so until it begins to crisp up. Fill with pipérade and replace the top of the loaf. Gently but firmly press the two halves together. Cut into slices and serve hot or cold.

POACHED EGGS

I have always marvelled at the way some people produce perfectly cooked poached eggs without having to rely on a poaching pan. My poached eggs taste good but don't look as visually appealing as those cooked by the traditional method, using a pan of hot water. Apparently the secret is to have the water hot but not boiling. Some people recommend adding a dessertspoon of vinegar to the pan to prevent the egg whites disintegrating.

To poach the eggs: bring a pan of water to the boil and add the vinegar. Reduce the heat and as soon as it stops boiling slide in the eggs. Keep the temperature the same or thereabouts until the egg has set. On no account must the water boil.

POTATO PURÉE WITH YOGHURT AND EGGS

SERVES 4
675 g (1½ lb) potatoes
150 ml (5 fl oz) natural yoghurt
freshly ground black pepper
100 g (4 oz) shelled peas, cooked
4 eggs

Peel the potatoes and cut into even-sized pieces. Cover with cold water, bring to the boil and cook until tender. Drain well. Rub the potatoes through a vegetable mouli or sieve and dry out over a gentle heat. Stir in the yoghurt and season with black pepper. Add the peas and heat through. Place in a shallow dish and keep warm. Poach the eggs as described above and lay them on top of the purée. Garnish with sprigs of parsley and serve immediately.

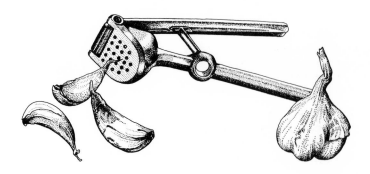

SCRAMBLED EGGS

This is one of the nicest ways of eating eggs; the only thing I object to is washing up the pan afterwards. Scrambled eggs should be soft and creamy, cooked slowly over a low heat. Take care not to overcook them as they then become tough and rubbery.

The eggs, usually two per person, are beaten and lightly seasoned with freshly ground black pepper. I prefer not to add milk or cream. Melt a knob of butter in a small pan and when thoroughly melted pour in the eggs. Cook over a low heat, stirring well with a wooden spoon. As soon as the eggs begin to set serve immediately.

Numerous savoury titbits can be added to the eggs to ring the changes. The most popular are pieces of ham, mushrooms, prawns, grated cheese, smoked fish, chicken livers, bacon and tomatoes.

MIRRORED EGGS

There are many recipes for this dish which is supposed to have been invented by Soyer for a dawn breakfast at a fashionable London party. He cooked the eggs, in front of the guests, on his new portable stove.

SERVES 4
a knob of butter
4 eggs
freshly ground black pepper

Melt a little butter in a flat enamel dish or shallow pan. Break in the eggs and season with pepper. Spoon some of the melted butter over the yolks. Cook slowly over a low heat until the whites are just set. Serve immediately.

EGG AND HERB PÂTÉ

4 hard-boiled eggs, chopped
225 g (8 oz) curd cheese
1 tsp fresh chives, finely chopped
1–2 tbsp natural yoghurt
seasoning

Mix all the ingredients together well until smooth and creamy or process briefly in a food processor or blender. Spoon into a small pot and leave in a cool place to firm up. Serve.

SPINACH ROULADE

350 g (12 oz) fresh spinach
2 tbsp sunflower oil
1 rounded tbsp unbleached white flour
275 ml (10 fl oz) milk
3 eggs, separated
50 g (2 oz) Cheddar cheese, grated
2 tbsp Parmesan cheese, grated
freshly grated nutmeg

Wash the spinach in several changes of water and trim off the stalks. Put into a saucepan and cover. Heat well until the spinach becomes limp and very soft – there should be no need to add any water but shake the pan occasionally to prevent the spinach from sticking to the bottom. Remove from the heat and chop the leaves well until they are almost reduced to a purée.

Heat the oil in a pan and stir in the flour. Cook for a minute or two until the mixture begins to bubble. Remove from the heat and gradually add the milk, stirring well after each addition. Return to the stove and heat until the sauce begins to thicken. Remove from the heat and stir in the spinach and the egg yolks. Beat the egg whites until stiff and peaked and fold into the mixture.

Line a swiss roll tin with greaseproof paper and brush with oil. Pour in the mixture and bake in a preheated oven, gas mark 5 (190° C/375° F) for 15–20 minutes until the centre begins to firm up. Remove from the oven, sprinkle the cheeses over the top and season with nutmeg. Roll up the roulade, using the paper to help you. Leave the paper in place for a minute while the roulade firms up. Then slide onto a hot dish and serve immediately.

YOGHURT

A little over 20 years ago yoghurt was a relatively uncommon product, eaten by 'health food cranks' who credited it with powers of longevity. It has now become, as a result of extensive advertising, a household name with sales in excess of two million pots a day.

Commercial yoghurt is made by adding a culture of lactobacillus bulgaricus, lactobacillus acidophilus or streptococcus thermophilus to low fat or skimmed milk. All yoghurts, unless pasteurised, sterilised or heavily sweetened after fermentation, contain live bacteria. These bacteria are reputed to be beneficial to our health, aiding digestion and inhibiting the growth of harmful micro-organisms in the intestines. They are especially valuable after intestinal disorders or the use of antibiotics.

Some yoghurts, particularly fruit varieties, contain preservatives, flavouring and colouring agents, emulsifiers, edible gums, gelatine and refined sugar. None of these additives improves the 'real' flavour or texture of yoghurt and must decrease its health giving properties. Most natural yoghurts are free from such additives but in order to be sure it is important to read the label on each pot. If there is no list of ingredients then the yoghurt must be additive free, in accordance with the Food Labelling Regulations. However, it is not so easy to tell whether a yoghurt is 'live' or whether it has been heat treated (pasteurised or sterilised) after fermentation.

A growing number of people are choosing to make their own yoghurt. There is no reason why home-made yoghurt should not be as good as that bought in the shops. It is both simple and cheap to make and can be used in its natural state in a wide variety of savoury dishes or it can be sweetened with fresh fruit, dried fruit purées or a little honey.

HOME-MADE YOGHURT

There are many gadgets on the market for making yoghurt. It is generally assumed that such equipment is necessary but excellent results can also be obtained simply by using an earthenware bowl or thermos flask. Nor is it necessary to buy expensive packets of yoghurt starter. A little commercial natural yoghurt, provided that it contains live bacteria, will do just as well.

575 ml (1 pint) milk
1 tbsp natural yoghurt
1 tbsp dried milk powder (*optional* – its inclusion makes the yoghurt thicker)

Put the milk in a pan and bring to the boil. Leave aside to cool. Fill the container (thermos flask or bowl) with boiling water. Test the milk by dipping in the little finger and counting to ten slowly. The milk should feel hot but not painfully so. If a thermometer is used the temperature should read 45° C/113° F. Stir in the natural yoghurt and the dried milk powder if you are using it. Discard the hot water in the container and pour in the warm milk mixture. Do not fill the thermos flask to the top or screw down the lid. Cover and leave in a warm place for 8–10 hours until the yoghurt has thickened.

There are a number of reasons why yoghurt may not thicken:
1. The temperature of the milk mixture is kept too low during the 8 hour period.
2. The bacteria may be killed if the milk is too hot.
3. The yoghurt starter may not have contained the necessary bacteria.
4. The milk may have contained antibiotics or preservatives which stop the bacteria growing.

EASTERN MUSHROOMS

1–2 tbsp sesame oil
225 g (8 oz) button mushrooms, halved if necessary
2 tsp dry white wine
2 tsp water
1 tsp soya sauce
$\frac{1}{2}$ tsp turmeric
5–6 tbsp natural yoghurt

Heat the oil in a pan, add the mushrooms and cook for 3–4 minutes. Remove them with a slotted spoon and place in a serving dish. Stir the remaining ingredients into the pan and heat through but do not boil. Pour over the mushrooms and leave to cool.

YOGHURT SOUP

350 ml (12 fl oz) natural yoghurt
2 tbsp gram flour
150 ml (5 fl oz) water
2 tbsp groundnut oil
$\frac{1}{2}$ tsp black mustard seeds
$\frac{1}{2}$ tsp cumin seeds
a pinch of asafoetida
$\frac{1}{2}$ tsp ground cumin
$\frac{1}{2}$ tsp turmeric
$\frac{1}{2}$ tsp ground coriander
1 ripe tomato
1.25 cm ($\frac{1}{2}$ in) fresh root ginger, peeled and grated
additional water if necessary
fresh coriander leaves, finely chopped

Whisk the yoghurt, gram flour and water together in a large bowl or blender.

Heat the oil in a large pan and stir in the spices. Fry lightly over a low heat for 2–3 minutes. Thinly slice the tomato and add to the pan. Cook gently until the tomato is very soft. Stir in the smooth yoghurt mixture and the root ginger. Bring to a slow boil and cook over a low heat until it begins to thicken. I generally add a further 150 ml (5 fl oz) water at this stage but it is very much a matter of personal taste. Heat through and sprinkle with fresh coriander leaves before serving.

For a smoother, more elegant soup pass through a sieve or vegetable mouli or process briefly in a blender or food processor.

POTATOES WITH YOGHURT

This excellent recipe is taken from a favourite book of mine, *In the Kitchen Garden* by George Seddon and Helena Radecka (Mitchell Beazley/Edenlite, 1975).

3 tbsp ghee or sunflower oil
1 onion, chopped
2.5 cm (1 in) fresh root ginger, peeled and grated
1 tbsp ground coriander
1 tsp turmeric
2 green chillies, finely chopped
3 tomatoes, blanched, peeled and chopped
275 ml (10 fl oz) natural yoghurt
$\frac{1}{4}$ tsp ground mace
4 tbsp raisins
675 g (1$\frac{1}{2}$ lb) small new potatoes, cooked
1 tbsp fresh coriander leaves, finely chopped

Heat the ghee or oil in a large frying pan. Add the onion and ginger and fry, stirring occasionally, until golden brown. Stir in the spices and chillies and cook for a further 3–4 minutes. Add the tomatoes and yoghurt and bring to the boil. Simmer until the sauce thickens. Add the remaining ingredients and heat through. Sprinkle with fresh coriander leaves before serving.

STUFFED COURGETTES WITH YOGHURT SAUCE

6–8 courgettes

FOR THE FILLING:
2–3 tbsp olive oil
1 aubergine, chopped
3 heaped tbsp cooked brown rice
2 ripe tomatoes, chopped
25 g (1 oz) pine kernels
25 g (1 oz) sultanas
1 tbsp fresh parsley, finely chopped
seasoning
a good pinch ground cinnamon

FOR THE SAUCE:
275 ml (10 fl oz) natural yoghurt
2 egg yolks

Cut the courgettes in half lengthways and scoop out the spongy centres. Steam for 5 minutes.

Heat the olive oil in a pan, add the aubergine and cook until it begins to soften. Add the remaining filling ingredients and adjust the seasoning to taste. Cook for a further 4–5 minutes, stirring occasionally.

Place the lightly cooked courgettes in a shallow ovenproof dish and pile the stuffing into the centre of each. Beat the yoghurt and egg yolks together in a bowl and pour over the top. Bake in a preheated oven, gas mark 6 (200° C/ 400° F) for 20–25 minutes.

CHEESE

I always thought there was a good deal of truth in the saying, 'there's nowt so queer as folk', but I never imagined anyone would be daft enough to give up the pleasures of eating a wedge of cheese with their apple pie simply because cheese was deemed to be unfashionable. Yet this was the situation in Britain until the nineteenth century, when its popularity had more to do with the problems of providing food for the new industrial towns than any sudden appreciation of its gastronomic qualities.

Unfortunately, as well as stimulating demand, the Industrial Revolution tolled the death knell for a good many varieties of traditional farmhouse cheeses. The advent of the railways and, a little later, motor transport, enabled farmers to send their surplus milk to the towns. In the 1870s the opening of the first factory creamery offered yet another outlet for their surplus milk and it became inevitable that farmers should stop the laborious and time-consuming process of making their own cheese and concentrate solely on milk production. By the end of the First World War over 50 types of English cheese had ceased to exist.

While factory creameries were able to produce cheese efficiently and on a large scale, the product tended to be characterless and in 1934 the Milk Marketing Board set up the Farmhouse Cheesemakers Scheme aimed at promoting cheese made in the traditional way. The Scheme has been in operation ever since and although farmhouse cheeses are slightly more expensive than the run-of-the-mill brands they are well worth the extra cost. Cheese-making is a complex and delicate process and the differences between cheeses can be as subtle and as varied as those between wines. It should be possible to note a seasonal change in their taste and texture as the quality of milk varies from month to month. In the past most cheese was made in the summer when the milk was rich and creamy. During the winter, when the cows were kept indoors, being fed on hay, farmers rarely bothered to make cheese except perhaps on the odd occasion when bad weather prevented them from getting the milk away.

When buying cheese it is best to look for a shop which seems to know how to store it and one which has a good turnover. Don't buy cheeses which look hard and dry, or are sweating, or showing signs of mould unless characteristic of the type. Avoid all cheeses which come prepacked as they have had little chance to ripen naturally and are generally rather bland and rubbery. There is also something particularly unattractive about cheeses which come in uniform rectilinear blocks and they do little to enhance the cheese board.

As cheese continues to mature throughout its life, correct storage is important. Temperature and humidity are critical in this process; if the cheese is too warm it will ferment, if too cold it will rot. A refrigerator is not the best place to keep cheese as it is too cold and dries it out but as few modern houses have either pantries or cellars we have very little choice, particularly in the summer. If you must use the fridge take the cheese out about an hour before it is to be eaten.

Cheese has been described as a 'splendid and noble food to be enjoyed at any time' and while not disagreeing with such sentiments I would like to add that it should be used judiciously. For although cheese is an excellent source of protein and contains moderate amounts of calcium, phosphorus and sodium it is also, unfortunately, high in saturated fats and calories (with the exception of skimmed milk varieties) and is thought to be incidental in many cases of food allergies and respiratory disorders owing to its mucous-forming properties. I think it is much better to enjoy a small amount of good farmhouse cheese with a salad or apple, or with biscuits at the end of a meal, rather than indiscriminately adding it to sauces and savoury dishes.

In recent years there has been a revival of farm-based creameries. This is particularly noticeable in the production of goat's milk cheese but there are also signs that some of our traditional cheeses such as the Blue Vinney of Dorset and the Cotherstone of Cleveland are being made once again, albeit in small amounts. More often than not, however, our choice is limited to the following.

Cheddar
An excellent all-purpose cheese good for eating on its own and for cooking. It is sweet and mild when young but becomes sharp and full of flavour when left to mature for months and even years. Choose a fairly mature cheese for cooking as young ones tend to become stringy and, as one writer described, can taste like a mixture of chewing gum and butter. As its name suggests it was first made in Cheddar, Somerset and owing to the benevolent and well-intentioned work of Joseph Harding, who toured the country giving instruction on how to make Cheddar cheese, no other variety has been so widely imitated. We even import the stuff from Canada and New Zealand, but they do not rival our own mature farmhouse Cheddar in either flavour or texture.

Cheshire
Thought to be the oldest English cheese, Cheshire is surprisingly popular abroad where it is sold under the name of 'Chester'. It is crumblier, saltier and slightly sharper than Cheddar and makes exceptionally good soufflés. When first made it had such a reputation that Welsh Border farmers tried to sell their slightly inferior cheese under its banner. In response the Cheshire farmers insisted that the Welsh colour their cheese with annatto but unfortunately their plan backfired, for the general public took a liking to the new 'red Cheshire' with the result that a true red Cheshire had to be produced to compete with the Welsh imposter. Some claim that there is no difference, apart from colour, between white and red Cheshires but I find the white has a cleaner taste. There is a blue Cheshire on the market too.

Lancashire
This cheese is similar to Cheshire in appearance and texture but is much sharper and is excellent for toasting. The best Lancashire cheese I have ever tasted came, not surprisingly, from a stall on Lancaster market. Three types were available, strong, mild and creamy and they were being sold as quickly as each piece could be cut from the large truckles.

Caerphilly
Another crumbly white cheese but this one is mild, soft and creamy and is particularly useful as a flavouring in delicate dishes. It is eaten very young and in 1940 the Minister of Food banned its production due to its short keeping properties. The Welsh cheesemakers never recovered and now most Caerphilly is made in Somerset.

Wensleydale
Often mistaken for Caerphilly, Wensleydale is a soft, light cheese with a slight taste of buttermilk. It was traditionally made from ewe's milk by the monks of Jervaux Abbey but these days cow's milk is used. Blue Wensleydale is said by some to taste even better than blue Stilton.

Gloucester
A close-textured straw-coloured cheese which comes from Somerset. Farmhouse double Gloucester requires full cream milk and is made in the summer and early autumn only when the grazing is good. I understand that several farms have recently started producing single Gloucester cheese again, known also as hay cheese because it was the staple fare of itinerant hay makers. As its name suggests it is not as rich as double Gloucester and is eaten much younger, being left to ripen for eight weeks as opposed to the nine months needed to produce a good double Gloucester. Both varieties slice well and are good for sandwiches and ploughmen's lunches.

Leicester
A moist, flaky cheese with a mild nutty flavour. It is dyed (using a natural colouring agent) a bright orange and is ideal for cheese sauces.

Stilton
Truly my favourite cheese but only when it is white. It has always been the custom in my family to buy a good wedge of white Stilton at Christmas to eat with the Christmas cake and mince pies. I find it odd that so many cookery books assume that Stilton cheese is blue. Is white Stilton a regional speciality? Certainly relatives living in the South are unable to buy it

in their local shops. To avoid disappointment, it is worth while asking the shopkeeper for a sample before making a purchase. Over-ripe Stilton can be so strong and overpowering that it would frighten away even the hungriest of mice but when under-ripe it is bland and rather boring.

The story goes that Stilton cheese was first made at Quenby Hall, near Leicester and was sold as Quenby cheese. When one of the daughters of the family married and moved to the Bell Inn at Stilton, a truckle of cheese was sent to her every Christmas. So popular did it prove to be with the locals that the pub soon became famous for its cheese and gradually Quenby was forgotten and the cheese became known as Stilton.

CHEESE FOUNDATION

This is one of my mother's recipes which, she says, keeps for a week in a cold pantry and for well over a month in a fridge. It can be used as the base for cheese sauces, flans, as a pancake filling or a sandwich spread.

1 egg
175 ml (6 fl oz) milk
1 dsp dry mustard powder
1 tsp Worcestershire sauce
15 g ($\frac{1}{2}$ oz) butter
225 g (8 oz) Cheddar cheese, grated

Break the egg into a small pan and mix in the other ingredients. Heat gently until the mixture thickens. I have been assured that it never curdles.

SAVOURY RICE

75 g (3 oz) long grain brown rice
a scant 225 ml (8 fl oz) water
25 g (1 oz) butter
1 large onion, finely chopped
4 heaped tbsp cheese foundation (see below left)
seasoning
fresh parsley, chopped
brown breadcrumbs
25–50 g (1–2 oz) grated cheese

Put the rice and water in a heavy pan and bring to the boil. Cover and simmer for 35–40 minutes, without stirring, until the rice is tender. Drain if necessary and leave covered until needed.

Melt the butter in a pan, add the onion and sauté until soft. Remove from the heat and work in the cheese foundation. When well-mixed add the cooked rice and parsley. Season to taste. Mix well and spoon into an ovenproof dish. Sprinkle the breadcrumbs and grated cheese over the top and bake in a preheated oven, gas mark 5 (190° C/375° F) for 20–25 minutes.

MOCK CHEESE AND TOMATO PIE

This was one of my stand-by recipes in my student days and has remained a firm favourite ever since.

SERVES 4
a knob of butter
8 slices of wholewheat bread, crusts removed
150 g (5 oz) red Cheshire cheese, thinly sliced
3 tomatoes, sliced
275 ml (10 fl oz) milk
1 egg
a good pinch or two of cayenne pepper

Butter a small casserole dish and place in the bottom alternate layers of bread, cheese and tomato, finishing with a layer of bread. Mix the milk and egg together and season with cayenne pepper. Pour over the dish and leave to stand for 10–15 minutes.

Meanwhile, preheat the oven to gas mark 5 (190° C/375° F) and then bake for 25–30 minutes.

TARTE À L'OIGNON (ONION TART)

The secret of making good onion tarts is to cook the onions slowly until they are meltingly soft and golden. Don't rush this, the onions mustn't brown or lose their shape. When cooked in this way the onions become surprisingly sweet and need to be countered by using a sharp cheese such as a mature Stilton or Lancashire.

225 g (8 oz) wholewheat shortcrust pastry (for method, see page 12)
2 tbsp olive oil
675 g (1½ lb) mild onions, thinly sliced
1 tbsp fresh parsley, finely chopped
2 tsp fresh mint, finely chopped
3 eggs
275 ml (10 fl oz) natural yoghurt
75 g (3 oz) grated cheese

Roll out the pastry on a lightly-floured board and use it to line a 25-cm (10-in) flan ring. Prick the base with a fork and blind bake in a preheated oven, gas mark 6 (200° C/400° F) for 10 minutes.

Heat the olive oil in a large frying pan, add the onions and sweat them for 15–20 minutes. Stir in the parsley and mint and then spoon the mixture into the pastry case. Beat the eggs and yoghurt together in a bowl and stir in the grated cheese. Pour over the onions, carefully mixing the two together. Return to the oven and bake for a further 25–30 minutes until the filling is lightly coloured and just setting in the centre.

LANCASHIRE RABBIT

SERVES 4
225 g (8 oz) Lancashire cheese, grated
2 tsp English mustard, ready-made
1 tbsp white wine vinegar
4 slices of wholewheat bread

Mix the cheese, mustard and vinegar together in a bowl. Toast one side of the bread and then spoon the cheese mixture over the untoasted side. Put the bread under a hot grill and cook until the cheese is bubbling and beginning to brown.

GALETTE AU FROMAGE

The French galette can take many forms. It can be a round flat cake made from flaky pastry and eaten on Twelfth night, a quiche or a crêpe. This galette is something of a hybrid; it is made with a rich batter mixture but is then baked in the oven like a pastry. It is delicious eaten warm from the oven.

100 g (4 oz) wholewheat flour
100 g (4 oz) unbleached white flour
225 g (8 oz) Gruyère cheese, grated
2 tsp Dijon mustard
freshly ground black pepper
6 eggs, beaten
1 egg yolk

Mix all the dry ingredients together in a bowl and season with mustard and black pepper. Gradually add the beaten eggs and stir well until the mixture is smooth.

Line a 25-cm (10-in) flan ring with grease-proof paper and pour in the fairly stiff batter. Brush with the remaining egg yolk and bake in a preheated oven, gas mark 4 (180° C/350° F) for 50–60 minutes.

BAKED RICE WITH COURGETTES AND CHEESE

225 g (8 oz) long grain brown rice
575 ml (1 pint) water
2 courgettes, grated
4 tbsp fresh parsley, finely chopped
175 g (6 oz) Cheddar cheese, grated
6 eggs, beaten
seasoning

Put the rice and water in a heavy pan and bring to the boil. Cover and simmer for 35–40 minutes, without stirring, until the rice is dry and tender. Remove from the heat but leave covered until needed.

Mix all the ingredients together in a bowl and season to taste. Spoon into an oiled oven-proof dish and bake in a preheated oven, gas mark 6 (200° C/400° F) for 30–40 minutes until firm to the touch and lightly browned.

COURGETTES WITH MOZZARELLA CHEESE

Originally Mozzarella cheese was made from buffalo's milk and no doubt tasted very different from our modern cow's milk version. Nonetheless it is still very useful, being one of the best cooking cheeses. It has a rubbery texture and bland flavour but melts beautifully.

1 tbsp olive oil
1 large onion, finely chopped
900 g (2 lb) tomatoes, chopped
2 tbsp dry white wine
2 tbsp fresh basil, finely chopped
a good pinch of dried basil (*optional*)
freshly ground black pepper
900 g (2 lb) courgettes, sliced
2–3 tbsp Parmesan cheese, grated
225 g (8 oz) Mozzarella cheese, sliced

Heat the oil in a heavy pan, add the onion and gently fry until soft. Add the tomatoes, wine and basil and stew until the tomatoes have softened and reduced to a thick purée. Season with black pepper.

Brush an ovenproof casserole with olive oil and lay half the sliced courgettes in the bottom. Sprinkle with some of the Parmesan and half the Mozzarella cheese. Spoon over half the tomato mixture. Repeat these layers with the remaining ingredients, finishing with a layer of tomatoes. Bake in a preheated oven, gas mark 6 (200° C/400° F) for 25–30 minutes. Serve with jacket potatoes and a green salad.

STUFFED MARROW – VEGETARIAN STYLE

1 tbsp sunflower oil
1 small onion, finely chopped
1 stick celery, finely chopped
75 g (3 oz) soft wholewheat breadcrumbs
2 large eggs, beaten
$\frac{1}{2}$ tsp dried oregano
$\frac{1}{2}$ tsp dried sage
$\frac{1}{2}$ tsp dried rosemary
$\frac{1}{2}$ tsp ground cumin
2–3 tbsp desiccated coconut
75 g (3 oz) grated Cheddar cheese
seasoning
1 medium marrow

Heat the oil in a frying pan, add the onion and celery and sauté until soft. Remove from the heat and mix in the breadcrumbs, eggs, herbs, coconut and cheese. Adjust the seasoning to taste.

Cut the marrow in half lengthways and scoop out the seeds and spongy centre. Fill the two halves with the stuffing and then place one on top of the other, the cut sides together. Tightly wrap in greaseproof paper so that it resembles a Christmas cracker and bake in a preheated oven, gas mark 6 (200° C/400° F) for 30 minutes.

CHICKEN ROMAGNA

SERVES 4
4 chicken breasts
8 slices of Parma ham
50 g (2 oz) Gruyère cheese, thinly sliced
wholewheat flour for dusting
2 eggs, beaten
75 g (3 oz) soft wholewheat breadcrumbs
50 ml (2 fl oz) sunflower oil
50 g (2 oz) unsalted butter

Working with one chicken breast at a time cut the meat from the bone, keeping it in one piece if possible. Press any small 'leftover' pieces down on top of the larger slice. Put two slices of Parma ham, side by side, on a chopping board or work surface with the long sides running from the right to the left. Lay the chicken breast down the middle of the ham so that its short sides are at the top and the bottom. Place a slice of cheese on top of the chicken and then wrap over the Parma ham so that the chicken and cheese are sealed in an open-ended parcel. If necessary turn the 'parcel' over so the two joins are underneath. Repeat with the other chicken breasts.

Carefully dip each 'parcel' first into flour, then beaten egg and finally into the bread-crumbs. Heat the oil and butter together in a large frying pan and when the fat begins to bubble add the chicken 'parcels'. The fat should come about halfway up each one. Fry over a moderate heat for 8–10 minutes on each side, turning down the heat if they brown too quickly. Drain on absorbent paper before serving.

GLOUCESTER CHEESE AND ALE

A traditional English dish which was popular with travellers and farmers alike. It was generally on the menu of roadside hotels and hostelries in the Cotswolds until the turn of the century.

SERVES 4
225 g (8 oz) Gloucester cheese, grated
2 tsp English mustard, ready-made
4 tbsp ale
4 slices of wholewheat bread

Put the grated cheese, mustard and ale in a small pan and heat gently until well mixed and bubbly. Meanwhile, toast the bread on one side only. Spoon the cheese mixture over the untoasted side and put under a hot grill until the cheese begins to melt. Serve immediately.

CROQUE MONSIEUR

Cheese and ham are a splendid combination. The proper way to cook croque monsieur is in the frying pan but I prefer to toast the sand-wich. Almost any type of cheese can be used.

SERVES 4
8 slices of wholewheat bread
Dijon mustard (*optional*)
100 g (4 oz) Wensleydale cheese, sliced
4 slices of cooked ham

Brush 4 slices of bread with mustard and then cover each with a slice of cheese and ham. Top with a second slice of bread, press gently together and toast on both sides under a hot grill.

CHEESE AND LENTIL SLICES

225 g (8 oz) red lentils
425 ml (15 fl oz) water
1–2 tbsp sunflower oil
2 large onions, chopped
175 g (6 oz) red Leicester, grated
2 tsp yeast extract
1 tsp mixed dried herbs
1 egg
50 g (2 oz) soft wholewheat breadcrumbs
seasoning

Sort through the lentils carefully and remove any small stones or pieces of grit. Put into a pan or pressure cooker with the water and cook until the lentils are soft and all the water has been absorbed. In a pan this will take about 50–60 minutes, but do check the contents of the pan regularly to make sure that they do not boil dry. Pressure cook for 10 minutes.

Meanwhile, heat the oil in a large frying pan, add the onions and sauté until soft and golden. Remove the onions with a slotted spoon and put them in a large bowl with the cooked lentils. Add three-quarters of the grated cheese, the yeast extract, dried herbs, the egg and half the breadcrumbs. Mix together well and season to taste.

Brush a shallow square tin with oil and spoon in the mixture. Mix the remaining breadcrumbs and grated cheese together and sprinkle over the top. Bake in a preheated oven, gas mark 6 (200° C/400° F) for 25 minutes. Cool slightly before cutting into slices. Serve hot or cold.

LENTIL AND SPINACH PIE

FOR THE FILLING:
225 g (8 oz) brown lentils
575 ml (1 pint) water
6 whole cloves
1 large onion
75 g (3 oz) Cheddar cheese, grated
freshly grated nutmeg
450 g (1 lb) spinach, cooked and chopped
seasoning

FOR THE PASTRY:
225 g (8 oz) wholewheat flour
100 g (4 oz) hard butter, grated
4 tbsp cold water
1 egg, beaten

Sort through the lentils carefully and remove any small stones or pieces of grit. Put into a pan or pressure cooker with the water. Push the cloves into the onion and add to the lentils. Bring to the boil and simmer for 45–55 minutes checking regularly that the pan is not boiling dry or pressure cook for 12 minutes. Drain. Take the cloves from the onion and then chop the onion finely. Mash the beans with a fork or rub through a sieve or vegetable mouli. Stir in the chopped onion, cheese, nutmeg and spinach. Season to taste.

To make the pastry put the flour in a bowl and mix in the grated butter with a fork. Add the water and knead to form a pastry dough. Divide the pastry in two and on a lightly-floured board roll out one piece slightly larger than a 25-cm (10-in) pie dish. Line the dish with the pastry and spoon in the filling. Roll out the remaining pastry to a circle large enough to cover the pie. Dampen the pastry rim and cover the pie with the pastry top. Press the edges together to seal. Brush with beaten egg and bake in a preheated oven, gas mark 6 (200° C/400° F) for 25–30 minutes.

FISH

FISH

One reason for our conservative taste in fish must surely be the fact that until recently it was extremely difficult to buy anything more exciting than a pair of kippers or some cod's roe. Such delicacies as smoked trout, scallops and crayfish are relatively new arrivals and I am sure that they and other more unusual fish have helped to stimulate our imagination.

Apart from having an amazing variety of flavours and textures, fish are also extremely nutritious. They are rich in protein and contain as little as 2 per cent unsaturated fat in the case of cod, haddock and plaice. The oilier fish such as herring and mackerel have fat levels between 10–20 per cent depending on the season. Shellfish are something of an exception being low in fat but containing twice as much cholesterol as other fish, poultry and game. Fish also contain many valuable vitamins and minerals including vitamins A and D, calcium and iodine.

Fish can almost be described as a 'convenience food' as it requires very little preparation and cooking. In spite of quick and simple cooking techniques half the fish eaten in this country is bought at the fish and chip shop. Perhaps this isn't a true reflection of our cooking skills but more a result of the demise of the wet fish shop. In some areas the only fish fillets available are the square varieties that come in boxes. Although the old-fashioned fishmonger, selling his wares from dripping boxes piled high with fish, is a less familiar sight these days, an increasing number of supermarkets have excellent fresh fish counters and it is hard to resist the displays of gleaming, colourful fish attractively arranged on trays of crushed ice.

Fish stocks

Admittedly cleaning and gutting fish is not everyone's cup of tea but it is impossible to make good stock without the trimmings – after all there are no fish stock cubes to fall back on. If you are in the habit of buying filleted fish ask the fishmonger for some bones, heads, tails etc with your fish. Sometimes he will be glad to give them away but even if you have to pay the amount will be small.

There are two basic types of stock, court bouillon and fumet. Court bouillon is the name given to the liquid in which fish is usually poached. It is used in preference to water as it enhances both the flavour and colour of the fish. Just enough is needed to cover the fish, the exact amount having as much to do with the size of the cooking pot as the size of the fish itself. Court bouillon is usually made from water, wine vinegar or wine, chopped vegetables and herbs and spices. However, it can be milk based. All the ingredients are simmered together for half an hour or so before being strained. It is always left to cool before being poured over the fish.

COURT BOUILLON 1

This court bouillon is excellent for poaching delicate white fish. For stronger flavoured fish, particularly freshwater eel, use red wine. In Normandy, cider takes the place of the wine.

1.2 litres (2 pints) water
150 ml (5 fl oz) dry white wine
1 onion, sliced
1 stick celery, sliced
1 carrot, sliced
10 black peppercorns, lightly crushed
2 sprigs of fresh parsley
2 sprigs of fresh thyme
2 sprigs of fresh fennel (*optional*)
1 bay leaf

Place all the ingredients in a large pan, bring to the boil and simmer for about 30 minutes. Strain and leave to cool.

COURT BOUILLON 2

A useful recipe for those occasions when there is no wine to spare. Red or white wine vinegar can be used.

1.2 litres (2 pints) water
3 tbsp wine vinegar
1 onion, stuck with 3 whole cloves
1 leek, sliced
1 carrot, sliced
6 black peppercorns, lightly crushed
2 sprigs of fresh parsley
1 sprig of fresh thyme
1 sprig of fresh tarragon
1 bay leaf

Cook as above.

FUMET (FISH STOCK)

The liquid left over after the fish has been removed from the poaching pan is known as a fumet. The word literally means a scent or bouquet of fish. It has a much better flavour than a court bouillon and is the basis of most fish soups and stews. If the fumet is reduced, by brisk boiling, from 850 ml ($1\frac{1}{2}$ pints) to 275 ml ($\frac{1}{2}$ pint), it can be served as a sauce or added to enrich and flavour thick creamy sauces.

A fumet can be made in two ways: simply use the court bouillon in which a piece of fish has been poached; or make it quickly and cheaply from fish trimmings. If a recipe calls for a certain amount of fish stock this is the liquid you need to use; few recipes call it by its proper name fumet.

450 g (1 lb) fish trimmings
850 ml ($1\frac{1}{2}$ pints) water
150 ml (5 fl oz) dry white wine (*optional*)
1 onion, sliced
1 medium carrot, sliced
10 black peppercorns
1 sprig of fresh parsley
1 sprig of fresh thyme
1 bay leaf

Remove any pieces of gut or gills from the trimmings before placing them in a large pan with the other ingredients. Cover and bring to the boil. Skim, cover again and simmer gently for 30–40 minutes. Pass through a sieve, pushing through as much of the solid mixture as you wish. If you intend to concentrate the fumet, to use it as an aspic or if you need a clear stock, simply strain through a muslin-lined sieve and discard all the solids. The fumet can be kept in the fridge for several days and in a freezer for up to 3 months.

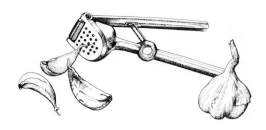

ZUPPI DI PESCE

A puréed fish soup from Italy, perfect for those who like fish but object to their bones.

1 kg (2–2$\frac{1}{2}$ lb) assorted white fish (red mullet,
conger eel, halibut, hake,
monkfish, haddock, cod)
1.5 litres (2$\frac{1}{2}$ pints) fumet or fish stock
olive oil
2 onions, chopped
2 cloves garlic, peeled and crushed
450 g (1 lb) ripe tomatoes, peeled and chopped
2 sprigs of fresh fennel (*optional*)
1 sprig of fresh parsley
1 sprig of fresh thyme
a good pinch of saffron strands
a good pinch of cayenne pepper
seasoning

Clean and trim the fish. Chop into large pieces. Place all the bones, skin and any heads and tails in a large pan with the stock. Bring to the boil, cover and simmer for 30 minutes. Strain and discard the solids.

Heat the oil in a large pan, add the onions and garlic and sauté for 8–10 minutes. Add the pieces of white fish and the tomatoes and cook for a further 5 minutes. Add the fumet, just enough to cover, and the remaining ingredients. Bring to the boil, cover and simmer for 35 minutes.

Strain the soup and remove the herbs and any bones left in the fish. Rub the soup through a vegetable mouli or coarse sieve back into the broth. Adjust the consistency and seasoning to taste. Heat through.

BOUILLABAISSE

Bouillabaisse is perhaps the most famous of all fishermen's stews. It is said to have originated in the coastal towns of southern France, and in particular Marseilles. Certainly its heady aroma and bright colouring are typical of Provençal cooking. An authentic bouillabaisse would contain: some rascasse (a small bony fish, also called the scorpion fish, and found mainly in the Mediterranean); John Dory; monkfish; bream; red mullet; whiting; sea bass; gurnard; weever fish; wrasse; lobster; and crab. Shellfish are included but they are invariably small and spiny and are used simply to strengthen the broth.

While it may be difficult to produce a true bouillabaisse in Britain don't be put off by the odd-sounding fish. Here is my own version.

900 g (2 lb) mixed fish (cod, haddock, whiting,
eel, prawns, monkfish, hake and scallops)
3–4 tbsp olive oil
2 onions, chopped
2 cloves garlic, peeled and crushed
225 g (8 oz) ripe tomatoes, chopped
2 sprigs of fresh thyme
2 sprigs of fresh fennel leaves
1 bay leaf
grated rind of $\frac{1}{2}$ orange
a good pinch of saffron strands
seasoning
1–2 tbsp fresh parsley, finely chopped

Clean and scale the firm-fleshed fish and cut into thick chunks. Prepare any shellfish you may be using.

Heat the olive oil in a large pan, add the onions and garlic and sauté for 8–10 minutes until soft and golden. Add the tomatoes, the herbs, orange rind and saffron. Sauté for 5 minutes more. Stir in the fish, except for any whiting or prawns, and barely cover with water. Bring to the boil and cook for 5 minutes. Add the remaining fish and boil briskly for a further 3–4 minutes. The fish should be cooked but still hold its shape. Remove the herbs and season to taste. Sprinkle with parsley. Serve with warm French bread.

MONKFISH CASSEROLE

groundnut oil
2 mild onions, chopped
1 green pepper, deseeded and sliced
450 g (1 lb) tomatoes, chopped
4 potatoes, scrubbed and sliced
1–2 tbsp tomato purée
575 ml (1 pint) fumet/fish stock
seasoning
675 g (1½ lb) monkfish, roughly chopped

Heat 1–2 tablespoons of oil in a large pan, add the onions and sauté until they begin to soften. Add the green pepper and the tomatoes and cook for 2–3 minutes more before adding the potatoes. Add the tomato purée and barely cover the vegetables with fish stock. Season to taste. Cover and simmer gently until the potatoes are almost done. Add the fish and continue to cook until that too is tender. Adjust the seasoning to taste before serving.

BAKED RED MULLET WITH ROSEMARY

SERVES 4
4 red mullet
olive oil
1 onion, finely chopped
8 tomatoes, finely chopped
2 tbsp fresh rosemary, chopped
freshly ground black pepper
juice of 1 lemon

Scale and clean the fish, leaving the heads on. Brush 4 pieces of foil, large enough to wrap each fish in, with olive oil and place a fish in the centre of each. Scatter the chopped onion and tomatoes over the top and sprinkle with rosemary. Season with black pepper and lemon juice. Fold the foil over the top of the fish, turning over the ends to keep in the juices.

Place the 4 neat parcels on a baking tray and bake in a preheated oven, gas mark 4 (180° C/ 350° F) for 25 minutes.

RED MULLET WITH FENNEL AND TOMATO

SERVES 4
olive oil
1 Florence fennel bulb, thinly sliced
225 g (8 oz) tomatoes, chopped
1 lemon
fresh parsley
freshly ground black pepper
4 red mullet (weighing approx.
175–225 g/6–8 oz each)

Heat a little olive oil in a pan, add the fennel and sauté for 3–4 minutes, until lightly coloured. Add the tomatoes, the grated rind and the juice of ½ the lemon and 1 tablespoon finely chopped parsley. Season with black pepper. Bring to the boil, stirring frequently. Cover and reduce the heat. Simmer gently for 10 minutes, stirring occasionally. Transfer the mixture to a large, shallow ovenproof dish.

Scale and clean the fish, leaving their heads on. Make 2–3 gashes on both sides of each fish. Put a small sprig of parsley into the cuts on one side of each fish. Place the fish on top of the fennel mixture, parsley side downwards. Brush with olive oil. Slice the remaining ½ lemon and cut each slice in half. Push a piece into each cut on the exposed side of the fish. Cover with foil and bake in a preheated oven, gas mark 4 (180° C/350° F) for about 20 minutes.

ROSY FISH PIES

The clean, refreshing taste of fennel is the perfect partner for conger eel which can be a little overpowering on its own.

SERVES 4
4 conger eel steaks
575 ml (1 pint) court bouillon (for method, see page 32)
olive oil
1 small Florence fennel bulb, finely chopped
2 cloves garlic, peeled and crushed
4 tomatoes, chopped
1–2 tbsp tomato purée

FOR THE SAUCE:
2 tbsp olive oil
a scant 25 g (1 oz) unbleached white flour
150 ml (5 fl oz) milk
150 ml (5 fl oz) fumet
freshly ground black pepper

FOR THE PASTRY:
350 g (12 oz) rough puff pastry (for method, see page 43)

Place the fish, skin uppermost, under a hot grill until they begin to toast. Carefully remove and discard the loosened skin. Bring the court bouillon to the boil in a large pan, add the steaks to the bubbling stock and simmer gently until tender. Lift out the steaks and boil the stock quickly to reduce it by a half to produce the fumet for the sauce.

Cut the fish into large pieces and remove the bones. Put in 4 individual pie dishes. Heat a little oil in a frying pan, add the fennel and garlic and sauté until they soften. Add the tomatoes and cook for 4–5 minutes more. Stir in the purée.

Heat the 2 tablespoons of oil in a saucepan and stir in the flour. Cook for 3–4 minutes. Gradually add the milk and fumet, stirring well after each addition. Bring to the boil and cook until the sauce begins to thicken. Season. Stir the tomato mixture into the sauce until well mixed and pour over the fish. Make the pastry, divide it into 4 and roll out each portion on a lightly floured board to a circle large enough to cover the pie. Cover the pies with the pastry tops and bake in a preheated oven, gas mark 6 (200° C/ 400° F) for 25 minutes.

FRESH SALMON QUICHE

FOR THE PASTRY:
175 g (6 oz) fine wholewheat flour
75 g (3 oz) butter, diced
6 tsp cold water

FOR THE FILLING:
175 g (6 oz) cooked salmon, flaked
1 tbsp fresh parsley, finely chopped
4 eggs
1 egg yolk
150 ml (5 fl oz) natural yoghurt
freshly ground black pepper
1 tbsp Parmesan cheese, grated

Put the flour in a bowl and rub in the butter, using your fingertips, until the mixture resembles breadcrumbs. Add sufficient water to form a pastry dough. Turn onto a lightly floured board, roll out and line a 25 cm (10 in) flan ring. Prick the pastry base with a fork and blind bake in a preheated oven, gas mark 6 (200° C/400° F) for 10–12 minutes.

Lay the cooked fish in the bottom of the pastry case and scatter the parsley over the top. Beat the eggs, egg yolk and yoghurt together and season with black pepper. Pour over the fish. Sprinkle with Parmesan and return to the oven. Bake for a further 25 minutes.

TRUITES AUX PIGNONS (TROUT WITH PINE KERNELS)

SERVES 4
4 trout, cleaned and trimmed
wholewheat flour
50–75 g (2–3 oz) butter
100 g (4 oz) pine kernels
1 lemon, cut into wedges
fresh parsley, chopped

Clean the fish, rinse and pat dry. Dust the trout lightly with wholewheat flour. Melt the butter in a large, heavy frying pan and cook the fish over a low heat for about 5 minutes on each side. When tender place on a serving dish and keep warm. Add the pine kernels to the frying pan and quickly brown them. Sprinkle the nuts over the fish and garnish with lemon and parsley.

GRILLED TROUT WITH SESAME SAUCE

SERVES 4
4 trout
2–3 tbsp fumet (fish stock)
2 tbsp sesame oil
25 g (1 oz) butter
25 g (1 oz) sesame seeds
3 tbsp lemon juice
2 tbsp red wine

Cut the heads and tails from the trout and use to make the fumet. Clean the fish, rinse and pat dry. Prepare the fumet as described on page 32.

Heat the oil and butter together in a small pan. Add the sesame seeds and lightly fry for several minutes, shaking the pan frequently to prevent them from burning. Pour over the lemon juice, wine and fumet and bring to the boil. Continue cooking until the liquid is reduced by a half.

Meanwhile, make 3 diagonal gashes on both sides of each trout. Brush with a little more sesame oil. Place under a hot grill and cook for about 5 minutes on each side, basting frequently with the sesame sauce. When tender lift the fish onto a serving dish and keep warm. Pour any juices which may have collected in the grill pan into the saucepan holding the remaining sesame sauce. Heat through and pour over the fish before serving.

CRAB SOUFFLÉ

250 ml (9 fl oz) milk
1 slice of onion
1 bay leaf
6 black peppercorns
40 g (1½ oz) butter
1 shallot, finely chopped
15 g (½ oz) unbleached white flour
2 tbsp natural yoghurt
4 eggs, separated
225 g (8 oz) brown crab meat
a pinch of cayenne pepper
freshly grated nutmeg

Put the milk, onion, bay leaf and black peppercorns in a saucepan and bring to the boil. Remove from the heat and leave to infuse for 10–15 minutes. Strain.

Melt the butter in another saucepan, add the shallot and sauté, taking care not to let it brown. Stir in the flour and cook for a minute or two over a low heat. Remove from the heat and gradually add the strained milk. Return to the heat and bring to the boil. Leave to cool for 5 minutes before beating in the yoghurt and egg yolks. Stir in the crab meat and season well with cayenne and nutmeg.

Whisk the egg whites until stiff and peaked and fold into the mixture. Spoon into a buttered soufflé dish and bake in a preheated oven, gas mark 7 (220° C/425° F) for 10–15 minutes. Serve immediately.

HADDOCK FRICASSÉE

A delicious, rich, creamy stew.
675 g (1½ lb) haddock fillets, skinned
225 ml (8 fl oz) water
2 tbsp dry white wine
a pinch of grated nutmeg
a pinch of ground mace
1 sprig of fresh thyme
1 sprig of fresh rosemary
1 sprig of fresh parsley
50 g (2 oz) peas
50 g (2 oz) button mushrooms, sliced
20 g (¾ oz) butter
15 g (½ oz) unbleached white flour
225 ml (8 fl oz) natural yoghurt
25–50 g (1–2 oz) white Stilton cheese, grated

Cut the fish into 2.5 cm (1 in) strips and place in a pan with the water, wine, spices, herbs, peas and mushrooms. Cover, bring to the boil and poach for 4–5 minutes until tender. Drain and reserve the cooking liquor. Remove the sprigs of herbs and place the fish and vegetables in a casserole dish. Keep warm until needed.

Work the butter and flour together to form a paste or beurre manié. Roll into small balls. Put the cooking liquor in a pan, heat gently and drop the balls of beurre manié into it, one at a time. Stirring frequently, add all the balls and cook until the stock begins to thicken. Pour in the yoghurt. Pour the sauce over the fish and sprinkle with cheese. Place under a hot grill until the stew begins to bubble and brown. Serve immediately with crisp French bread and a green salad.

MACKEREL STUFFED WITH GRAPEFRUIT AND WATERCRESS

I have often read that the definitive way to serve mackerel is with gooseberry sauce. The relationship between the two seems to have been made in heaven for the French actually call the gooseberry 'groseille a maquereau'. But don't be misled into thinking that this is the only accompaniment for mackerel; most acidic foods will improve the digestibility and flavour of this oily fish. In Ireland it is cooked with rhubarb while the Scots enjoy it stuffed with orange and baked in dry cider or wine.

SERVES 4
4 mackerel
1 grapefruit, peeled
1 stick celery, finely chopped
2 tbsp fresh parsley, chopped
1 bunch of watercress, trimmed and chopped
4 tbsp soft wholewheat breadcrumbs
freshly ground black pepper

Clean the fish, leaving the heads and tails on. Rinse and pat dry. Remove the white pith from the grapefruit and cut into small pieces. Place the grapefruit in a bowl with the remaining ingredients. Mix together well.

Stuff each fish with the filling and then press back into shape. Brush the fish with olive oil. Wrap 'en papillote' in greaseproof paper, twisting the ends securely. Bake in a preheated oven, gas mark 5 (190° C/375° F) for 20–25 minutes.

WHITEBAIT

Whitebait are small fish, no more than 5 cm (2 in) long, which are cooked and eaten whole.

SERVES 4
groundnut oil for frying
450 g (1 lb) fresh whitebait
100 g (4 oz) seasoned flour

Heat 7.5–10 cm (3–4 in) of oil in a large deep pan. Roll the fish in the seasoned flour. Deep fry, a few at a time until crisp and golden – this should take 2–3 minutes. Drain on absorbent paper and serve immediately with twists of lemon and slices of fresh brown bread and butter.

HALIBUT IN COCONUT SAUCE

FOR THE MARINADE:
2 tbsp fresh lime juice
$\frac{1}{2}$ tsp dried oregano
$\frac{1}{2}$ tsp dried dill weed

REMAINING INGREDIENTS:
675 g ($1\frac{1}{2}$ lb) halibut steaks
1 tbsp groundnut oil
1 small onion, chopped
275 ml (10 fl oz) fish stock (including the liquor in which the fish has marinated)
1 bay leaf
$\frac{1}{2}$ tsp dried oregano
$\frac{1}{2}$ tsp dried dill weed
1 tbsp fresh lime juice
2 tbsp tomato purée
75 g (3 oz) creamed coconut
freshly ground black pepper

FOR THE GARNISH:
small red pepper, deseeded and thinly sliced

Put the marinade ingredients in a small bowl and mix together well. Arrange the fish in a large shallow ovenproof dish and pour over the marinade. Leave in a cool place for 8–10 hours. Keeping the fish in the dish, drain off the liquid and reserve it to use in the stock.

Heat the oil in a frying pan, add the onion and gently sauté until soft. Add the stock and marinade liquor, bay leaf, the remaining oregano, dill weed and lime juice, tomato purée, creamed coconut and some black pepper. Bring to the boil and cook gently, stirring frequently, until the creamed coconut has dissolved.

Pour the sauce over the fish and garnish with red pepper. Bake in a preheated oven, gas mark 5 (190° C/375° F) for 25–30 minutes.

MEAT

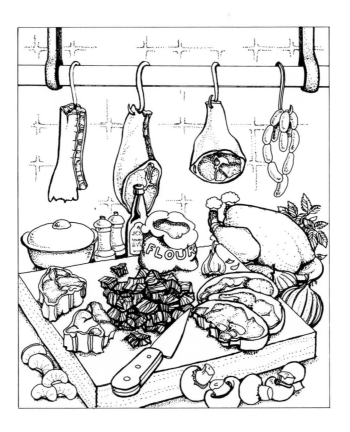

MEAT

Old friends and colleagues will be astonished to see a collection of recipes under the bold heading 'meat' for I have been a vegetarian for many years. I use the word vegetarian loosely for there has been a gradual re-introduction of animal foods into my diet. On each occasion curiosity got the better of me. After all who could refuse the offer of a beautifully-speckled quail's egg, a pot of goat's milk yoghurt or a garfish with its amazing electric blue bones. Surprisingly my first taste of meat was not so glamorous – it happened to be a piece of pork pie served with a ploughman's lunch in Wensleydale. Not an auspicious start but nonetheless I thoroughly enjoyed it and was much relieved to find that I didn't feel ill as a result of my rash behaviour.

Having taken the first tentative steps back down the road to meat eating I felt no qualms about buying a brace of wood pigeon I saw in my greengrocer's one day. Fortunately they were already plucked and drawn as I am still not sure whether I am ready to face that gruesome experience yet. Not having prepared a meat dish for over eight years I was surprised at how ill equipped I was for the task. My knives weren't strong enough, my pans were too small and I was very reluctant to use my chopping board which had previously dealt with nothing stronger in flavour than a clove of garlic. I was surprised at the time involved in preparing the dish and felt that vegetarian cooking is often unfairly criticised on this score, although I appreciate that making a pigeon pie is slightly different from an everyday meal of 'bangers and mash'.

Before friends and relations begin plying me with plates of steak and kidney pie, roast beef and Yorkshire pudding and Cumberland sausage, let me hasten to add that I still prefer vegetarian food and anticipate my appreciation of meat dishes to be the exception rather than the rule.

There are many reasons why people choose to restrict the amount of meat they consume and it must be appreciated that it never requires any great feat of will power or self discipline. Quite often it is simply a question of preference – believe it or not but many vegetarian dishes are much more interesting and appetising than meat dishes. Other issues to be taken into consideration are:

Cost A vegetarian diet is generally much cheaper than one relying on meat and fish.

Economic In 1979 two-thirds of the world's grain supplies and three-quarters of its fish stocks went to feed the animal and human population in western industrialised countries (one-quarter of the total world population). It has been said that: 'the average western man eats 1 cow, 7 bullocks, 36 pigs and 550 poultry in his life time. If instead people ate the equivalent in plant food necessary to sustain these animals it would keep five times as many people healthy and well fed.'

Humanitarian Many believe it to be morally wrong and uncivilised to take animals' lives simply to satisfy their hunger.

Additives Almost all animal products contain additives, chemicals etc. A campaign for free range meat has sprung up and there are several shops, principally in the south, displaying the red and white Organic Butchers' sign.

Health The fact that there are many instances of vegetarian and vegan peoples throughout the world who have prospered for generations proves that meat, fish and dairy products are not in themselves necessary for good health. Evidence is coming to light in support of the idea that vegetarians are in fact healthier than meat eaters and that they are protected against some of the chronic degenerative diseases.

As you can see there are many different reasons why people choose to become vegetarians. Some avoid the consumption of all animal foods while others adopt a more flexible approach. For those of you who have no wish to become fully fledged vegetarians let me first reassure you that total abstinence from animal products, in particular meat, is not an essential prerequisite for good health. However, having said that, it is widely agreed in medical circles that we, in western industrialised countries, eat far more meat and animal foods than is necessary and that a little restraint would be beneficial.

BEEF WITH MARJORAM AND YOGHURT SAUCE

2 tbsp olive oil
2 onions, chopped
1 clove garlic, peeled and crushed
675 g (1½ lb) beef steak, fillet, rump or sirloin
225 g (8 oz) smoked bacon, trimmed and chopped
2 tbsp fresh marjoram, chopped
275 ml (10 fl oz) dry white wine
2 level tbsp unbleached white flour
575 ml (1 pint) natural yoghurt
2 tbsp fresh chives, chopped

Heat the oil in large heavy pan, add the onions and garlic and sauté until golden brown. Trim the fat from the beef and cut into chunks about 1.25 cm (½ in) thick. Add the pieces of beef and bacon to the cooking pot and fry for a few minutes, stirring frequently. Add the marjoram and white wine and bring to the boil. Reduce the heat and simmer for 15–20 minutes. Mix the flour and yoghurt together and stir in a tablespoon or two of cooking juices from the pan. Then pour the yoghurt mixture into the pan and stir well. Simmer gently for 25–30 minutes until the meat is tender. Stir occasionally to prevent the sauce sticking to the pan. Sprinkle with chives before serving.

This recipe is based on a traditional Hungarian dish which I first saw in *The Yoghurt Book* by Arto der Haroutunian (Penguin Books, 1983).

BEEF AND BEAN CASSEROLE

175 g (6 oz) butter beans, soaked overnight in plenty of water
675 g (1½ lb) chuck steak
2–3 tbsp sunflower oil
1 onion, chopped
1 clove garlic, peeled and crushed
2 carrots, chopped
2 tomatoes, chopped
1 sprig of fresh thyme
1 sprig of fresh marjoram
1 sprig of fresh parsley
1 bay leaf
275 ml (10 fl oz) red wine
bean stock
freshly ground black pepper

Drain the beans and put them in a pan with 850 ml (1½ pints) of fresh water. Simmer for 2 hours until tender checking regularly that the contents of the pan are not boiling dry; or cook in a pressure cooker for 20–25 minutes. Drain and reserve the stock.

Trim the meat and cut into cubes. Heat the oil in a large pan, add the meat and brown it on all sides. Stir in the onion and garlic and sauté for 5–6 minutes more. Add the carrots, tomatoes, herbs, wine and cooked beans. Pour in sufficient bean stock to cover the ingredients. Season with black pepper. Cover and bring to the boil. Simmer gently on top of the stove for 1½–2 hours until the meat is tender.

SPICY STUFFED MARROW

100 g (4 oz) long grain brown rice
275 ml (10 fl oz) cold water
1–2 tbsp olive oil
1 onion, chopped
2.5 cm (1 in) fresh root ginger, peeled and grated
1 clove garlic, peeled and crushed
1 green chilli, finely chopped
2 tsp turmeric
2 tsp ground coriander
450 g (1 lb) minced beef
2 large tomatoes, chopped
1 tbsp tomato purée
2 tbsp fresh parsley, finely chopped
2 tsp fresh mint, finely chopped
50 g (2 oz) raisins
1½ kg (3 lb) marrow

Put the rice in a heavy pan with the water and bring to the boil. Cover and simmer gently, without stirring, for 35–40 minutes until the rice is tender and all the water has been absorbed.

Meanwhile, heat a little olive oil in a large pan, add the onion, ginger and garlic and sauté for 8–10 minutes. Stir in the chilli, turmeric and ground coriander and cook for a minute or two more, stirring constantly. Add the mince and lightly brown before mixing in the tomatoes, tomato purée, parsley, mint, raisins and cooked rice. Add 15 ml (1 tablespoon) of water if the mixture looks very dry. Season to taste and remove from the heat.

Wash the marrow and trim off the ends. Cut in half lengthways and scoop out the seeds and spongy centre. Stuff the two halves with the mixture and carefully place one on top of the other, the cut sides together. Wrap tightly in greaseproof paper and bake in a preheated oven, gas mark 6 (200° C/400° F) for 35–40 minutes until the marrow is tender.

MARINATED BEEF WITH VEGETABLES

675 g (1½ lb) braising steak, trimmed and chopped

FOR THE MARINADE:
1 tbsp olive oil
150 ml (5 fl oz) red wine
1 small onion, chopped
1 stick celery, chopped
1 bay leaf
1 sprig of fresh thyme
1 sprig of fresh parsley
6 black peppercorns

REMAINING INGREDIENTS:
wholewheat flour for dusting
olive oil
1 onion, chopped
2 sticks celery, chopped
3 carrots, chopped
1 small swede, chopped
150 ml (5 fl oz) beef stock
freshly ground black pepper
2 tsp soya sauce

Put the meat in a small deep dish and add the marinade ingredients. Cover and leave in a cool place for 3–4 hours, turning the meat occasionally. Drain and reserve the stock. Pat the meat dry and dust with flour.

Heat 1–2 tablespoons of oil in a large, heavy, casserole-type dish, add the onion and celery and sauté until they begin to soften. Remove the vegetables with a slotted spoon and set aside. Add the meat to the pan and brown it on all sides, adding more oil if necessary. Return the onion and celery to the pan with the other vegetables. Pour over the stock and the strained marinade. Cover with a tight-fitting lid and simmer gently for 45–55 minutes until the meat and vegetables are tender. Season to taste with black pepper and soya sauce.

BEEF IN BEER

675 g (1½ lb) chuck steak
2–3 tbsp sunflower oil
2 onions, chopped
1 clove garlic, peeled and crushed
1 tbsp wholewheat flour
275 ml (10 fl oz) beer (bitter)
1 bay leaf
1 sprig of fresh parsley
1 small swede, chopped
2 carrots, chopped
seasoning

Trim the meat and cut into chunks. Heat the oil in a heavy flameproof casserole, add the onions and garlic and sauté until soft and golden. Remove them with a slotted spoon and toss in the meat. Cook gently, turning frequently until it is brown on all sides. Return the onions to the pan and stir in the flour. Let it bubble for a minute or two and then gradually stir in the beer. Bring to the boil, stirring all the time until it thickens. Add the remaining ingredients. Cover and put into a preheated oven, gas mark 3 (160° C/325° F) for 1½–2 hours until the meat is tender.

BEEF STEW

675 g (1½ lb) topside of beef
2 tbsp olive oil
a pinch of ground cinnamon
a pinch of ground cloves
freshly ground black pepper
1 bay leaf
2 tbsp red wine vinegar
2 tbsp tomato purée
425 ml (15 fl oz) beef stock
225 g (8 oz) button onions
225 g (8 oz) button mushrooms

Trim the meat and cut into cubes. Heat the oil in a pan, add the meat and brown it on all sides. Stir in the spices, pepper, bay leaf, vinegar and tomato purée. Just cover with stock. Cover the pan and simmer gently for 30 minutes. Add the onions and mushrooms and continue to cook for 50–60 minutes until the meat is tender.

SPAGHETTI WITH PARMA HAM AND YOGHURT

Parma ham is one of my favourite foods. It is lightly cured and salted compared with many hams and is generally sold in wafer thin slices. Like smoked salmon, the slicing is all important for the ham is not usually cooked and if the pieces are too thick they do not melt in the mouth and instead become extremely difficult to chew and swallow. When I am preparing this dish I generally trim the slices of ham and roll each one up into a cigar shape. Each roll is then cut into thin rings which either unfurl during cooking or stay looking like mini catherine wheels.

225 g (8 oz) French beans, sliced
175 g (6 oz) Parma ham
450 g (1 lb) wholewheat spaghetti (fresh pasta if possible)
olive oil
225 g (8 oz) button mushrooms
425 ml (15 fl oz) natural yoghurt
1 tbsp unbleached white flour

Cook the beans in a small pan of boiling water for 3–4 minutes. Drain.

Trim the ham and cut into delicate strips. Put the pasta in a large pan of water to which you have added 1 tablespoon of olive oil. Boil briskly, uncovered, for 8–10 minutes and drain as soon as the spaghetti is al dente.

Meanwhile, heat 1–2 tablespoons of oil in a large frying pan, add the ham and mushrooms and sauté for 3–4 minutes. Add the parboiled beans. Mix the yoghurt and flour together before pouring into the pan. Bring to the boil, reduce the heat and cook gently until the sauce thickens. Put the cooked pasta in a serving dish and pour over the sauce. Serve immediately.

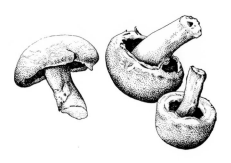

STEAK AND KIDNEY PIE

The traditional English steak and kidney pie always contained a dozen or so oysters. It must be remembered that in the nineteenth century they were very common and were probably cheaper than either the steak or kidneys. This modern recipe omits the oysters but is nonetheless delicious, though there is no reason why, should you happen to have a glut of oysters, you couldn't toss some into the filling.

FOR THE FILLING:
450 g (1 lb) stewing steak
225 g (8 oz) ox kidney
2 tbsp sunflower oil
1 onion, chopped
40 g (1½ oz) wholewheat flour
100 g (4 oz) mushrooms, halved
1 bay leaf
575 ml (1 pint) beef stock
1–2 tbsp soya sauce
seasoning

FOR THE PASTRY:
150 g (5 oz) strong wholewheat bread flour
1.25 ml (¼ tsp) cream of tartar
90 g (3 oz) butter
90–105 ml (6–7 tbsp) cold water
additional flour

Trim the meat, removing any excess fat and cut into cubes. Slice the kidneys and remove the tubes.

Heat the oil in a pan, add the onion and sauté for 5 minutes. Dust the meat with flour before adding it to the pan. Cook until it is lightly browned on all sides. Add the remaining flour and all the filling ingredients. Cover and bring to the boil. Simmer gently for 2–2½ hours until tender. Remove the bay leaf and season to taste. Leave to cool.

To make the pastry, mix the flour and cream of tartar together in a bowl. Add 20 g (¾ oz) butter and rub in with the fingertips. Add the water and, with a fork, mix to form a soft dough. Turn onto a floured board and knead lightly until smooth and pliant. Wrap in polythene and put in a cool place to rest for 30 minutes.

Meanwhile, sprinkle the remaining butter with a little additional flour, and with a rolling pin, beat out to form a neat oblong about 1.25 cm (½ in) thick. Roll the rested dough to an oblong a little larger than the butter shape, and long enough for the two ends of the dough to fold over the butter and slightly overlap. Place the butter in the centre of the dough and fold the pastry over to cover it completely. Press the edges together to seal. Give the dough a half turn to bring the open ends to the top and bottom. With the rolling pin press the dough gently, from the centre to the top and bottom, and then quickly and lightly roll out the dough to an oblong three times as long as it is wide. (Don't roll out too thinly or the layers of dough and butter will merge.) Mark the pastry into thirds but don't cut through the dough, and fold the bottom third over the centre and the top third down over both. Seal the edges and give the pastry a half turn. Repeat the rolling, folding and turning once more, then wrap in polythene and chill for 30 minutes.

After two further rolls, folds and turns the pastry must rest again. Roll, fold and turn twice more. The pastry is now ready for use. Roll out and cover the pie dish. Trim the edges and brush with milk or beaten egg, without allowing the glaze to run down the sides as this will stop the pastry rising evenly. Bake in a preheated oven, gas mark 8 (230° C/450° F) for 20–25 minutes.

BARBECUED PORK CHOPS

SERVES 4
4 pork chops
15 g ($\frac{1}{2}$ oz) butter
1 small onion, chopped
1 stick celery, chopped
1 tbsp Worcestershire sauce
1 tbsp wine vinegar
2 tsp tomato purée
$\frac{1}{2}$ tsp paprika
150 ml (5 fl oz) chicken stock or water
juice of 1 lemon

Place the chops in a casserole and cook, uncovered, for 30 minutes in a preheated oven, gas mark 6 (200° C/400° F) for 30 minutes. Strain off any fat. Melt the butter in a pan, add the onion and celery and sauté until soft. Mix all the remaining ingredients together in a bowl and pour over the chops. Add the sautéed vegetables. Cover and bake for a further 45 minutes.

LIVER WITH MUSTARD SAUCE

675 g ($1\frac{1}{2}$ lb) lamb's liver
2–3 tbsp sunflower oil

FOR THE SAUCE:
1 small onion, chopped
150 ml (5 fl oz) dry white wine
2 tbsp Dijon mustard
40 g ($1\frac{1}{2}$ oz) butter
1 tbsp lemon juice
freshly ground black pepper
2 tbsp fresh parsley, finely chopped

Heat the oil in a pan, add the liver and cook until tender. Remove with a slotted spoon and stand on absorbent paper in a warm place until needed.

Put the onion into the pan and cook until it softens. Add the wine and bring to the boil. Reduce the stock by a half. Remove from the heat. Cream the mustard and butter together and stir into the stock. Pour in the lemon juice and season with black pepper. Return to the stove and heat through gently. Place the liver in a serving dish and pour over the sauce. Sprinkle with parsley before serving.

LIVER WITH FENNEL AND CIDER

450 g (1 lb) lamb's liver, trimmed and sliced
40 g ($1\frac{1}{2}$ oz) wholewheat flour
2 tbsp sunflower oil
1 large Florence fennel bulb, trimmed and chopped
275 ml (10 fl oz) dry cider
seasoning

Dust the liver with a little of the flour. Heat the oil in a pan, add the liver and brown. Remove the liver from the pan with a slotted spoon and keep aside. Fry the fennel in the remaining oil until it begins to soften. Stir in the rest of the flour and gradually add the cider, stirring frequently. Bring to the boil and cook until the sauce begins to thicken. Return the liver to the pan and simmer until it is heated through and tender. Season to taste and serve.

KIDNEYS IN MUSHROOM SAUCE

8 lamb's kidneys
1–2 tbsp sunflower oil
100 g (4 oz) mushrooms, chopped
1 tbsp wholewheat flour
275 ml (10 fl oz) stock / water
3 tbsp red wine
1 tbsp tomato purée
2 tsp soya sauce

Remove the skins from the kidneys and cut them in half, removing any tubes. Heat the oil in a large pan, add the kidneys and brown quickly, taking care not to overcook them or they will become tough. Remove the kidneys from the pan with a slotted spoon and keep warm. Add the mushrooms and cook for 3–4 minutes before stirring in the flour. Let the flour bubble and then gradually add the stock/water and wine, stirring frequently until it begins to boil. Stir in the tomato purée and soya sauce. Simmer gently for 5 minutes. Pour over the kidneys and serve.

CHICKEN IN WINE SAUCE

$1\frac{1}{2}$ kg (3 lb) chicken
3–4 tbsp olive oil
1 onion, finely chopped
1 clove garlic, peeled and crushed
2–3 tbsp unbleached white flour
275 ml (10 fl oz) chicken stock
150 ml (5 fl oz) dry white wine
a good pinch of saffron strands
1 bay leaf
2 tbsp fresh parsley, finely chopped
1 tbsp fresh thyme, finely chopped
2 red peppers, deseeded and sliced
seasoning

Joint the chicken and use the carcass and giblets to make 275 ml (10 fl oz) of stock.

Heat the oil in a large pan, add the chicken pieces and lightly brown them on all sides. Remove from the pan with a slotted spoon, add the onion and garlic and sauté. Stir in the flour and cook until the flour begins to bubble. Gradually stir in the stock and wine and simmer until it thickens. Thin with a little more stock and wine if necessary. Add the remaining ingredients and the chicken pieces. Cover and simmer gently for 35–45 minutes until the chicken is tender. Season to taste.

CHICKEN LUBERON

SERVES 4
2 tbsp olive oil
4 chicken pieces
1 onion, chopped
1 red pepper, deseeded and chopped
4 tomatoes, chopped
225 g (8 oz) button mushrooms, halved if necessary
1 tbsp tomato purée
275 ml (10 fl oz) dry white wine
150 ml (5 fl oz) stock/water
1 sprig of fresh thyme
1 sprig of fresh parsley
1 sprig of fresh rosemary
10 black olives
freshly ground black pepper

Heat the oil in a heavy flameproof casserole, add the chicken pieces and brown them on all sides. Remove them from the pan with a slotted spoon and add the onion and red pepper. Cook gently until they begin to soften. Add the remaining ingredients and the chicken pieces and bring to the boil. Cover and place in a preheated oven, gas mark 4 (180° C/350° F) for $1\frac{1}{4}$ hours. Season to taste with black pepper. Serve.

COQ AU VIN

olive oil
$1\frac{1}{2}$ kg (3 lb) roasting chicken
100 g (4 oz) button onions
275 ml (10 fl oz) red wine
2 cloves garlic, peeled and crushed
1 sprig of fresh thyme
1 sprig of fresh parsley
1 sprig of fresh marjoram
1 bay leaf
seasoning

Heat some olive oil in a large heavy pan, add the bird and brown it on all sides. Remove the chicken, add the onions to the pan and fry until golden. Return the chicken to the pan and add the remaining ingredients. Cover the pan and simmer gently for 1 hour, or until the chicken is tender. Remove the herbs, adjust the seasoning to taste and serve.

CHICKEN HOTPOT

1½ kg (3 lb) chicken
2–3 tbsp olive oil
seasoned flour
1 onion, chopped
1 clove garlic, peeled and crushed
425 ml (15 fl oz) chicken stock approx.
150 ml (5 fl oz) dry white wine
a good pinch of saffron strands
freshly grated nutmeg
seasoning

TO GARNISH:
25 g (1 oz) fresh wholewheat breadcrumbs
olive oil
2 hard-boiled eggs, chopped
1 tbsp fresh chives, chopped

Joint the chicken. Heat the oil in a large pan. Dust the pieces with seasoned flour, add to the pan and brown them on all sides. Remove the chicken from the pan with a slotted spoon, add the onion and garlic to the pan and sauté until soft and golden. Return the chicken to the pan and barely cover with stock. Add the wine, saffron and a little nutmeg. Bring to the boil. Cover and simmer for 35–45 minutes until the chicken is tender. Season to taste. Lift the chicken from the pan, put into a serving dish and keep warm. Briskly boil the juices left in the pan until slightly reduced and pour over the chicken.

Meanwhile, heat a little olive oil in another pan, add the breadcrumbs and fry until crunchy. Sprinkle over the chicken with the chopped eggs and chives. Serve.

ROAST DUCKLING

2.2 kg (5 lb) duckling, oven-ready

FOR THE STOCK:
giblets
1 onion, chopped
1 carrot, chopped
1 stick celery, chopped
575 ml (1 pint) water
1 lemon, chopped
3 sprigs of fresh thyme
3 sprigs of fresh marjoram

REMAINING INGREDIENTS:
1 tbsp wholewheat flour
freshly ground black pepper

Put the giblets, vegetables, water, lemon and herbs in a large pan. Bring to the boil, skim the fat from the surface and simmer for 1 hour. Strain the stock.

Set the duckling on a wire rack and stand over a baking tray. Prick the skin all over with a sharp fork or skewer. Roast in a preheated oven, gas mark 7 (220° C/425° F) for 15 minutes. Reduce the oven temperature to gas mark 4 (180° C/350° F) and cook for a further 45 minutes, basting occasionally.

Remove the duckling and the wire tray and drain off the excess fat that has collected in the baking tray. Stand the duckling in the baking tray and pour over 425 ml (15 fl oz) stock. Return to the oven and cook for 40 minutes, basting every now and then. When tender place the bird on a serving dish and keep warm. Remove the stock and strain off any surplus fat. Sprinkle the flour into the bottom of the baking tray, place over a moderate heat and gradually stir in the stock. Season with black pepper. Serve with the bird.

GAME

GAME

I am a relative beginner when it comes to cooking game and make no claims to being an authority on the subject. I am not particularly skilful at or keen on hanging, skinning, plucking or gutting and whenever possible buy my game 'oven-ready'.

Game originally referred to any edible creature which had not been domesticated or reared for food. The term is used more loosely today as many game animals and birds are reared specifically for the table. Apart from its good flavour and texture, game is widely considered to be among the healthiest of meats. As a general rule when in prime condition it is best roasted, provided that it is adequately trussed, larded and basted. Older, more sinewy animals are better cooked slowly in stews and casseroles, sometimes being marinated beforehand. Although the ingredients vary from recipe to recipe a marinade usually consists of a little vinegar to break down the fibres and tenderise the meat, oil to add succulence and wine, herbs and spices to give flavour.

Venison

Venison is a rich dark meat. I am told that the modern preference is for fresh venison which has not developed the strong gamey flavour of hung meat. The saddle and haunch are the best cuts, ideal for roasting, the loins are often cut into chops and the rest of the animal is used for stewing, braising, pâtés, pies and sausages. Allow 20–25 minutes per lb when roasting and $1\frac{1}{2}$–2 hours for stewing. Cook until the juices run clear and the meat is tender. Sharp piquant flavours go particularly well with venison, and rowanberry sauce is a traditional accompaniment. Cranberries, juniper berries and Seville oranges are also good flavourings.

Mallard

Mallard (wild duck) is the most common variety of wild fowl. One plump bird will serve two to three people. The meat is leaner and drier than that of ordinary domestic duck and needs to be carefully larded and basted when being roasted. Don't worry if the uncooked bird has a blue or greenish tint to its skin, as it is not difficult to tell the difference between a high and a bad bird. The former smells distinctly gamey while the latter smells rotten.

Some mallard, especially those that have been feeding on aquatic life, may taste reminiscent of lambs' liver. Like venison, mallard needs to be served piping hot. It goes well with sharp, crisp salads.

Pigeon

All types of pigeon, from the grey wood pigeon to the turtle dove, can be eaten. They were an extremely important source of food from the Middle Ages until the early part of the twentieth century and no self-respecting farmhouse or manor was without a dovecote. Nowadays the only people to keep them on any scale are pigeon fanciers, breeding the birds for winning races rather than for the table.

Pigeons have a pleasant beefy flavour and when young are succulent and tender. Unfortunately older birds tend to be tough and stringy and can defy even the sharpest knife. It is difficult to judge the age of a pigeon and older birds do not look significantly different from their siblings; they even give off the same delicious, mouth-watering aromas while being cooked. Experts suggest studying the bird's feet before making a purchase because those of younger birds are soft, supple and free from scales. This may be sound advice but I have never had the occasion to put it to the test. At my local shops pigeons are sold trussed up like chickens and one simply has to take pot luck. Although I have never had reason for complaint I do play safe, always cooking the birds slowly in stews, pies and casseroles and sometimes marinating them beforehand in red wine.

Very young pigeons, about a month old, are sold as squabs and are considered to be a great delicacy. They are best roasted, needing only 10–15 minutes.

Rabbit

Myxomatosis has tended to keep the rabbit

population in check but rabbits are still economically priced. Presumably the price is related, to some extent, to demand for the rabbit which has never regained the popularity it had in the seventeenth and eighteenth centuries.

Rabbits do not need to be hung and are best eaten within a few days of being caught. Many of those on sale in our shops have been frozen, some coming all the way from China. Frozen rabbit meat tends to be on the dry side and is best marinated or cooked in juicy casseroles. There are many splendid traditional English recipes for rabbit including rabbit pie, rabbit and cider casserole, rabbit pâté and rabbit and mushroom pudding.

Wild rabbits are believed by some to have a better flavour than those fed on lettuce leaves and cabbages. In France, particularly in Provence and the Cevennes, rabbit meat is still held in high regard and the countryside is dotted with wild rabbit farms. The animals are allowed to run freely over the surrounding fields and their diet of young tender sprigs of rosemary and thyme is thought to give the meat a delicate and intriguing flavour.

Grouse

The finest and most coveted of all game birds. Their diet of moorland berries, heather buds and young shoots gives them an incomparable flavour. Grouse used to be hung for anything between 3 and 14 days but modern palates prefer them fresher and many birds are not hung at all. This explains why, on the afternoon of the Glorious Twelve, there is a rush to provide the top restaurants with a few birds so that they may appear on the menu that very night.

Young birds need plain cooking. Cover their breasts with slices of bacon before roasting them in a hot oven for 15–20 minutes. Some cookery books recommend serving them with a sauce made from rowanberries. Older birds should be used to make pies, pâtés or gently stewed in wine.

VENISON WITH SOUR CREAM AND MUSTARD

2 tbsp sunflower oil
675 g (1½ lb) stewing venison, trimmed and chopped
1 large onion, chopped
1 clove garlic, peeled and crushed
350 g (12 oz) button mushrooms
425 ml (15 fl oz) beer (bitter)
425 ml (15 fl oz) water
freshly ground black pepper
1 sprig of fresh thyme
1 sprig of fresh marjoram
1 sprig of fresh parsley
1 bay leaf
2 tbsp sour cream
2 tsp Dijon mustard

Heat the oil in a large pan, add the venison, onion and garlic and carefully brown. Wipe the mushrooms, add them to the pan and sauté for 2–3 minutes. Pour over the beer and water. Season liberally with black pepper and add the herbs. Cover and bring to the boil. Simmer gently for 1½–2 hours until the meat is tender. Boil briskly to reduce if necessary – the stock should thicken during cooking. Remove the herbs.

Mix the sour cream and mustard together and stir into the pan immediately before serving.

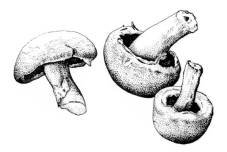

VENISON CASSEROLE

SERVES 4
450 g (1 lb) stewing venison, trimmed and chopped

FOR THE MARINADE:
2 tbsp olive oil
150 ml (5 fl oz) red wine
1 onion, chopped
1 clove garlic, peeled and crushed
1 tsp coriander seeds, lightly roasted and crushed
freshly ground black pepper
2 sprigs of fresh oregano

REMAINING INGREDIENTS:
2 tbsp olive oil
1 onion, chopped
2 sticks celery, chopped
wholewheat flour
150 ml (5 fl oz) marinade stock
2 carrots, sliced
1 sprig of fresh oregano
1 sprig of fresh parsley
1 tbsp tomato purée
freshly ground black pepper

Put the venison in a bowl and add the marinade ingredients. Cover and leave in a cool place overnight. Next day drain and reserve the stock.

Heat the olive oil in a heavy flameproof casserole, add the onion and celery and sauté until soft and golden. Dry the venison and dust with flour. Add the meat to the pan and lightly brown it on all sides. Pour over 150 ml (5 fl oz) of the marinade. Bring to the boil, stirring frequently. Add the carrots, herbs and tomato purée. Season with black pepper. Cover and cook in a preheated oven, gas mark 4 (180° C/350° F) for 1–1½ hours until tender. Serve with baked potatoes and a green salad.

VENISON WITH RED CABBAGE

675 g (1½ lb) stewing venison, trimmed and chopped

FOR THE MARINADE:
275 ml (10 fl oz) red wine
275 ml (10 fl oz) stock/water
1 carrot, chopped
1 small onion, chopped
1 bay leaf
6 juniper berries
6 black peppercorns

REMAINING INGREDIENTS:
flour for dusting
2–3 tbsp olive oil
1 onion, chopped
½ small red cabbage, shredded
1 level tsp cayenne pepper
2 level tsp paprika
50 g (2 oz) sultanas
1 tbsp red wine vinegar
freshly ground black pepper

Put the venison in a bowl and add the marinade ingredients. Cover and leave in a cool place overnight. Next day drain and reserve the stock. Dry the meat and dust with flour.

Heat the olive oil in a pan, add the onion and soften it for 10 minutes before adding the venison. Cook until the meat is lightly browned. Add the remaining ingredients and pour over the marinade. Cover and simmer gently until the meat and cabbage are tender, approximately 1½–2 hours.

WILD DUCK WITH PEPPERS

This dish is especially good served in the centre of a ring of brown rice accompanied by a watercress, lettuce and chicory salad.

2 wild duck (mallards), oven-ready

FOR THE STOCK:
1 sprig of fresh thyme
1 sprig of fresh parsley
1 bay leaf
10 black peppercorns
½ carrot, sliced
2 slices of onion
850 ml (1½ pints) water

REMAINING INGREDIENTS:
wholewheat flour for dusting
freshly ground black pepper
olive oil
2 cloves garlic, peeled and crushed
2 onions, chopped
4 tomatoes, diced
2 red peppers, deseeded and diced
575 ml (1 pint) stock
150 ml (5 fl oz) dry white wine
1 sprig of fresh parsley
1 sprig of fresh thyme
1 level tsp paprika

Cut the birds into joints and remove the meat from the bones. Trim away and discard the skin and yellow fat. Cut the meat into chunks.

To make the stock put the carcasses into a large pan with the herbs, peppercorns, vegetables and water. Bring to the boil. Skim, reduce to a simmer and gently cook for 30 minutes. Drain and reserve the stock.

Meanwhile dust the meat with a little wholewheat flour seasoned with black pepper. Heat the olive oil in a large heavy pan, add the meat a little at a time, and brown it on all sides. Lift out the meat and place it in a colander lined with absorbent paper.

Sauté the garlic and onions in the same pan until soft but without allowing them to brown. Add the tomatoes and red peppers. Cook gently until soft. Pour over the stock and wine and add the meat, herbs and paprika. Cover and simmer gently for 1½–2 hours until tender. Remove the herbs before serving.

ROAST GROUSE

SERVES 3–4
a brace of grouse, oven-ready
a knob of butter
freshly ground black pepper
olive oil

Roll the butter in black pepper and break in half. Place a piece inside each bird. Brush the birds and a roasting tin with olive oil and put the birds into a preheated oven, gas mark 7 (220° C/425° F) for 10 minutes. Brush the birds with a little more oil and reduce the oven temperature to gas mark 4 (180° C/350° F). Roast for a further 15 minutes, basting occasionally. Serve with baked onions, baked potatoes and a green vegetable or salad.

LEFTOVER GROUSE PIE

SERVES 4
175 g (6 oz) wholewheat shortcrust pastry (for method see page 35)
1–2 tbsp olive oil
1 onion, chopped
350 g (12 oz) mushrooms, chopped
225 g (8 oz) cooked grouse meat, chopped
275 ml (10 fl oz) dry white wine
275 ml (10 fl oz) stock
seasoning

Make the pastry and set aside while preparing the filling. Heat the oil in a pan, add the onion and sauté until soft and golden. Wipe the mushrooms, add them to the pan and cook for a minute or two more. Remove from the heat, mix the vegetables with the meat and place in a pie dish. Pour over the wine and stock. Season to taste.

Roll out the pastry to a circle large enough to cover the pie and about 0.75 cm ($\frac{1}{4}$ in) in thickness. Dampen the pie dish rim and cover the pie with the pastry top. Press around the edges to seal. Bake in a preheated oven, gas mark 6 (200° C/400° F) for 25–30 minutes.

CASSEROLE OF GAME WITH BUTTER BEANS

This dish was regularly served at the Garrick Club during the nineteenth century.

100 g (4 oz) butter beans, soaked overnight in plenty of water
575 ml (1 pint) water
sunflower oil
1 onion, chopped
100 g (4 oz) unsmoked (green) bacon, trimmed and chopped
1 pheasant, jointed
1 mallard, jointed
wholewheat flour for dusting
2 carrots
100 g (4 oz) flat mushrooms, chopped
2 sprigs of fresh thyme
2 sprigs of fresh parsley
2 sprigs of fresh marjoram
275 ml (10 fl oz) red wine
275 ml (10 fl oz) stock (made from the birds' carcasses)

Drain the beans and put into a pan with the measured water. Bring to the boil and simmer for 2 hours until the beans are tender. Check the pan regularly to make sure that the contents do not boil dry. Add more water if necessary. If using a pressure cooker cook for 20 minutes. Drain, reserving the stock and keep on one side until needed.

Heat 1–2 tablespoons of oil in a large heavy casserole-type pan, add the onion and bacon and sauté for 8–10 minutes. Remove with a slotted spoon. Dust the meat with flour and brown it in the pan, adding more oil if necessary. Return the onion and bacon to the pan along with the remaining ingredients. If the meat is not covered top up the pan with the bean stock. Bring to the boil and simmer for $1\frac{1}{2}$–$1\frac{3}{4}$ hours until the meat is tender. Remove the herbs and season with black pepper before serving.

SALMI OF GAME

Another popular Victorian dish. Any selection of game birds can be used.

1 pheasant
2 pigeons
olive oil
1 bay leaf
1 sprig of fresh thyme
1 sprig of fresh parsley
1 onion, chopped
1 clove garlic, peeled and crushed
2 carrots, roughly chopped
2 tomatoes, chopped
40 g (1½ oz) wholewheat flour
100 g (4 oz) button mushrooms, halved if necessary
juice of 1 orange
150 ml (5 fl oz) red wine
freshly ground black pepper

Brush the birds with olive oil and roast in a preheated oven, gas mark 6 (200° C/400° F) for 20 minutes. Leave to cool and then cut into neat joints and pieces. Keep aside. Place the carcasses in a pan with the bay leaf, thyme and parsley and just cover with water. Bring to the boil and simmer for 30–40 minutes. Strain and reserve the stock.

Heat 1–2 tablespoons of oil in a large heavy pan, add the onion and garlic and sauté for several minutes. Add the carrots and tomatoes and cook until the tomatoes are soft. Stir in the flour and gradually add 575 ml (1 pint) of the stock. Bring to the boil, stirring frequently until the sauce begins to thicken.

Here my recipe departs from those of a hundred years ago. In the past cooks were advised to strain the sauce at this point, discarding all the vegetables. I, however, prefer to leave them in.

Wipe the mushrooms and add them to the pan along with the orange juice and wine and stir well. Season with black pepper. Arrange the pieces of meat in the pan and cover with a lid. Simmer gently for 15–20 minutes until tender. Turn the meat occasionally while it is cooking, particularly if it is not all covered with stock. Remove the herbs and serve.

RABBIT AND POTATO CASSEROLE

1–2 tbsp olive oil
2 onions, chopped
1 rabbit, jointed
1 clove garlic, peeled and crushed
3 medium carrots, chopped
5 tomatoes, chopped
1 tbsp white wine vinegar
150 ml (5 fl oz) dry white wine
275 ml (10 fl oz) stock or water
freshly ground black pepper
450 g (1 lb) potatoes, scrubbed and chopped

Heat the oil in a large frying pan, add the onions and sauté until soft and golden brown. Remove them from the pan with a slotted spoon, add the rabbit joints and brown on all sides, adding more oil if necessary.

Place the nicely browned rabbit, the cooked onions, garlic, carrots, tomatoes, wine vinegar and wine in a heavy pan. Rinse the frying pan with the stock or water before pouring it over the rabbit. Season with black pepper.

Cover and bring to the boil. Simmer for 30 minutes and then add the potatoes. Continue cooking until both the rabbit and potatoes are tender. Serve with crusty bread and a green salad.

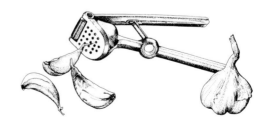

NUTS
AND BEANS

NUTS

Nuts have always been a popular addition to savoury and sweet dishes and until recently gathering nuts in the late autumn was an important part of country life. Kent is still famous for its cobnuts and my husband, who was brought up in West Sussex, remembers family outings to the woods to collect sweet chestnuts which were then taken home and roasted by an open fire.

The very best nuts are those sold in their shells in the late autumn, when they are fresh, milky and sweet tasting. Whole nuts have a better flavour and texture than shelled ones and keep reasonably well in a cool dry dark place, or in the freezer. They are, however, time-consuming to shell and are usually eaten as dessert nuts before or after a meal, traditionally with cocktails or port. It has been suggested that the Romans were the first to eat nuts with alcoholic drinks. This was due not to gastronomic considerations but to the belief that six almonds prevented drunkenness.

It makes good ergonomic sense to buy nuts for use in the kitchen already shelled, but it should be remembered that once nuts have lost their protective covering they deteriorate fairly quickly and they should be bought in small amounts as and when needed. Whole, shelled brazils do not keep as well as hazels or almonds because of their high fat content which soon becomes rancid and stale when exposed to heat, light and air. Similarly, ground, flaked and chopped nuts are best bought from a shop with a high turnover and used fairly soon after purchase.

The cuisines of many countries use nuts to good effect in traditional dishes. There are rice dishes, decorated with almonds and cashews from India, the peanut soups, sauces and stews of Central Africa and the Far East, the walnut soups of France, the rich cakes of Eastern Europe made with eggs, butter, sugar and ground hazelnuts and the widespread use of pine kernels throughout the Mediterranean. By comparison British nut recipes are rather limited, both in number and imagination. We tend to think of nuts either as flavouring and decoration for cakes and biscuits or as a snack food to be nibbled between meals. This is particularly true at Christmas when, instead of nuts being served at the end of the meal with the port as was the custom until the end of the nineteenth century, a large bowl of mixed nuts is now strategically placed next to the fruit bowl to help keep the hunger pangs at bay between meals.

Nibbling nuts is a pleasant enough pastime. However, they are concentrated storehouses of energy, being rich in unsaturated fat, protein, vitamins B and E, iron and calcium, and unfortunately also contain a large number of calories. I much prefer to use nuts in the kitchen where their distinctive flavour, texture and nutritional content can be used to the full in nut roasts and rissoles, pâtés, salads, savoury rice dishes, impressive raised pies, salads and decorative cakes and pastries.

PEANUT BURGERS

MAKES 6–8
175 g (6 oz) peanuts, coarsely ground
75 g (3 oz) soft wholewheat breadcrumbs
100 g (4 oz) carrots, grated
100 g (4 oz) celery, finely chopped
2 eggs, beaten
2 tsp mixed dried herbs
2 tsp yeast extract
2 tsp tomato purée
seasoning

FOR THE COATING:
soft wholewheat breadcrumbs or wheatgerm

Mix all the ingredients together in a bowl and adjust the seasoning to taste. Leave the mixture to stand for 30 minutes in a cool place to firm up. Shape into burgers about 2 cm ($\frac{3}{4}$ in) thick and coat in either breadcrumbs or wheatgerm. Fry in shallow oil or place on a greased baking tray and bake in a preheated oven, gas mark 6 (200° C/400° F) for 15 minutes on both sides.

CASHEW NUT RISOTTO

2 tbsp olive oil
1 onion, chopped
1 clove garlic, peeled and crushed
1 green pepper, deseeded and sliced
100 g (4 oz) button mushrooms, halved if necessary
5 tomatoes, chopped
225 g (8 oz) long grain brown rice, cooked
75 g (3 oz) cashew nuts, lightly roasted and chopped
freshly ground black pepper
2 tbsp Parmesan cheese, grated

Heat the oil in a large frying pan, add the onion and garlic and sauté until soft. Add the pepper and cook for 5 minutes more. Wipe the mushrooms and stir into the pan along with the tomatoes and rice and heat through. Add the cashews and season to taste with black pepper. Sprinkle with Parmesan before serving.

BEETROOT SALAD WITH ORANGES AND CASHEWS

225 g (8 oz) grated raw beetroot
2 oranges, peeled and sliced
juice of $\frac{1}{2}$ orange
50 g (2 oz) roasted cashew nuts

Put the beetroot in a mixing bowl. Stir in the slices of orange and the juice. Leave to stand for 1 hour or so. Drain well and put into a serving dish. Sprinkle with cashews.

COURGETTE AND WALNUT SOUP

An excellent way of using up a surfeit of courgettes from the garden.

675 g (1$\frac{1}{2}$ lb) yellow courgettes, chopped (you could use green ones)
1 onion, chopped
1 litre (1$\frac{3}{4}$ pints) water
75 g (3 oz) walnuts
1 tbsp pine kernels
freshly ground black pepper
150 ml (5 fl oz) natural yoghurt

Put the courgettes and onion in a large pan and pour over half the water. Bring to the boil and simmer until the courgettes are tender. Add the nuts and purée the mixture in a food processor or blender until fairly smooth. Stir in the remaining water until the consistency is slightly thicker than that of single cream. Season with black pepper. Return to the pan and reheat. Ladle into a soup bowl and swirl some yoghurt into each. Serve.

SUPER MUESLI

A slightly extravagant breakfast food but well worth the expense for the occasional treat.

4 tbsp porridge oats
4 tbsp jumbo oats
4 tbsp water
juice of 4 oranges
4 apples, grated
7–8 tbsp ground almonds

Mix the porridge and jumbo oats together in a bowl and pour over the water. Leave to soak overnight. Stir in the remaining ingredients and serve.

SAVOURY NUT LOAF

175 g (6 oz) mixed ground nuts
75 g (3 oz) soft wholewheat breadcrumbs
1 small onion, finely chopped
1 carrot, finely grated
2 large eggs, beaten
1 level tbsp fresh rosemary, finely chopped
1 level tbsp fresh sage, finely chopped
1 tbsp tomato purée
1–2 tsp yeast extract
seasoning

FOR THE TOPPING:
1 tomato, sliced
15 g ($\frac{1}{2}$ oz) butter

Mix all the ingredients together in a bowl and adjust the seasoning to taste. Line a 450 g (1 lb) loaf tin with oiled greaseproof paper and spoon in the mixture. Press down lightly. Arrange the tomato slices on the top and dot with butter. Bake in a preheated oven, gas mark 6 (200° C/ 400° F) for 30–35 minutes. Leave to cool in the tin for 5 minutes before turning out. Serve hot or cold.

VEGETABLES WITH SPICY PEANUT SAUCE

The sauce is very easy to make and delicious especially served with vegetables or rissoles.

1 tbsp groundnut oil
1 onion, sliced
1 yellow pepper, deseeded and sliced
1 small cauliflower, cut into pieces and lightly steamed
225 g (8 oz) shelled peas

FOR THE SAUCE:
15 g ($\frac{1}{2}$ oz) creamed coconut
225 ml (8 fl oz) water
50 g (2 oz) peanuts
$\frac{1}{2}$ tsp ground cumin
$\frac{1}{2}$ tsp turmeric
$\frac{1}{2}$ tsp garam masala
$\frac{1}{2}$ tsp ground coriander
1 tbsp lemon juice

Heat the oil in a pan, add the onion and pepper and soften. Stir in the cauliflower and peas and cook until all the vegetables are tender. Remove from the heat and keep warm.

Meanwhile, put the creamed coconut in a small pan with the water. Simmer until the coconut has dissolved. Put the coconut and all the remaining sauce ingredients into a blender and mix until smooth and creamy. Return to the pan and heat through. Pour over the vegetables and serve.

NUT PÂTÉ

50 g (2 oz) walnuts, ground
50 g (2 oz) roasted hazelnuts, ground
75 g (3 oz) low fat cream cheese
1 tbsp natural yoghurt
1–1$\frac{1}{2}$ tbsp dry white wine
1 level tsp ground cumin
seasoning

Mix all the ingredients together in a bowl. Adjust the seasoning to taste. Leave in a cool place to firm up. Serve.

VEGETABLE RAGOÛT WITH WALNUTS

2 tbsp olive oil
1 large onion, chopped
1 clove garlic, peeled and crushed
225 g (8 oz) leeks, sliced
2 courgettes, sliced
$\frac{1}{4}$ cauliflower, broken into florets
225 g (8 oz) tomatoes, chopped
$\frac{1}{2}$ tsp dried basil
$\frac{1}{2}$ tsp dried oregano
150 ml (5 fl oz) vegetable stock or water
seasoning
100 g (4 oz) walnuts

Heat the oil in a large heavy pan, add the onion and garlic and sauté for 8–10 minutes. Add the remaining vegetables and stir-fry for several minutes more. Mix in the herbs and pour over the stock or water. Bring to the boil, cover with a lid and cook gently for 8–10 minutes until the vegetables are tender. Towards the end of the cooking time remove the lid and boil briskly to reduce the cooking stock if necessary. The mixture should be moist rather than wet. Season to taste and stir in the walnuts before serving.

HAZELNUT RISSOLES

MAKES 5–6
1 onion, finely chopped
2 carrots, finely grated
1 green pepper, deseeded and finely chopped
75 g (3 oz) roasted hazelnuts, coarsely ground
4–5 tbsp soft wholewheat breadcrumbs
1 tsp mixed dried herbs
1 tsp soya sauce
1 tbsp natural yoghurt
1 tbsp tomato purée
1 large egg
freshly ground black pepper

FOR THE COATING:
soft wholewheat breadcrumbs
1 egg, beaten

Mix all the ingredients together in a bowl and adjust the seasoning to taste. Turn the mixture onto a clean working surface and, using your hands, roll into sausage-shape rissoles about 2 cm ($\frac{3}{4}$ in) thick. Brush with beaten egg and roll in the breadcrumbs. Place on an oiled baking tray and bake in a preheated oven, gas mark 5 (190° C/375° F) for 25 minutes.

BRAZIL NUT ROAST

Brazil nuts make wonderfully rich nut roasts and this one is no exception.

75 g (3 oz) millet
1 large cooking apple
175 g (6 oz) carrots
2 tbsp tahini
100 g (4 oz) brazil nuts, ground
1–2 tsp dried basil
1 tbsp mugi miso
1 tbsp water
1 egg, beaten
freshly ground black pepper

FOR THE GARNISH:
1 tomato, sliced
a knob of butter

Put the millet into an old pan and heat fiercely, shaking the pan frequently until the grains begin to smell deliciously nutty and turn slightly darker in colour. Remove from the pan and leave to cool for several minutes. Then return to the pan and pour over 275 ml (10 fl oz) water and bring to the boil. Cover and simmer for 10–15 minutes until all the water has been absorbed and the grain is soft and fluffy.

Wash, core and quarter the apple and trim the carrots. Grate both into a bowl. Add the tahini, ground nuts and basil. Mix the miso with the water before stirring into the other ingredients. Mix in the cooked millet and egg and season with black pepper. When well mixed spoon into a lined 900 g (2 lb) loaf tin. Press down lightly with the fingertips. Arrange the tomato slices on top and dot with butter.

Bake in a preheated oven, gas mark 5 (190° C/375° F) for 40 minutes. Leave in the tin for 5 minutes before turning out. Serve hot or cold.

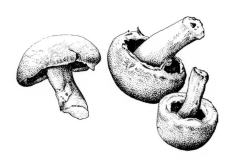

NUT ROAST EN CROÛTE

A more sophisticated version of a nut roast. I usually bake it in a rectangular tin with fold-down sides. This makes serving so much easier. You could use a loaf tin but do be careful how you take the pie out.

275 g (10 oz) wholewheat shortcrust pastry (for method, see page 12)
1 tbsp olive oil
1 small onion, finely chopped
1 large tomato, finely chopped
50 g (2 oz) mushrooms, finely chopped
1 level tbsp wholewheat flour
125 ml (4 fl oz) water
1–2 tsp soya sauce
1 tsp dried mixed herbs
50 g (2 oz) ground almonds
50 g (2 oz) ground brazil nuts
100 g (4 oz) soft wholewheat breadcrumbs
1 egg, beaten
freshly ground black pepper

FOR THE GLAZING:
1 egg, beaten

Make the pastry and set aside while you prepare the filling. Heat the oil in a pan, add the onion and sauté for 10 minutes. Add the tomato and mushrooms and cook for a further 3–4 minutes. Stir in the flour, water, soya sauce and mixed herbs. Bring to the boil and bubble for 2–3 minutes until the mixture begins to thicken. Add the remaining ingredients and adjust the seasoning to taste. Leave to cool.

Oil well a 450 g (1 lb) loaf tin. Divide the pastry in two, making one piece larger than the other. Roll out the larger piece, line the loaf tin and spoon in the filling. Roll out the remaining pastry to an oblong large enough to cover. Dampen the pastry rim and cover with the pastry top. Press the edges together to seal and brush with beaten egg. Bake for 25–30 minutes in a preheated oven, gas mark 6 (200° C/400° F).

Leave to cool in the tin for 5–10 minutes before turning out and serving.

COURGETTES IN WINE SAUCE WITH ALMONDS

FOR THE SAUCE:
25 g (1 oz) butter
25 g (1 oz) unbleached white flour
125 ml (4 fl oz) dry white wine
175 ml (6 fl oz) milk
seasoning

REMAINING INGREDIENTS:
3 courgettes
15 g ($\frac{1}{2}$ oz) ground almonds
15 g ($\frac{1}{2}$ oz) flaked almonds

Melt the butter in a pan and stir in the flour. Cook until the mixture begins to bubble. Remove from the heat and gradually add the wine and milk, stirring well after each addition. Return to the heat and cook, stirring all the time, until the sauce thickens. Season to taste. Keep to one side until needed.

Trim and slice the courgettes and steam for 3–4 minutes until barely tender. Place in the bottom of an au gratin dish and pour over the sauce. Sprinkle the top first with the ground almonds and then with the flaked almonds.

Put under a hot grill or in a hot oven until the nuts begin to brown and the sauce is hot and bubbling.

SICILIAN COURGETTES

1–2 tbsp olive oil
900 g (2 lb) courgettes, sliced
1 clove garlic, peeled and crushed
2 tbsp wine vinegar
2 tbsp water
50 g (2 oz) pine kernels
50 g (2 oz) sultanas
1 tbsp fresh basil, finely chopped

Heat the olive oil in a large heavy pan, add the courgettes and sauté until they begin to brown. Add the garlic and fry for a few minutes more. Pour over the wine vinegar and water and add the pine kernels and sultanas. Cover and simmer gently until the courgettes are tender. Sprinkle the basil over the top before serving.

CHESTNUTS

Chestnuts are available in greengrocers from the middle of October through to January. When buying them check the nuts carefully to ensure that they are of the highest quality. Really fresh wholesome nuts should feel firm and solid when pressed between the finger and thumb. Those that give slightly under pressure may be rotten and are best avoided. I look for large-sized nuts, for though they may be a penny or two dearer they are generally of a better quality and are quicker to peel than the smaller ones.

There are several methods of peeling chestnuts – they can be roasted beside an open fire, baked in the oven or cooked in boiling water. I use the last method. First make a cross with a sharp knife in the outer skin of each nut. Put them in a pan of cold water and bring to the boil. Simmer gently for 20 minutes and then immerse in cold water. Take them out of the water one at a time and carefully remove both the outer and inner shells. If the inner skins are particularly stubborn try frying the shelled chestnuts in a little butter or oil. The inner skin soon becomes crisp and can be rubbed off with a cloth. On some occasions, notably when the chestnuts are to be cooked in a casserole-type dish, I reduce the cooking time to 5–10 minutes, taking the chestnuts from the pan as soon as the cross has opened.

If the preparation sounds arduous and is putting you off let me end on a note of encouragement – the effort is always worth while for chestnuts are one of the most delicious of foods. In an effort to make life easier I have experimented with the dried, shelled chestnuts which can be bought throughout the year. Unfortunately the poor flavour and texture of this type of nut did not make up for the time and effort saved in its preparation.

CHESTNUT AND VEGETABLE AU GRATIN

A delicious vegetarian dish which has a much wider appeal. Sufficient as a main course for 3 people.

450 g (1 lb) chestnuts

FOR THE SAUCE:
575 ml (1 pint) milk
3 slices of onion
3 slices of carrot
10 black peppercorns
1 bay leaf
40 g (1½ oz) butter
a scant 40 g (1½ oz) unbleached white flour
1 level tsp Dijon mustard
50 g (2 oz) Cheddar cheese (optional)

REMAINING INGREDIENTS:
2 leeks
225 g (8 oz) Brussels sprouts
1 tbsp sunflower oil
100 g (4 oz) button mushrooms, halved if necessary
freshly grated nutmeg
350 g (12 oz) buckwheat spaghetti

Cook and peel the chestnuts as described on page 60. Chop in half and keep aside until needed.

To make the sauce put the milk, onion, carrot, peppercorns and bay leaf in a pan and bring to the boil. Remove from the heat and leave to infuse for 20–30 minutes. Strain and reserve the flavoured milk.

Meanwhile, wash, trim and slice the leeks and Brussels sprouts. Steam until tender. Heat the sunflower oil in a pan and sauté the mushrooms for 4–5 minutes stirring frequently. Add the other vegetables and the chestnuts. Season liberally with nutmeg. Keep warm.

Bring a large pan of water to the boil and add 1 tablespoon of olive oil and the pasta. Boil briskly, uncovered, for 10–12 minutes and drain as soon as it is al dente.

Melt the butter in a saucepan and stir in the flour. Cook gently over a low heat until the mixture begins to bubble. Remove from the heat and gradually add the flavoured milk, stirring well after each addition. Return to the stove and bring to the boil, stirring constantly, until the sauce thickens. Mix in the mustard and grated cheese.

Place the cooked and drained spaghetti in the bottom of an ovenproof dish. Next add the vegetables and chestnuts and finally pour over the sauce. Either serve straightaway or place in a hot oven for 15 minutes to heat through.

CHESTNUT SOUP

450 g (1 lb) chestnuts
2 tbsp olive oil
1 stick celery, chopped
1 carrot, chopped
1 clove garlic, peeled and crushed
1 onion, chopped
425 ml (15 fl oz) water
425 ml (15 fl oz) milk
seasoning
2 tbsp fresh lemon thyme, finely chopped

Cook and peel the chestnuts as described on page 60. Chop coarsely.

Heat the oil in a large pan, add the vegetables and sauté for 8–10 minutes. Add the water and cook gently until soft. Then add the milk and chopped chestnuts. Using a blender or food processor, process until smooth and creamy. Heat through and season to taste. Ladle into serving bowls and sprinkle with thyme. Serve with crusty bread.

CHESTNUTS WITH RICE

450 g (1 lb) chestnuts
1 tbsp sunflower oil
1 small onion, chopped
225 g (8 oz) long grain brown rice
a scant 575 ml (1 pint) milk
seasoning

Cut a cross in the outer skin of the chestnuts, put them in a pan of cold water and bring to the boil. Simmer until the crosses open. Test to see if the outer and inner skins will come away easily, if not cook for a little longer. The chestnuts themselves need not be soft. Cut the peeled chestnuts in half. Set aside until needed.

Heat the oil in a large heavy pan, add the onion and sauté until soft and golden. Stir in the rice and cook for a minute or two more. Add the chestnuts and pour over the milk. Cover and bring to the boil. Simmer for 35–40 minutes, without stirring, until the rice is tender and all the milk has been absorbed. Season to taste and serve.

CHESTNUTS WITH SPROUTS

Very much a traditional dish and one that I particularly enjoy making at Christmas.

900 g (2 lb) chestnuts
2–3 tbsp sunflower oil
450 g (1 lb) mild onions, chopped
2 sticks celery, chopped
575 ml (1 pint) stock
675 g (1½ lb) Brussels sprouts, trimmed
freshly ground black pepper
lemon juice to taste

Prepare the chestnuts as in the recipe for Chestnuts with Rice on page 61. Set aside until needed.

Heat the oil in a pan, add the onions and celery and sauté until soft. Add the chestnuts and stock. Cook over a low heat until almost all the liquid has been absorbed. Add the sprouts and cover with a tight-fitting lid. Continue to cook until the sprouts are tender and all the liquid has been absorbed by the chestnuts. Season to taste with black pepper and lemon juice.

CHESTNUT STROGANOFF

A richly coloured and flavoured dish ideal for serving in the winter with game.

4 large prunes
150 ml (5 fl oz) red wine
350 g (12 oz) chestnuts
2 tbsp olive oil
1 large onion, chopped
350 g (12 oz) red cabbage, shredded
1 cooking apple, cored and sliced
1 tbsp lemon juice
a pinch of cayenne pepper
a pinch of chilli powder
a pinch of paprika
seasoning

Put the prunes in a bowl, pour over the wine and leave to soak overnight. Drain and reserve the juice. Stone and chop the prunes. Prepare the chestnuts as in the recipe for Chestnuts with Rice on page 61.

Heat the oil in a large pan, add the onion and sauté until soft and golden. Add the remaining ingredients, including the chopped prunes, juice, and the prepared chestnuts. Transfer to a flameproof casserole and cover. Simmer on top of the stove for 45–50 minutes. Season to taste. Serve with sour cream.

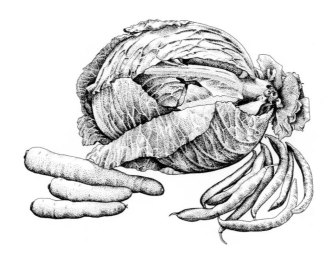

BEANS

'Pulses' is the collective name for the wide range of dried beans and lentils that play an important role in many types of cooking. Throughout man's history pulses have been used as a staple food and almost every country has a traditional bean dish. The Indians have dhal, the Americans Boston baked beans, the French cassoulet, the Egyptians ful medames and the Mexicans frijoles refritos. Here in Britain the word bean has become synonymous with the 'Heinz' variety although more and more shops are beginning to stock dried pulses and there can be few kitchens without jars of beans brightening up the shelves. The reason for this renewed enthusiasm include economic considerations (pulses are generally between 40 and 60 pence per pound and bearing in mind that they double and even triple in weight when reconstituted they are an extremely cheap protein food), the trend towards natural healthy foods and the growing number of cooks who are prepared to be adventurous.

Beans are good sources of vitamins A and B, protein and essential minerals such as iron, potassium and calcium. They contain very little saturated fat and can be used to supplement or augment meat dishes, providing a good supply of protein without any intake of animal fats which are thought to be a principal factor in the incidence of coronary heart disease. However, only the soya bean contains all the amino acids that make up a complete protein needed in a balanced diet. The other pulses should be eaten with whole grain products, such as brown rice, wholewheat bread and wholewheat pasta, with nuts and seeds or with dairy products to ensure that the body's needs are fully met.

There are many types of pulse, each with its own distinctive colour, shape and flavour; for example the shiny red kidney bean, the creamy butter bean, the wrinkled chick pea, the delicate flageolet bean, the marrowfat pea and many types of lentil. My own favourites are butter beans and chick peas. Chick peas have a distinctive, fairly robust flavour that is not to everyone's liking, but nonetheless they are becoming increasingly popular, particularly with those who holiday abroad. The chick pea or garbanzo is eaten widely in Spain, Greece and North Africa. The brown lentil is probably the most versatile pulse as it can be used to replace or extend meat in many recipes. I use it successfully in moussaka, bolognese sauce, shepherd's pie and pâtés.

In my experience many people are now aware that pulses are highly nutritious and extremely cheap but have great difficulty using them in attractive and appetising ways. An attempt to plan a meal round a plateful of boiled beans would tax the imagination of even the greatest cook. However, beans are seldom cooked and served on their own. Vegetables and seasonings play a very important role and can turn even a simple dish of beans into a meal fit for a king.

It is generally thought that beans need lengthy soaking and cooking but the lentils, split peas and the delicious blackeye bean need no soaking and cook fairly quickly, particularly in a pressure cooker. Pressure cooking is the best method of cooking all beans; it reduces both soaking and cooking times, saves fuel and gives the cook greater flexibility in selecting and making appetising dishes in the minimum of time.

Basic Preparation of Pulses
1. Pulses will more or less double in weight when soaked and cooked. Approximately 225 g (8 oz) dry weight of beans will be sufficient for 4–6 people in a main dish.
2. Always wash the beans and remove any stones that may remain from harvesting. This is particularly important when preparing lentils.
3. The flatulence problem often associated with eating beans is caused by sugars called oligosaccharides which need to be broken down into a more digestible form before they can be properly assimilated by the body. Soaking the harder beans not only reduces the cooking time but also removes a proportion of

these gaseous substances. Cooking to the point of tenderness ensures complete digestibility.

4. Do not add baking powder during cooking as it destroys the valuable B vitamins.

5. Pulses should not be seasoned with salt or salty products until they are tender. The osmotic effect of the brine prevents the proper absorption of the water, considerably lengthening the cooking time and making the skins hard and tough.

ADUKI BEAN LASAGNE

Aduki beans are grown throughout the Far East and are very popular in China and Japan where they are known as the 'King of the Beans'. They are small, round, reddish-brown beans with a light, nutty flavour and can be used in sweet and savoury dishes. To cook aduki beans soak overnight in plenty of cold water. If using a pressure cooker soak for a minimum of 6 hours. Drain and put into a pan with 575 ml (1 pint) water to every 225 g (8 oz) dried beans. Simmer until tender adding more water if necessary. Drain. They will cook in 1 hour if simmered in a pan and in 12–15 minutes in a pressure cooker.

FOR THE FILLING:
225 g (8 oz) aduki beans
1–2 tbsp olive oil
1 onion, chopped
1 green pepper, deseeded and chopped
2 cloves garlic, peeled and crushed
4 tomatoes, chopped
2 tbsp tomato purée
1 level tsp dried basil
1 level tsp dried oregano
freshly ground black pepper

FOR THE SAUCE:
1 bay leaf
1 slice of onion
3 slices of carrot
850 ml (1½ pints) milk
6 black peppercorns
4–5 tbsp olive oil
50 g (2 oz) unbleached white flour

REMAINING INGREDIENTS:
225 g (8 oz) wholewheat lasagne, cooked
175 g (6 oz) Mozzarella cheese, sliced

Prepare the beans as described above, reserving the stock in which the beans were cooked. Heat the olive oil in a large pan, add the onion, pepper and garlic and sauté until soft. Add the tomatoes and cook until they too soften. Stir in the cooked beans, tomato purée and herbs and season to taste. Moisten with a little bean stock or water if the mixture is too dry.

To make the sauce put the bay leaf, onion, carrot, milk and peppercorns in a pan and bring to the boil. Remove from the heat and leave to infuse for 15–20 minutes. Strain. Heat the oil in a small pan and stir in the flour. Cook until the mixture begins to bubble. Remove from the heat and stir in the milk, a little at a time. Return to the stove and bring to the boil, stirring frequently until the sauce thickens.

Put a layer of the bean mixture in a large shallow ovenproof dish and cover with some of the sauce. Arrange a few slices of cheese over the top, followed by a layer of lasagne. Repeat the layers finishing up with a layer of cheese on top. Bake in a preheated oven, gas mark 6 (200° C/400° F) for 25 minutes.

CREAM OF LENTIL SOUP

225 g (8 oz) red lentils
2 tbsp soya oil
2 sticks celery, chopped
2 large carrots, chopped
2 onions, chopped
1 clove garlic, peeled and chopped
1.1 litres (2 pints) water
1 tbsp soya sauce
freshly ground black pepper

Wash the lentils and carefully remove any stones or pieces of grit. Put them into a large pan. Heat the soya oil in another pan, add the celery, carrots, onions and garlic and sauté until soft. Remove them with a slotted spoon and add to the lentils. Pour over the water and bring to the boil. Cover and simmer for 45–50 minutes until the lentils are very soft. If using a pressure cooker cook at high pressure for 10 minutes. Purée the soup by passing it through a vegetable mouli or process it briefly in a food processor or blender until smooth. Return to the pan, and adjust the consistency if necessary by adding more water. Season with soya sauce and black pepper. Heat through and serve.

BEAN PÂTÉ

225 g (8 oz) blackeye beans
1–2 tbsp tahini
1–2 tbsp lemon juice
1 clove garlic, peeled and crushed
1 tsp ground cumin
1 tbsp fresh mint, finely chopped
seasoning

Place the beans in a pan with 575 ml (1 pint) water and bring to the boil. Cover and simmer for 45–55 minutes until tender, adding more water if necessary. If using a pressure cooker cook for 10–12 minutes. Drain and discard the stock.

Rub the beans through a sieve or vegetable mouli and then mix with the remaining ingredients. Adjust the seasoning to taste. Leave in a cool place to firm up.

BLACK BEAN AND MUSHROOM QUICHE

Black beans are used extensively in South American and Caribbean cooking. They are shiny, black and kidney shaped and taste faintly of mushrooms. They are also known by the names 'turtle soup bean', 'Mexican Blacks' and 'frijoles negros'.

FOR THE PASTRY:

225 g (8 oz) wholewheat flour
75 g (3 oz) butter, diced
2 tbsp sunflower oil
1 egg yolk
50 g (2 oz) Cheddar cheese, grated
a little cold water

FOR THE FILLING:

100 g (4 oz) black beans, soaked overnight in plenty of water and then drained
275 ml (10 fl oz) water
1 tbsp sunflower oil
1 stick celery, chopped into small pieces
100 g (4 oz) button mushrooms, sliced
3 eggs
200 ml (7 fl oz) milk
1 tbsp fresh parsley, finely chopped
a good pinch of paprika

To make the pastry put the flour in a bowl and rub in the butter and oil until the mixture resembles breadcrumbs. Add the egg yolk and cheese and mix together with the fingertips. Pour in a tablespoon or two of water and knead to form a pastry dough. Turn onto a lightly floured board, roll out and line a 25 cm (10 in) flan ring. Prick the pastry base with a fork and blind bake in a preheated oven, gas mark 6 (200° C/400° F) for 10 minutes.

Put the beans in a pan with the measured water. Bring to the boil and simmer for $1\frac{1}{4}$–$1\frac{1}{2}$ hours until tender. Add more water if necessary. Cook in a pressure cooker for 15–20 minutes. Drain as soon as they are soft.

Heat the oil in a frying pan, add the celery and sauté for 5 minutes. Add the mushrooms and cook for a further 2–3 minutes. Stir in the cooked beans and spoon into the pastry case. Beat the eggs and milk together and stir in the parsley and paprika. Pour over the beans and vegetables. Return to the oven and bake for a further 25 minutes until firm to the touch.

RED KIDNEY BEAN CASSEROLE

Red kidney beans are perhaps the most popular and widely used bean. Rich in flavour and colour they feature in all types of cuisine. The most famous dish is the South American chilli con carne. If cooking them in a slow cooker remember to boil briskly for 10 minutes before putting them into the crock.

1–2 tbsp sunflower oil
1 onion, chopped
3 sticks celery, chopped
3 carrots, chopped
$\frac{1}{2}$ small swede, chopped
3 tomatoes, chopped
100 g (4 oz) flat mushrooms, chopped
1–2 tbsp fresh sage, finely chopped
175 g (6 oz) red kidney beans, cooked
275–425 ml (10–15 fl oz) bean stock
1 tbsp soya sauce
freshly ground black pepper

To cook the beans soak them overnight in plenty of water (if using a pressure cooker soak for a minimum of 6 hours). Drain and put into a pan with 850 ml ($1\frac{1}{2}$ pints) of fresh water. Cover, bring to the boil and simmer for $1\frac{1}{2}$ hours until tender. Make sure that the pan does not boil dry. If using a pressure cooker, cook for 20 minutes. Drain again and reserve the bean stock.

Heat the oil in a pan, add the onion and celery and sauté for 10 minutes until they begin to soften. Stir in the remaining vegetables and cook for 4–5 minutes more. Add the sage and cooked beans. Pour over the stock and top up with water if necessary. The stock should cover three-quarters of the vegetable and bean mixture. Cover and simmer gently for 35–40 minutes until the vegetables are tender.

BLACKEYE BEANS WITH CORN TOPPING

As their name suggests these beans are creamy-white in colour and have a black mark at the sprouting point. This easily recognisable marking has resulted in them being known as 'blackeyed suzies'. Like members of the lentil and split pea families, blackeye beans require no preliminary soaking. They will cook, straight from the packet, in 45–55 minutes if simmered and in 10–12 minutes in a pressure cooker. Unlike the lenticular lentil and split pea, 'blackeyed suzies' are definitely bean shaped and do not disintegrate to a purée during cooking.

FOR THE FILLING:
100 g (4 oz) blackeye beans, cooked (reserve the cooking stock)
1–2 tbsp olive oil
1 onion, chopped
1 clove garlic, peeled and crushed
100 g (4 oz) flat mushrooms, chopped
100 g (4 oz) sweetcorn
2–3 tsp soya sauce
1 tbsp fresh thyme, finely chopped
freshly ground black pepper

FOR THE TOPPING:
100 g (4 oz) maize meal
150 ml (5 fl oz) natural thick set yoghurt
2 medium eggs
25 g (1 oz) butter, melted
150 ml (5 fl oz) milk

To cook the blackeye beans place in a pan with 275 ml (10 fl oz) water and bring to the boil. Cover and simmer for 45–55 minutes until tender, adding more water if necessary. If using a pressure cooker cook for 10–12 minutes. Drain and reserve the stock.

Heat the oil in a pan, add the onion and garlic and sauté until soft. Stir in the mushrooms and cook for a further 4–5 minutes. Add the remaining filling ingredients and season to taste with black pepper. The mixture should be moist, add a tablespoon or two of stock if it looks too dry. Leave to cool.

To make the topping place all the ingredients in a liquidiser and blend until smooth. Spoon the filling into a large ovenproof dish or 4 individual ones. Pour over the topping and bake in a preheated oven, gas mark 8 (230° C/ 450° F) for 25–30 minutes. The corn topping will become golden brown and will come away from the sides of the dish.

BLACKEYE BEANS EN COCOTTE

Serve with a selection of hors d'oeuvres or salad dishes.

100 g (4 oz) blackeye beans
25 g (1 oz) butter
100 g (4 oz) flat mushrooms, finely chopped
1 small green pepper, deseeded and finely chopped (*optional*)
1 tsp fresh sage, finely chopped
1 tsp fresh rosemary, finely chopped
3 tbsp dry white wine
1–2 tsp tomato purée
$\frac{1}{2}$ tsp Dijon mustard
$\frac{1}{2}$ tsp soya sauce
freshly ground black pepper
2 small eggs, beaten

To cook the blackeye beans place in a pan with 275 ml (10 fl oz) water and bring to the boil. Cover and simmer for 45–55 minutes until tender, adding more water if necessary. If using a pressure cooker cook for 10–12 minutes. Drain and discard the stock.

Melt the butter in a pan, add the mushrooms and pepper and sauté for 4–5 minutes. Add the cooked beans and the herbs. Remove from the heat. Mix the wine, tomato purée, mustard and soya sauce together and stir into the vegetables and beans. Season with black pepper. Mix in the beaten eggs. Pour the mixture into two buttered ramekin dishes and stand in a dish of warm water. Cover with greaseproof paper and bake in a preheated oven, gas mark 4 (180° C/350° F) for 20–25 minutes until firm. Serve cold.

HARICOT BEANS À LA PROVENÇALE

Haricot beans are probably the best known of all the beans, popularised by H. J. Heinz. In their natural state they are white, oval-shaped beans and feature in the national cuisine of Middle Eastern countries, Italy, France and Greece.

50 g (2 oz) haricot beans
1–2 tbsp olive oil
1 onion, chopped
100 g (4 oz) unsmoked (green) bacon, chopped
225 g (8 oz) carrots, roughly chopped
225 g (8 oz) small new potatoes, scrubbed
1 sprig of fresh mint
1 sprig of fresh parsley
1 tsp Dijon mustard
225 g (8 oz) French beans, sliced
freshly ground black pepper

Soak the beans overnight in cold water, if using a pressure cooker soak for a minimum of 6 hours. Drain and put into a pan or pressure cooker with 575 ml (1 pint) of fresh water. Cook until tender. If simmered they will take about 1 hour but they will cook in 12–15 minutes in a pressure cooker. Drain again and reserve the stock.

Meanwhile, heat the olive oil in a large heavy pan, add the onion and bacon and sauté for 8–10 minutes. Add the carrots, potatoes, mint, parsley, mustard and cooked haricot beans. Barely cover with the bean stock and bring to the boil. Simmer for 10 minutes and then add the French beans. Cook until all the vegetables are tender. Season with black pepper. Remove the herbs before serving.

BUTTER BEAN AND MISO CRUMBLE

The butter bean is one of my favourites, particularly the small baby butter bean. It has the same taste, smooth texture and creamy-white colour as its bigger brother but cooks in half the time. Soak both types of bean in plenty of water overnight or if using a pressure cooker for a minimum of 6 hours. Drain and put into a pan with 575 ml (1 pint) of fresh water to every 225 g (8 oz) dried beans. Cover, bring to the boil and cook until tender. The larger beans will take approximately 2 hours (20 minutes in a pressure cooker) and the smaller ones $1-1\frac{1}{4}$ hours (10–12 minutes in a pressure cooker). When cooking the beans in a pan of water make sure that it does not boil dry. Add more water as and when necessary.

1–2 tbsp sunflower oil
2 onions, chopped
175 g (6 oz) mushrooms, chopped
175 g (6 oz) butter beans, cooked (reserve the stock)
1 tbsp wholewheat flour
1 tbsp mugi miso
1 tbsp fresh rosemary, chopped

FOR THE TOPPING:
100 g (4 oz) porridge oats
75 g (3 oz) wholewheat flour
5 tbsp sunflower oil
2–3 tsp soya sauce

Prepare the beans as described above, reserving the stock.

Heat the oil in a large frying pan, add the onions and sauté until soft. Add the mushrooms and cook for a further 2–3 minutes. Stir in the drained beans and the flour. Cook for a minute or two more. Blend the miso with 2–3 tablespoons of stock and add to the pan. Season with rosemary. Spoon the mixture into a pie dish. Pour over sufficient stock to cover half the filling.

To make the topping mix the porridge oats and flour together. Rub in the oil, using your fingertips, and season with soya sauce. Sprinkle over the vegetable and bean mixture and press down lightly with the fingertips. Bake in a preheated oven, gas mark 5 (190° C/375° F) for 25–30 minutes.

LEEK AND BEAN COBBLER

1–2 tbsp sunflower oil
2 onions, chopped
3 leeks, chopped
1 large cooking apple, peeled, cored and sliced
25 g (1 oz) wholewheat flour
2–3 tsp soya sauce
100 g (4 oz) haricot beans, cooked with stock reserved
1 level tbsp fresh sage, finely chopped
freshly ground black pepper
bean stock

FOR THE TOPPING:
225 g (8 oz) wholewheat self-raising flour
2 tsp mustard powder
40 g ($1\frac{1}{2}$ oz) butter, diced
150 ml (5 fl oz) milk

Heat the oil in a pan, add the onions and sauté for 5 minutes before adding the leeks. Fry for another 5 minutes and then mix in the apple slices. Stir in the flour and cook for a minute or two before removing from the heat. Add the soya sauce, the cooked haricots and sage. Season with black pepper. Spoon into an ovenproof dish and pour over sufficient bean stock to barely cover the mixture.

To make the topping mix the flour and mustard powder together. Rub in the butter and add the milk. Mix to form a fairly soft dough. Turn onto a lightly-floured board, roll out and, using a pastry cutter, cut into circles, approximately 1.25 cm ($\frac{1}{2}$ in) thick. Arrange them, slightly overlapping, on top of the bean and vegetable mixture and brush with a little milk. Bake in a preheated oven, gas mark 6 (200° C/400° F) for 25–30 minutes.

FLAGEOLET BEAN PIE

Flageolet beans are generally thought to be the aristocrats of beans, and this is reflected in their price. Removed from the pod when immature they are tender and have a light refreshing taste. Grown mainly in France and Italy they are traditionally eaten cold after being tossed in a herby vinaigrette dressing.

FOR THE FILLING:
1–2 tbsp groundnut oil
1 onion, chopped
1 stick celery, chopped
100 g (4 oz) French beans, lightly steamed
100 g (4 oz) sweetcorn
100 g (4 oz) button mushrooms, halved if necessary
100 g (4 oz) flageolet beans, cooked and drained
seasoning

FOR THE SAUCE:
25 g (1 oz) butter
25 g (1 oz) wholewheat flour
350 ml (12 fl oz) milk
1 tsp Dijon mustard
1–2 tbsp fresh parsley, finely chopped

FOR THE PASTRY:
175 g (6 oz) wholewheat flour
75 g (3 oz) butter, diced
6 tsp cold water
1 egg, beaten or milk to glaze

To cook the beans soak overnight in plenty of cold water (if using a pressure cooker soak for a minimum of 6 hours). Drain and put into a pan with 575 ml (1 pint) of fresh water. Cover, bring to the boil and simmer for $1-1\frac{1}{2}$ hours until tender, adding more water if necessary. Cook in a pressure cooker for 12–15 minutes. Drain well.

Heat the oil in a pan, add the onion and celery and sauté until soft. Add the remaining vegetables and the cooked beans and season to taste. Spoon into a pie dish.

To make the sauce melt the butter in a small pan and stir in the flour. Cook for 2–3 minutes, stirring all the time. Remove from the heat and gradually add the milk. Return to the stove and bring to the boil, stirring constantly until the sauce thickens. Add the mustard and parsley and mix well. Pour over the vegetable mixture.

To make the pastry put the flour in a bowl and rub in the butter, using your fingertips, until the mixture resembles breadcrumbs. Add the water and knead to form a pastry dough. Turn onto a lightly-floured board and roll out the pastry to a circle large enough to cover the pie and about 0.75 cm ($\frac{1}{4}$ in) in thickness. Dampen the pie dish rim and cover with the pastry top. Press around to seal and trim the edges. Brush with beaten egg or milk to glaze. Bake in a preheated oven, gas mark 6 (200° C/400° F) for 25–30 minutes.

NAPOLITANA BEANS

1–2 tbsp olive oil
1 onion, finely chopped
100 g (4 oz) flat mushrooms, chopped
225 g (8 oz) tomatoes, chopped
1 tbsp tomato purée
100 g (4 oz) haricot beans, soaked overnight and then drained
425 ml (15 fl oz) water
1 level tsp dried basil
1 level tsp cayenne pepper
1 level tsp paprika
seasoning

Heat the oil in a pan, add the onion and sauté until soft and golden. Add the remaining ingredients and bring to the boil. Cover and simmer for approximately $1\frac{1}{2}$ hours until the beans are soft, adding more water if necessary. If using a pressure cooker cook for 15–18 minutes.

When the beans are tender remove the pan lid and boil briskly to reduce the stock. The beans should be coated in a thick, rich sauce. Adjust the seasoning to taste. Serve hot or cold.

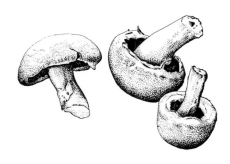

SALADS

SALADS

Salads are generally quick and easy to prepare and can be made from almost every conceivable ingredient, from the simple green salad served as an accompaniment to a main meal, to the more substantial salad composée which may contain fish, poultry, meat, cheese, eggs, beans, rice and potatoes. The ingredients must be in peak condition, chosen for their variety of colour, texture and flavour and tossed in a complementary dressing. I prefer to use three or four basic ingredients so that the special qualities of each one can be fully appreciated.

To prepare salad greens wash them quickly but thoroughly in cold running water and remove any discoloured or wilted leaves. Drain and remove surplus moisture by shaking them gently in a lettuce basket or spinning them in a rotary salad drier. Handle them carefully to avoid unnecessary bruising. Place the whole leaves in a plastic bag and store in the refrigerator until needed. Tear into even pieces and mix with the other ingredients just before tossing with the dressing. This ensures that the salad is fresh and crisp when it reaches the table.

The choice of dressing is almost as varied as the salad ingredients themselves, but as a general rule green salads are best with a light French dressing whereas some types of salad composée are delicious served with rich, creamier sauces. I prefer using white wine vinegar or lemon juice but cider vinegar, lime juice, orange juice and soya sauce can also be used. The choice of oil is important too as the indifferent flavour of a poor quality oil can have disastrous effects. Try using cold pressed oils, containing all the goodness and flavour of the original fruit or seed. Sunflower oil is especially suited to salads whose delicate flavour can easily be masked. Richer, green olive oil is best with heartier salads and those including Mediterranean ingredients such as olives, beefsteak tomatoes, basil, courgettes, peppers and Feta or Mozzarella cheese.

I make a light salad dressing from three parts sunflower oil to one part lemon juice seasoned with freshly ground black pepper and a more robust version from three parts olive oil to one part white wine vinegar seasoned with garlic, Dijon mustard and pepper. I like the distinctive flavour of garlic but many people find it rather pungent. A mere hint of garlic can be given to a salad by rubbing a peeled clove around the inside of the salad bowl.

Toss the salad in the dressing immediately before serving, using just sufficient to coat all the leaves. When using cooked vegetables, rice, beans or potatoes toss these ingredients in the dressing while they are warm and leave them to marinate and cool before adding the remaining ingredients.

An important aspect of making salads is their visual appearance. Use yellow or red peppers, radishes, spring onions, green and black grapes, yellow courgettes, twists of orange and lemon peel, carrots, olives, sweetcorn and tomatoes to add colour. Fresh herbs can also provide colour as well as giving a boost to the flavour of a dish. Tomatoes and basil, cucumber and mint and carrots and thyme are particularly good combinations.

There is really no limit to the number of different salads that you can make. It is well worth experimenting with a variety of ingredients, dressings and garnishes.

ORANGE SALAD

2 heads chicory
1 lettuce heart
1 box mustard and cress
2 oranges
4 tbsp natural yoghurt
1 tsp Dijon mustard
a pinch of cayenne pepper

Wash and shred the chicory and lettuce. Place in a bowl with the mustard and cress. Peel the oranges leaving only the orange flesh. Cut away the white pith from the peel and finely shred the peel. Put the peel into a pan of boiling water for 5–6 minutes. This helps to remove the bitter taste. Drain and leave to cool. Chop the orange segments and put them in the salad bowl.

Mix the yoghurt and mustard together and season with a pinch of cayenne pepper. Pour over the salad and toss. Sprinkle with the shredded orange peel and serve.

HAZELNUT AND ORANGE SALAD

1 bunch of watercress
$\frac{1}{4}$ cucumber
50 g (2 oz) hazelnuts
1 large orange

Wash and drain the watercress and trim away the coarse stalks. Dice the cucumber and place in a salad bowl with the watercress. Put the hazelnuts on a baking tray and roast in a preheated hot oven for 10 minutes, turning them occasionally so that they brown evenly. Rub them in a clean tea towel while they are still hot to remove their skins. Put the cleaned nuts into the salad bowl. Peel the orange and, working over the bowl, cut away the white pith and membrane and discard. Put the segments in with the other ingredients and toss well before serving.

TOMATO AND GOAT'S MILK CHEESE SALAD

450 g (1 lb) tomatoes
100 g (4 oz) goat's milk cheese
3 tbsp olive oil
1 tbsp white wine vinegar
1 tbsp fresh thyme, finely chopped

Slice the tomatoes and the cheese. Arrange on an attractive dish. Mix the oil and wine vinegar together and pour over the tomatoes. Sprinkle with thyme and serve.

GUACAMOLE

Guacamole makes an excellent starter, served with wholewheat toast fingers.

2 large avocados
1 tomato, finely chopped
3 spring onions, finely chopped
1 green chilli, finely chopped
1 tbsp fresh coriander, chopped
juice of 1–2 lemons
freshly ground black pepper

Peel, stone and mash the avocados. Stir them into a bowl containing the chopped tomato, spring onions, chilli and coriander. Season to taste with lemon juice and black pepper. Chill slightly before serving.

CRUDITÉS

One of the best ways of preparing young tender vegetables is to serve them as crudités, accompanied by a light sauce. Little or no cooking is required, all one needs is an attractive serving dish and a selection of vegetables that complement each other in colour and texture. They should be cleaned carefully before being sliced or chopped into delicate bite-sized pieces and arranged in groups on the dish. Cucumber, radishes, celery, carrots, courgettes, green beans, chicory, beetroot, spring onions, peppers and tomatoes can be used. Hard root vegetables such as cauliflower and small new potatoes are best lightly cooked and served hot or cold.

It is customary to eat crudités with one's fingers, dipping them into a sauce before popping them in the mouth. They may be served as a simple first course or with freshly baked bread as a lunch or supper dish.

Here are some sauces to serve with crudités.

SPICY PEANUT SAUCE

100 g (4 oz) creamed coconut
275 ml (10 fl oz) water
1 tsp turmeric
1 level tsp curry powder
1 level tsp cayenne pepper
100 g (4 oz) ground peanuts
1–2 tbsp lemon juice
1–2 tsp soya sauce (*optional*)

Place the creamed coconut and water together in a pan and heat gently until the coconut has dissolved. Stir in the spices and bring to the boil. Simmer gently and stir in the ground peanuts. Continue cooking for a few minutes more, stirring all the time. Season to taste with lemon juice and soya sauce. Leave to cool before serving.

CREAMED TAHINI SAUCE

Tahini or sesame cream has become very popular in recent years and can be bought in most high-class grocers', delicatessen and wholefood shops. It is an oily paste made from sesame seeds and can be used as a spread or to add flavour and interest to sauces and dips. It is a principal ingredient in the Middle Eastern dish known as hummus. A jar of tahini will keep almost indefinitely in a cool place or refrigerator. Don't worry if a thin film of oil collects on top of the jar, this is an indication that no artificial emulsifying agents have been added and that the tahini is of a good quality. Simply stir the oil back into the tahini before using.

Tahini has a deliciously nutty flavour but is very rich in oils and calories and should be used in moderation.

5 tbsp tahini
4 tbsp lemon juice
1 clove garlic, peeled and crushed
5 tbsp natural yoghurt

Blend all the ingredients together until smooth and creamy. Place in a small bowl and chill slightly before serving.

The sauce can be made without yoghurt. Mix the tahini, garlic and lemon juice together, thinning it down with water if the sauce becomes too sharp.

FETA CHEESE SAUCE

275 ml (10 fl oz) thick set natural yoghurt
75 g (3 oz) Feta cheese, grated
1 clove garlic, peeled and crushed
freshly ground black pepper
1 tbsp fresh chives, chopped

Mix together the yoghurt, cheese, garlic and black pepper. Pour into a small bowl and sprinkle with chives before serving.

AÏOLI

A classic French mayonnaise.

> 3–4 cloves garlic, peeled and crushed
> 1 egg yolk
> $\frac{1}{2}$ tsp Dijon mustard
> 150 ml (5 fl oz) olive oil
> 1 tbsp lemon juice
> freshly ground black pepper

Mix the garlic, egg yolk and mustard together. Work in the oil, a teaspoon at a time, beating well after each addition. As the mayonnaise begins to thicken add the oil in larger amounts. When the mixture becomes too thick thin down by adding a few drops of lemon juice. Season with black pepper before beating in the last of the oil.

Use immediately or keep cool in a refrigerator. If left for more than a few hours whisk lightly before serving.

LEMON AND PARSLEY SAUCE

Tofu has been heralded as a wonder food. It is extremely low in fat and calories and yet contains first-class proteins. It has a smooth texture and bland flavour and I find it most useful as a substitute for yoghurt in creamy sauces and fillings.

> 200 g (7 oz) silken tofu
> 2 tbsp sesame oil
> 2 tbsp lemon juice
> 1 tbsp fresh parsley, finely chopped
> 1 clove garlic, peeled and crushed
> 1 tsp soya sauce (*optional*)

Blend all the ingredients together until smooth and creamy.

MOCK GRELETTE SAUCE

The use of tofu in place of double cream and fromage blanc makes this nouvelle cuisine sauce even more acceptable to those trying to reduce their waistlines.

> 3 ripe tomatoes, peeled and chopped finely
> 1 level tsp Dijon mustard
> 4 tsp lemon juice
> 2 heaped tsp fresh parsley, finely chopped
> 1 tbsp tomato purée
> 100 g (4 oz) silken tofu
> pinch of cayenne pepper
> freshly ground black pepper

Blend all the ingredients together until smooth and creamy.

CASHEW NUT SALAD

> 1 cucumber, diced
> 1 lettuce heart, shredded
> 1 red eating apple, chopped
> 1 bunch of watercress, trimmed and chopped
> 50 g (2 oz) cashew nuts
> 4 tbsp sunflower oil
> 2 tbsp white wine vinegar

Place the salad ingredients in a bowl. Mix the oil and vinegar together well and pour into the bowl. Toss before serving.

WALNUT SALAD

> 1 head chicory, sliced
> 1 bunch of watercress, trimmed and chopped
> 1 flat lettuce, shredded
> 1 red pepper, deseeded and sliced
> 3 carrots, grated
> $\frac{1}{4}$ cucumber, diced
> 50 g (2 oz) walnuts
> wholewheat croûtons
> 4 tbsp walnut oil
> 1 tbsp lemon juice
> 1 clove garlic, peeled and crushed

Place all the salad vegetables, the walnuts and croûtons in a bowl. Mix the oil, lemon juice and garlic together well before pouring over the salad. Toss and serve.

BEANSPROUT WARDORF

3 sticks celery
2 crisp red apples
50 g (2 oz) walnuts
175 g (6 oz) beansprouts
1 tsp lemon juice
freshly ground black pepper
250 ml (9 fl oz) natural yoghurt
2 tsp fresh mint, finely chopped

Chop the apples, celery and walnuts and mix with the beansprouts in a bowl. Season with lemon juice and black pepper. Mix the yoghurt and mint together and pour over the salad. Toss lightly before serving.

BEANSPROUT SALAD

175 g (6 oz) beansprouts
2 apples, peeled, cored and chopped
2 sticks celery, chopped
$\frac{1}{4}$ cucumber, chopped
50 g (2 oz) sultanas
1 tbsp fresh mint, chopped
4 tbsp tahini
6 tbsp fresh orange juice

Place all the salad ingredients together in a bowl. Sprinkle over the chopped mint and toss. Mix the tahini and orange juice together and pour over the salad. Toss well and serve.

TABOULI

Tabouli or tabbouleh is a refreshing salad from the Lebanon. The principal ingredient is a cracked wheat product known as bulgur or burghul which requires very little cooking. It is pleasantly filling without being heavy or stodgy and is ideal for hot weather.

225 g (8 oz) bulgur
850 ml (1$\frac{1}{2}$ pints) boiling water
a bunch of spring onions, chopped
a scant teacup chopped fresh parsley
3 tbsp fresh mint, chopped
5 tbsp olive oil
5 tbsp lemon juice
freshly ground black pepper
lettuce
tomatoes

Place the bulgur in a saucepan and dry fry over a high heat until it becomes golden brown. Shake the pan frequently to ensure even cooking. Turn out immediately into a heat resistant bowl and cover with the boiling water. Leave for 1 hour. The bulgur will become light and fluffy but still have a little resistance to the bite. Drain well and spread the bulgur in the middle of a clean tea towel then fold it in half. Fold in half again, sandwiching the bulgur in the middle. Press firmly to remove any excess moisture. Repeat with another dry cloth if necessary.

Put the 'cooked' bulgur in a large bowl and add the spring onions, parsley and mint. Mix the olive oil and lemon juice together and pour over. Season with black pepper and toss.

Arrange a few lettuce leaves on a serving dish and spoon on the tabouli. Cut the tomato into wedges and use to decorate the dish.

CHICK PEA COLESLAW

100 g (4 oz) chick peas
575 ml (1 pint) water
$\frac{1}{4}$ small white cabbage, shredded
1 medium carrot, grated
1 small Spanish onion, thinly sliced
5 tbsp natural yoghurt
1 tbsp tahini

Soak the chick peas overnight in plenty of cold water. Next day drain and put into a large pan with the measured water. Bring to the boil, cover and simmer for 2 hours, or until tender. Check to make sure that the pan doesn't boil dry. If using a pressure cooker cook for 20–25 minutes. Drain.

When cool mix the beans with the other vegetables in a bowl. Beat the yoghurt and tahini together and pour over. Mix well before serving.

SUNFLOWER SEED SALAD

50 g (2 oz) roasted sunflower seeds
1 cucumber, chopped
1 small head Chinese leaves, shredded
1 yellow pepper, sliced
100 g (4 oz) button mushrooms, halved
3 tbsp peanut oil
1 tbsp lemon juice
1 tsp soya sauce

To roast the sunflower seeds either place on a baking tray and put into a moderate oven for 10 minutes, turning occasionally, or heat in a pan over a high flame for 4–5 minutes, shaking frequently.

Put the vegetables and seeds in a salad bowl. Mix the oil, lemon juice and soya sauce together thoroughly and pour over. Toss before serving.

LAYER SALAD

This salad looks particularly attractive in a glass bowl.

100 g (4 oz) shredded cabbage
175 g (6 oz) grated carrot
75 g (3 oz) chopped peanuts
100 g (4 oz) chopped celery
2 red apples, chopped
75 g (3 oz) chopped dates
100 g (4 oz) cooked brown rice
25 g (1 oz) sesame seeds
1 box mustard and cress
garnish with a few slices of tomato

Arrange the ingredients in a salad bowl, one layer on top of another.

MARINATED CARROTS

FOR THE MARINADE:
200 ml (7 fl oz) water
200 ml (7 fl oz) dry white wine
200 ml (7 fl oz) white wine vinegar
1 sprig of fresh thyme
1 sprig of fresh parsley
1 bay leaf
1 clove garlic, peeled and crushed
a pinch of cayenne pepper
6 tbsp olive oil

REMAINING INGREDIENTS:
450 g (1 lb) carrots, roughly chopped
2 tsp Dijon mustard

Place the marinade ingredients in a pan and bring to the boil. Toss in the carrots and boil briskly until they begin to soften. Remove the carrots with a slotted spoon and place in a serving dish. Stir the mustard into the marinade before pouring over the carrots. Leave to cool.

PLAT DE PROVENCE

1 crisp lettuce
1 clove garlic, peeled and crushed
2 tomatoes, cut into wedges
$\frac{1}{3}$ cucumber, sliced
4 spring onions, chopped
100 g (4 oz) seedless grapes
50 g (2 oz) white crumbly cheese
4 tbsp olive oil
$1\frac{1}{2}$ tbsp white wine vinegar
freshly ground black pepper

Wash and drain the lettuce and separate into leaves. Tear the leaves into smaller pieces if large. Place the lettuce in a bowl with the garlic, tomatoes, cucumber, spring onions and grapes. Crumble the cheese on top. Mix the olive oil and wine vinegar together and season with black pepper. Pour over the salad and toss before serving.

FENNEL SALAD

1 crisp lettuce
1 head chicory
1 Florence fennel bulb
1 apple
3 eggs (boiled for 5 minutes)
2 tbsp natural yoghurt
2 tbsp fresh parsley, chopped

Shred the lettuce and chicory, slice the fennel and apple and place in a salad bowl. Shell and mash the eggs in another bowl and stir in the yoghurt and parsley. Spoon the egg mixture into the salad bowl and toss with the other ingredients. Serve.

ARTICHOKES IN HERB DRESSING

6–8 small globe artichokes
juice of 1 lemon
6 tbsp olive oil
4 tbsp white wine vinegar
1 clove garlic, peeled and crushed
2 tsp fresh chives, finely chopped

Trim the stalks from the artichokes and cut the head into quarters. Remove the inner leaves and the choke and place them in a large pan of boiling water to which the lemon juice has been added. Cook for 10–15 minutes. Drain well.

Mix the remaining ingredients together and pour over the warm artichokes. Leave to cool. Drain again and serve.

ARTICHOKE AND VEGETABLE SALAD

Place 2 or 3 cooked, trimmed and sliced globe artichoke hearts in a salad bowl with some cooked new potatoes, cooked French beans and cooked carrots. Sprinkle with fresh chopped herbs (parsley, basil, thyme, chives etc) and pour over a vinaigrette dressing. Toss well and serve.

MUSHROOMS À LA GRECQUE

Coriander seeds are small, round and brittle and vary in colour from cream through to shades of brown and green. They have a lovely scent which is vaguely reminiscent of oranges and is enhanced by dry frying. Coriander is an essential ingredient in curried dishes and vegetables à la grecque.

3 tbsp olive oil
3 tbsp water
1 large ripe tomato, chopped
5 coriander seeds, crushed
1 bay leaf
1 sprig of fresh thyme
seasoning
225 g (8 oz) button mushrooms, trimmed

Put all the ingredients, except for the seasoning and mushrooms, in a small pan. Simmer gently for 4–5 minutes and then add the mushrooms. Continue cooking for another 4–5 minutes, stirring frequently. Remove the mushrooms with a slotted spoon and place in a serving dish. Boil the pan juices until reduced by a half and then strain. Adjust the seasoning. Pour over the mushrooms and leave to cool before serving.

MUSHROOMS WITH CORIANDER AND LEMON

450 g (1 lb) button mushrooms
olive oil
$\frac{1}{2}$ tsp ground coriander
juice of 1 lemon

Wipe and trim the mushrooms. Heat a little olive oil in a large frying pan and add the mushrooms and coriander. Cook them for several minutes, stirring frequently but be careful not to overcook them – they want to be on the firm side. Squeeze the lemon juice over the top and serve hot or cold.

CREAMED MUSHROOMS

225 g (8 oz) very fresh small button mushrooms
2 tbsp olive oil
2 tsp lemon juice
freshly ground black pepper
1–2 tsp Dijon mustard
4 tbsp sour cream

Wipe and trim the mushrooms. Place in a serving dish. Mix the remaining ingredients together in a bowl and pour over the mushrooms. Serve.

VEGETABLES

VEGETABLES

Contrary to popular belief vegetables have not always been neglected and ill-treated by the British and in the sixteenth century we were considered to be even finer vegetable cooks than the French. Cookery books were beginning to give precise instructions as to when vegetables should be added to carbonades and ragoûts so that they would not be overcooked and it was even suggested that salads should be eaten before the main course.

It was at this time too that the first market gardens were springing up around London growing peas, carrots, turnips, kale, parsnips, lettuce and cucumbers for the tables of merchants, gentlemen and the nobility. The rich liked to eat the vegetables when young and tender so that their delicate, fresh flavours could be appreciated to the full. Cottagers and labourers, on the other hand, grew what they could, sticking in the main to onions, garlic and cabbages, and letting them grow as big as possible. Not for them the dainty dishes of sweet, immature vegetables. They had mouths to feed and needed as many vegetables as possible to fill out stews, pies, hotpots and the like.

As trade with foreign lands increased, more and more unusual vegetables were introduced into Britain. Potatoes, maize, French and runner beans, Jerusalem artichokes and tomatoes came over from the Americas; asparagus and globe artichokes from France; improved celery from Italy and cauliflowers from Spain. Interest in vegetables, both in the kitchen and in the garden, continued to grow until the nineteenth century.

The Victorian era was something of a Golden Age in terms of architecture, inventions and industrial development but it did little to improve the reputation of English food. Queen Victoria's own chef Francetelli seemed more concerned with presentation than taste and specialised in creating fancy moulds out of mashed potatoes and sculpting rice into curious shapes. He had little regard for vegetables and in one recipe recommended boiling chicory (*endive*) until tender, squeezing out the water, stewing it for ten minutes in melted butter before adding double cream and sugar and then simmering 'until sufficiently reduced so as to be able to pile them on a dish when sending to table'.

Other Victorian cooks recommended cooking fresh peas for 40 minutes and boiling cabbage and carrots for between one and two hours. It is hardly surprising that vegetables became unpopular and were gradually relegated to the role of garnish or accompaniment to the main meat dish. The situation did not improve and by the 1920s foreigners were beginning to believe the saying: 'the English only have three vegetables and two of them are cabbage'. Today they must think we eat nothing but chips and peas!

Gradually, helped by the increase in foreign travel and a renewed interest in food and cooking, vegetables are once again being treated with the respect they deserve. I would, however, like to suggest to those restauranteurs who cannot cope with preparing and cooking vegetables properly that a bowl of crisp fresh salad would be much nicer than the standard tureens of soggy overcooked vegetables (frozen or otherwise).

Most vegetables can be eaten from the freezer every day of the year but the loss of flavour and texture makes them a poor substitute for fresh varieties. I prefer to eat vegetables according to their natural season and look forward to tasting the first garden peas, 'real French beans' and new potatoes. Frozen vegetables are, of course, more convenient and much easier to prepare but they simply don't taste as good as when fresh. I suppose I am lucky because I actually love everything about fresh vegetables – their shape, colour, texture, smell and taste – and I don't resent spending time buying, chopping or cooking them. For those of you who don't share my enthusiasm I would suggest that you first find a good greengrocer, then buy a sharp knife and try again. If this does not work you could follow the example set by a friend of American cookery writer,

M. F. K. Fisher. Apparently she hated vegetables and refused to eat them choosing instead to: 'live excitedly for about 20 years on strong tea and hard-boiled eggs. THEN she died.'

CARROT SOUP

2 tbsp sunflower oil
1 small onion, chopped
450 g (1 lb) carrots, coarsely grated
3 potatoes, scrubbed and diced
2–3 sprigs of fresh parsley
850 ml (1½ pints) water
seasoning

FOR THE GARNISH:
finely chopped parsley
wholewheat croûtons

Heat the oil in a large pan, add the onion and sauté for 8–10 minutes. Add the carrots, potatoes and parsley and cook for a few minutes more over a low heat, stirring frequently. Cover and cook for a further 10–15 minutes, checking occasionally to make sure that the vegetables are not catching on the bottom of the pan.

Pour over the water and bring to the boil. Simmer gently for 30 minutes and then pass through a sieve or vegetable mouli, or process briefly in a food processor or blender. Return to the pan and adjust the consistency and seasoning to taste. Heat through and garnish with croûtons and parsley before serving.

For a richer soup stir in a knob of butter.

BUTTERED CARROTS WITH THYME

450 g (1 lb) young carrots
15 g (½ oz) butter
1 tbsp fresh thyme, finely chopped

Scrub and trim the carrots. If they are small leave them whole, otherwise cut into halves or quarters lengthways. Place them in a saucepan, cover with cold water and cook quickly until the carrots are just tender. Drain. Dot the butter over the hot carrots and sprinkle with thyme. Toss and serve immediately.

SUMMER PEAS AND CARROTS (PETIT POIS AUX CAROTTES)

225 g (8 oz) carrots
450 g (1 lb) peas, shelled
1 onion, quartered
1 crisp lettuce, shredded
a knob of butter

Scrub and trim the carrots and cut them into julienne strips. Place in a pan with the remaining ingredients and barely cover with water. Bring to the boil, cover and cook gently for 8–10 minutes until the vegetables are tender. Drain and toss in the butter before serving.

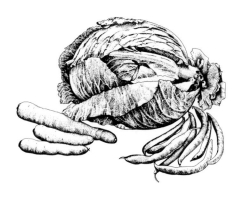

RATATOUILLE

It is difficult to make a first-class ratatouille away from the sun-drenched shores of the Mediterranean. The main problem is finding a good tomato, one which has ripened slowly under a hot sun and is full of colour and flavour. All too often, here in Britain at least, tomatoes are pale imitations of the real thing, and it would seem as if they are grown more for uniformity of size than any culinary qualities. The large, ridged beefsteak tomato seems to be the nearest equivalent to the large, misshapen blood red tomato found in the markets of southern France but they must be ripe. If beefsteaks are unavailable or ridiculously expensive and it is too early or late for good, local grown tomatoes you may find it necessary to add a little tomato purée to the ratatouille to bolster up the flavour. This applies equally to other dishes in which the flavour of the tomato is a significant feature.

1 aubergine
225 g (8 oz) courgettes
1 green pepper
225 g (8 oz) mild onions
2 beefsteak tomatoes
2–3 tbsp olive oil
1 clove garlic, peeled and crushed
2 tbsp fresh thyme, chopped
1 bay leaf
150 ml (5 fl oz) dry white wine
seasoning

Cut the aubergine in half lengthways and cut it into 0.75 cm ($\frac{1}{4}$ in) slices. Slice the courgettes, pepper, onions and tomatoes.

Heat the olive oil in a large heavy pan, add the onions and garlic and sauté until soft, but without allowing them to brown. Add the pepper and cook for 5 minutes more. Then add the aubergine, followed by the courgettes and finally the tomatoes, frying each for a few minutes before adding the next vegetable. Stir in the herbs and pour over the wine. Season to taste and cover with a lid. Simmer over a low heat for 30–40 minutes until the vegetables are soft.

Serve with baked potatoes or wholewheat rolls. The addition of a bowl of grated cheese would make a substantial meal.

BAKED AUBERGINES WITH FETA CHEESE

2 large aubergines
1 beefsteak tomato
1 red pepper
freshly ground black pepper
2 tbsp fresh marjoram, chopped
100 g (4 oz) Feta cheese, sliced

Slice the aubergines and lay half of them in the bottom of an oiled casserole dish. Remove the core and seeds from the pepper, chop with the tomato and arrange on top. Sprinkle with black pepper and marjoram. Lay the rest of the aubergine slices on top of that and cover with cheese.

Cover with a lid or foil and bake in a preheated oven, gas mark 4 (180° C/350° F) for 50–60 minutes until the aubergines are soft.

ARTICHOKES WITH PEAS

SERVES 4 AS A FIRST COURSE
1–2 tbsp olive oil
1 small onion, finely chopped
1 clove garlic, peeled and crushed
2 globe artichokes
1 lemon
100 g (4 oz) shelled peas
2 tbsp fresh parsley, finely chopped

Heat the oil in a pan, add the onion and garlic and sauté until soft and golden.

Meanwhile, prepare the artichokes. Cut off and discard the stalks and any tough outer leaves. Cut each head into six segments and remove and discard the choke. As you work remember to rub all the cut edges with lemon juice to prevent them discolouring.

Add the artichoke wedges to the pan of sautéed onion and pour over 150 ml (5 fl oz) water and the juice of $\frac{1}{2}$ the lemon. Bring to the boil. Cover and simmer gently for 10 minutes. Add the peas (and more water if necessary) and cook for a further 10–15 minutes until the vegetables are tender. To test if the artichokes are done, with a sharp knife, check that the base is tender enough to eat. Drain and sprinkle with parsley before serving.

ARTICHOKE CASSEROLE

3 globe artichokes
juice of 1 lemon
olive oil
1 onion, chopped
1 clove garlic, peeled and crushed
2 sticks celery, chopped
12 small new potatoes, scrubbed
3 carrots, roughly chopped
1 sprig of fresh thyme
1 sprig of fresh parsley
1 bay leaf
100 g (4 oz) French beans, sliced
100 g (4 oz) mangetouts or shelled garden peas
seasoning

Trim the stalks from the artichokes and cut the head into quarters. Remove and discard the purple inner leaves and the down-like choke. Cook in a large pan of boiling water to which the lemon juice has been added. Boil fairly briskly for 10 minutes, then drain and reserve the vegetable water.

Meanwhile, heat a tablespoon or two of oil in another pan, add the onion, garlic and celery and sauté for 10 minutes, without allowing them to brown. Add the potatoes, carrots and herbs and barely cover with the vegetable water. Cover and simmer until the vegetables are almost tender. Add the parboiled artichokes, the beans and mangetouts or peas. Cover again and continue to cook until all the vegetables are tender. (There should be no need to add more water or stock after the addition of these last vegetables – they will cook just as well in steam, provided that the pan is covered with a tight-fitting lid.) Season to taste before serving.

TEMPURA VEGETABLES

Tempura dishes are very popular in Japan and are deep-fried foods that have first been coated in a light batter. Special tempura pans are now available in this country but any deep pan or wok will suffice.

Any vegetable can be used such as carrots, cauliflower, broccoli, leeks, Brussels sprouts, mushrooms, courgettes and peppers. Root vegetables may need to be parboiled before being coated. The batter must be sufficiently thin to allow the food underneath to cook and yet it must coat the food evenly without becoming heavy and stodgy. To make the batter you will need:

50 g (2 oz) unbleached white flour
50 g (2 oz) chick pea flour (also known as gram or besan flour)
2 eggs, beaten
150–175 ml (5–6 fl oz) milk
1 tsp soya sauce
1 tsp white wine vinegar

Mix the flours together and stir in the eggs. Gradually beat in the milk until the batter has the consistency of single cream. Add the soya sauce and vinegar.

Heat a pan of oil to 180° C/350° F. If you have no thermometer wait until the oil gives off a *faint* blue smoke and then dip one piece of vegetable into the batter and drop it into the hot fat. It should sink to the bottom and then, after a few seconds, come bubbling to the surface. The fat is now ready for use. Dip the rest of the chopped vegetables into the batter and drop them into hot fat a few at a time. They will become crisp and brown in 4–5 minutes. Remove with a slotted spoon and put into a dish lined with absorbent paper. Keep warm while frying the remaining vegetables. Serve immediately.

CREAM OF GREEN PEA SOUP

This really is a deliciously refreshing summer soup and is an excellent way of using up a glut of peas from the garden. It freezes very well.

1½ kg (3 lb) garden peas, shelled
1 small lettuce, shredded
3 spring onions, chopped
3 slices of bacon, chopped
1.7 litres (3 pints) water
freshly ground black pepper
3–4 sprigs of fresh mint

Put the peas, lettuce, spring onions and bacon in a large pan and pour over the water. Bring to the boil, cover and simmer gently for 15–20 minutes until the peas are soft. Purée the soup by passing it through a sieve or vegetable mouli, or process it briefly in a food processor or blender until smooth and creamy. Return to the pan and season with black pepper and toss in the mint. Heat through and leave the mint to infuse for several minutes. Then discard and serve.

SCALLOPED POTATOES WITH ROSEMARY

450 g (1 lb) potatoes, scrubbed and thinly sliced
1 onion, thinly sliced
3–4 sprigs of fresh rosemary
150 ml (5 fl oz) water
2 tsp tomato purée
seasoning

Arrange the potatoes and onions in alternate layers in an ovenproof casserole, remembering to place a sprig of rosemary between each layer. Blend the water and tomato purée together and season to taste. Pour over the potatoes and bake in a preheated oven, gas mark 7 (220° C/425° F) for 50–60 minutes until the potatoes are soft and lightly browned on top.

POTATO SCONES

SERVES 4
225 g (8 oz) mashed potato
50 g (2 oz) wholewheat flour
4 spring onions, finely chopped
oil for frying

Gradually mix the flour into the potatoes until the mixture is fairly stiff. Add the spring onions and roll out the mixture on a lightly floured board thinly. Cut into rounds. Brush a heavy frying pan with oil and when fairly hot cook the scones until lightly browned on both sides.

POTATOES EN PAPILLOTE

Nicholas Soyer, grandson of the great chef Alexis Soyer, spent many years perfecting the paper bag method of cooking and indeed published a book extolling the virtues of his discovery. Cooking 'en papillote' is now a common enough practice, particularly useful when cooking fish but I was surprised to read that new potatoes could be cooked in this way too. At first I was a little dubious but was pleasantly surprised for they really do bake well inside their paper case. They are particularly good when cooked with fresh herbs.

Wash some small new potatoes, do not scrape them as their skins prevent them from sticking to the paper. Put them on a large piece of oiled greaseproof paper with a sprig of rosemary or mint. Fold the paper so that the potatoes are completely sealed inside, wrapping the ends underneath. Place in a preheated oven, gas mark 6 (200° C/400° F) for 45–50 minutes until soft.

SPINACH AND COTTAGE CHEESE QUICHE

It took me a long time to appreciate the flavour of spinach but now I use it regularly in savoury fillings, casseroles and tarts. Sorrel, which grows robustly in most gardens, can be used when fresh spinach is unavailable.

FOR THE PASTRY:
225 g (8 oz) wholewheat flour
75 g (3 oz) butter, diced
2 tbsp sunflower oil
8 tsp cold water

FOR THE FILLING:
450 g (1 lb) spinach
100 g (4 oz) cottage cheese
2 eggs
150 ml (5 fl oz) natural yoghurt
freshly ground black pepper
25 g (1 oz) Gruyère cheese, grated (*optional*)

Put the flour in a bowl and, using your fingertips, rub in the butter and oil until the mixture resembles breadcrumbs. Stir in the water and mix to form a pastry dough. Turn onto a lightly-floured board, roll out and line a 25 cm (10 in) flan ring. Press down lightly with the fingertips and prick the pastry base with a fork. Blind bake in a preheated oven, gas mark 6 (200° C/400° F) for 10–12 minutes.

Meanwhile, wash the spinach carefully in several changes of water to remove any dirt and grit. Chop off the stalks and shred the leaves. Place in a large pan, cover and cook gently over a low heat until much reduced and tender. There should be no need to add any water to the pan, the spinach will exude sufficient while it is cooking. But shake the pan occasionally to prevent the spinach from sticking to the bottom. Drain well, pressing down on the leaves to get rid of any excess liquid.

Mix the cooked spinach and cottage cheese together and spoon into the blind baked pastry case. Beat the eggs and yoghurt together and pour over the spinach filling. Sprinkle with grated cheese and black pepper. Return to the oven and bake for a further 25 minutes until firm to the touch.

BROWN RICE WITH GREEN BEANS AND PEAS

1 sprig of fresh parsley
225 g (8 oz) long grain brown rice
a scant 575 ml (1 pint) chicken stock or water
juice of $\frac{1}{2}$ lemon
50 g (2 oz) shelled green peas
50 g (2 oz) sliced French beans
seasoning

Put the parsley, rice, stock and lemon juice in a heavy pan and bring to the boil. Cover and simmer for 15 minutes. Add the peas and beans and continue cooking for a further 20–25 minutes, without stirring, until the rice is dry and tender. Remove from the heat and leave to stand with the lid on for a further 5–10 minutes. Season and stir gently before serving.

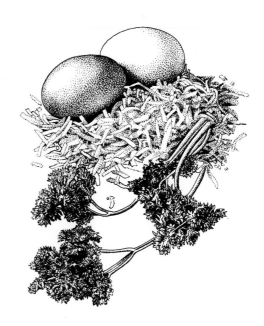

FRENCH ONION SOUP

I have only to see the words 'French Onion Soup' chalked up on a menu for my mouth to water. It is as if I can actually smell the onions cooking in the kitchen and can see the bowl of rich, velvety soup topped with crusty bread and melting cheese set down on the table in front of me. But alas all too often I have to let my imagination suffice for in many cafés and restaurants the dish masquerading as onion soup is a pale shadow of the real thing.

The very best onion soup is made with a rich beef stock and, perhaps, a dash of brandy. These days it is often easier to lay your hands on the alcohol than it is to find a reasonable amount of good stock. Here are two recipes, one in the traditional style and a second requiring neither stock nor alcohol.

450 g (1 lb) mild onions
40 g (1½ oz) butter
1.1 litres (2 pints) rich beef stock
1 tbsp brandy
freshly ground black pepper
1 stick of French bread
100 g (4 oz) Gruyère cheese

Peel and slice the onions thinly. Melt the butter in a large pan, add the onions and sauté slowly until very soft and golden brown. This can take up to 20 minutes. Pour over the stock and bring to the boil. Reduce the heat, cover and simmer for a further 30 minutes. Add the brandy and season to taste with black pepper.

Just before serving cut the bread into thick slices and toast on both sides. Ladle the soup into individual bowls and float a slice or two of toast on top. Lay thin slices of cheese on the toast and put under a hot grill until the cheese is bubbling. Serve immediately.

ONION SOUP WITH SOYA SAUCE

450 g (1 lb) mild onions
1 tbsp sunflower oil
25 g (1 oz) butter
3 level tbsp wholewheat flour
1.1 litres (2 pints) water
1 bay leaf
2 tsp soya sauce
a pinch of dried sage
freshly ground black pepper
1 stick of French bread
50 g (2 oz) Gruyère cheese
2–3 tbsp Parmesan cheese, grated

Peel and slice the onions thinly. Heat the oil and butter together in a large pan, add the onions and sauté slowly until very soft and golden brown. Stir in the flour and cook for a minute or two. Remove from the heat and gradually add the water. Return to the heat and bring to the boil, stirring all the time. Add the bay leaf. Cover and simmer for 30 minutes. Discard the bay leaf and season to taste with soya sauce, sage and black pepper.

Just before serving cut the bread into thick slices and toast on both sides. Ladle the soup into individual bowls and place a slice of toast in each. Grate the Gruyère and mix with the Parmesan. Sprinkle over the toast and put under a hot grill until the cheese is bubbling. Serve immediately.

FENNEL AND TOMATO PIE

This is one of my favourite pies. You can make it with shortcrust pastry but if you have time try this version with puff pastry. It uses much less butter than most recipes and yet when it is baked the pastry is light, soft and flaky.

FOR THE PASTRY:
225 g (8 oz) wholewheat self-raising flour
100 g (4 oz) butter
3–4 tbsp cold water
milk or beaten egg to glaze

FOR THE FILLING:
1–2 tbsp sunflower oil
1 onion, sliced
1 Florence fennel bulb, sliced
225 g (8 oz) tomatoes, chopped
2 hard-boiled eggs

FOR THE SAUCE:
25 g (1 oz) butter
a scant 25 g (1 oz) wholewheat flour
275 ml (10 fl oz) milk
2 tbsp fresh parsley, finely chopped
freshly ground black pepper

To make the pastry put the flour in a bowl. Cut the butter into small walnut-sized pieces and mix into the flour with a knife. Add sufficient water to form a dough, again mixing with a knife or spoon so as not to rub in the butter. Roll out to form a rectangle about three times as long as it is wide. Fold the pastry by bringing the top third and the bottom third into the centre. Press the edges of this pastry stack together and put into a plastic bag.

Chill for 25–30 minutes. Repeat this rolling, folding and chilling three more times. The pastry is now ready for use and should be kept in a cool place until needed.

To make the filling heat the oil in a pan, add the onion and fennel and soften. Add the tomatoes and cook for a further 5 minutes. Spoon the mixture into an oiled pie dish and slice the eggs over the top.

To make the sauce melt the butter in a saucepan and stir in the flour, cooking it until it begins to bubble. Remove from the heat and gradually stir in the milk. Return to the heat and slowly bring to the boil, stirring until the sauce begins to thicken. Season with parsley and pepper. Pour over the filling in the pie dish.

Roll out the pastry to a circle large enough to cover the pie. Dampen the pastry rim and cover the pie with the pastry top. Trim the edges and brush with milk or beaten egg. Bake in a preheated oven, gas mark 6 (200° C/400° F) for 25–30 minutes.

FENNEL CASSEROLE

A rich vegetable stew from France, closely related to the ratatouille.

2–3 tbsp olive oil
2 mild onions, chopped
2 Florence fennel bulbs, trimmed and sliced
450 g (1 lb) tomatoes, chopped
4 courgettes, sliced
1 sprig of fresh thyme
1 sprig of fresh parsley
1 bay leaf
seasoning

Heat the oil in a large heavy-bottomed pan or casserole. Add the onions and sauté for 8 minutes before stirring in the fennel. Continue cooking, stirring occasionally, for a further 5 minutes. Add the remaining ingredients and cover with a tight-fitting lid. Simmer gently over a low heat until all the vegetables are soft. If the stew is too watery, uncover and boil briskly until the stock is reduced. The casserole should be moist when it is taken to the table.

SPICY RED CABBAGE

1 small red cabbage
150 ml (5 fl oz) red wine vinegar
150 ml (5 fl oz) water
150 ml (5 fl oz) red wine
2 apples, chopped
50 g (2 oz) sultanas
2 onions, chopped
1 bay leaf
1 sprig of fresh thyme
1–2 tsp paprika
seasoning

Quarter the cabbage, cut away the central stalk and shred the leaves finely. Place the cabbage in a bowl with the vinegar, water and wine. Marinate for 1–2 hours. Put the cabbage and liquid into a large pan and add the remaining ingredients. Bring to the boil and cook for 10 minutes. Transfer to an ovenproof dish and cover. Bake in a preheated oven, gas mark 3 (150° C/300° F) for $1\frac{1}{2}$ hours. Season to taste before serving.

MUSHROOM RAGOÛT

2–3 tbsp sunflower oil
1 onion, chopped
2 sticks celery, chopped
450 g (1 lb) mushrooms, chopped
1 tbsp wholewheat flour
150 ml (5 fl oz) water approx.
1 tsp yeast extract
1 sprig of fresh thyme, finely chopped
1 sprig of fresh parsley, finely chopped
1 bay leaf
a pinch of cayenne pepper
freshly ground black pepper

Heat the oil in a large heavy pan, add the onion and celery and sauté until soft and golden. Add the mushrooms and cook for a further 3–4 minutes. Stir in the flour and continue to cook for a minute or two. Pour over the water, stir well and bring to the boil. Add the yeast extract, herbs and cayenne pepper. Simmer gently for 5–10 minutes. Season with black pepper. Serve.

MIXED VEGETABLES WITH GOLDEN MILLET

SERVES 6–8
1 tbsp sunflower oil
1 onion, sliced
175 g (6 oz) millet
1 large potato, scrubbed and chopped into small pieces
100 g (4 oz) white cabbage, shredded
2 sticks celery, chopped
100 g (4 oz) sweetcorn
575 ml (1 pint) water
2 tbsp fresh parsley, finely chopped
2 tbsp fresh mint, finely chopped
1 tbsp lemon juice
seasoning

Heat the oil in a heavy pan, add the onion and sauté for 8–10 minutes. Add the millet and cook until golden brown, stirring all the time. Stir in the remaining ingredients and bring to the boil. Cover and simmer gently for 30 minutes until the vegetables and millet are tender. Add more water if necessary but the pan should be dry at the end of cooking. Adjust the seasoning before serving.

VELVET SOUP

2 tbsp light olive oil
25 g (1 oz) butter
2 onions, chopped finely
1 clove garlic, peeled and crushed
675 g (1$\frac{1}{2}$ lb) tomatoes, chopped
75 g (3 oz) ground almonds
850 ml (1$\frac{1}{2}$ pints) water
2 level tsp dried basil
seasoning

Heat the oil and butter together in a pan, add the onions and garlic and sauté until soft and golden. Add the tomatoes and cook for 3–4 minutes more, stirring frequently. Mix the almonds and water together and pour over the tomatoes. Bring to the boil and simmer gently for 15–20 minutes. Purée the soup by passing it through a sieve or vegetable mouli or process it briefly in a food processor or blender. Add the basil and season to taste. A dash of lemon juice can be added. Return the soup to the pan, heat through and serve.

DEVILLED LEEKS

8 leeks, trimmed and sliced
1 sprig of fresh parsley
1 sprig of fresh thyme
75 ml (3 fl oz) dry white wine
75 ml (3 fl oz) stock or water
freshly ground black pepper
1 bay leaf
2 tsp Dijon mustard

Put all the ingredients in a pan and bring to the boil. Stir and simmer for 15–20 minutes until the leeks are tender. Remove the leeks with a slotted spoon and place in a serving dish. Keep warm. Discard the herbs and boil the stock briskly until it is reduced by a half. Pour over the leeks and serve.

PASTA, PIZZAS AND PANCAKES

PASTA

Although pasta is generally associated with Italy it has also been a staple food in the Far East for thousands of years. At one time it was thought that Marco Polo brought it back to Italy from the courts of Kublai Khan. Before every Italian reaches for pen and paper let me hasten to add that this is no longer believed to be the case. Pasta-making equipment has since been excavated from the ruins of Pompeii, proving that eating pasta was a popular Italian pastime long before their famous compatriot reached China. In fact, the word pasta, which is used to describe such foods as spaghetti, macaroni, ravioli, cannelloni and lasagne is derived from an Italian word meaning dough.

The quality of the dough is of key importance when making pasta. The best pasta is always made from high protein durum wheat which gives the dough an elastic consistency so that it is not only easy to handle but also retains its shape during cooking. Much of the pasta available is made from refined white durum flour and in recent years an increasing amount has been produced from 100 per cent wholewheat durum flour.

I prefer to use these wholewheat varieties as they have a delicious flavour and contain many vitamins (especially the B group) and minerals into the bargain. They also have eight times more fibre than refined white pasta. Wholewheat spaghetti, spaghetti rings, macaroni and lasagne are readily available in most supermarkets, high-class grocers' and wholefood shops. When buying wholewheat pasta don't be put off by its rather drab khaki colour. When cooked it changes to a more appetising creamy hue.

There is also an increasing number of Italian shops springing up in our major cities. They are generally very attractive, decorated in the colours of the Italian flag, and selling anything from wine, cheese, ham, sausage, fresh pasta, oil, gateaux, breads, savoury sauces to made-up pasta dishes. Most of them make their own pasta fresh every morning, and its flavour and texture are superior to those of the dried varieties.

Most of us are familiar with the thin sticks of spaghetti and the short, stumpy tubes of macaroni but there are over 200 different shapes to choose from. Cappelletti is shaped like little hats, farfalle like butterflies, fiori di sambuc is star shaped, ruote looks like wheels and conchiglie resembles conch shells. Some are merely decorative while others are specially shaped for functional reasons and it is important to choose the right pasta for a dish. Here are a few guidelines:
1. Pasta for thin soups and broths should be small enough to enable it to be eaten easily (and politely) with a soup spoon.
2. In more substantial soups, such as minestrone, containing beans and chopped vegetables the pasta should be a similar size to the other main ingredients.
3. Thin tubes of pasta lose their shape and become squashed when a sauce is poured over them. Thicker macaroni is most robust and better for such dishes.
4. Large hollow shapes can be rather overwhelming on their own but are delicious filled with a moist, tasty stuffing. A fiddly job but well worth the trouble for special occasions.

Yet another type of pasta is made from buckwheat flour and is generally sold as buckwheat spaghetti or soba. It has a lovely nutty flavour and a smoother, creamier texture than other whole grain pastas. I serve it with stir-fried vegetables, which have been quickly sautéed in sesame oil and seasoned with soya sauce.

Pasta is many people's idea of a cheap and easy meal. It is a convenient food, capable of being stored for a reasonable length of time (apart from fresh varieties which are best eaten on the day of making) and can be cooked simply and quickly. Those of you who enjoy experimenting in the kitchen should try making it for yourself, particularly if you are unable to buy fresh pasta locally. Mixing the dough is easy, and if you have plenty of time and patience so too is the rolling out. There are a number of gadgets on sale to help the amateur pasta maker; they help speed up the process and make interesting shapes.

BASIC WHOLEWHEAT PASTA DOUGH

250–275 g (9–10 oz) finely ground strong bread flour
a pinch of salt (*optional*)
3 eggs

Put the flour and salt in a bowl and make a well in the centre. Break in the eggs. Using the fingertips, mix the eggs with the flour in the centre of the bowl. Gradually draw more flour into the mixture until it becomes a moist pliant dough. It should not be sticky. The amount of flour needed will vary and it may not be necessary to use all that in the bowl.

Place the dough on a clean, dry work surface and knead for several minutes. Lightly dust the surface with flour if the dough becomes sticky. Divide the dough in half and roll into two balls. Roll out each piece of dough very thinly. You can now cut the pasta sheets into all kinds of shapes.

To make lasagne cut the dough into strips measuring 5 x 15 cm (2 x 6 in). For tagliatelle roll the sheet up loosely and cut into strips about 0.75 cm ($\frac{1}{4}$ in) wide, then unwind them immediately. Hang over a chair or cupboard door until needed.

COOKING PASTA

The golden rule when cooking pasta is to use a large pan and plenty of water. Generally 450 g (1 lb) of pasta needs 3 litres (6 pints) of water. When the water is boiling briskly, add the pasta and stir well with a fork to prevent it sticking together. A tablespoon or two of oil added to the water will help and will also stop the pan boiling over. Boil, uncovered, until the pasta is soft on the outside and slightly firm on the inside. This is known as 'al dente'. Cooking times vary depending on the type of pasta used. Fresh pasta cooks quicker than dried varieties.

Fresh wholewheat lasagne will cook in 10–12 minutes
Fresh wholewheat spaghetti in 8–10 minutes
Fresh wholewheat tagliatelle in 8–10 minutes

When cooked drain the pasta and serve as soon as possible. If using pasta shells drain them thoroughly and make sure that no water is trapped inside.

SAUCES TO SERVE WITH PASTA
CREAMY TOMATO SAUCE

2 tbsp olive oil
450 g (1 lb) ripe tomatoes, chopped
1 onion, chopped
1 clove garlic, peeled and crushed
$\frac{1}{2}$ tsp dried mixed herbs
3 tbsp red wine or water
seasoning
a knob of butter (*optional*)

Heat the olive oil in a frying pan, add the tomatoes, onion and garlic and sauté for 8–10 minutes. Mix in the herbs and wine and season to taste. Bring to the boil, cover and simmer gently until the mixture has been reduced to a pulp. Either rub the mixture through a sieve or process briefly in a blender or food processor, adding a tablespoon or two of tomato purée if necessary. Return to the pan and cook gently. Stir frequently until the sauce is heated through and has thickened. Stir in the knob of butter before serving.

PESTO

A classic pasta sauce from Genoa. The French make a similar sauce known as *pistou*, the only difference being that their version does not contain any pine kernels.

Pesto is an excellent way of preserving the wonderful flavour of basil into the depths of winter. It lasts very well and should be made in late summer when the basil plants are flourishing. (Perhaps flourishing is a little too grand a word to describe my basil plants – in these northern latitudes it takes them all their energy to survive.)

2 tbsp fresh basil, chopped
2 tsp dried basil
1 large clove garlic, peeled and crushed
4 tbsp pine kernels
50 g (2 oz) Parmesan cheese, grated
2 tbsp olive oil

If using a pestle and mortar, pound the fresh basil, dried basil, garlic and pine kernels together to form a smooth paste. Stir in the Parmesan cheese and then the olive oil, a little at a time, until the sauce has the consistency of creamy butter. If using a blender drop the pine kernels onto the rotating blades and when ground put into a small bowl. Add the finely chopped fresh basil, the dried basil and crushed garlic and mix together well. Continue as in the recipe above. For those of you lucky enough to have a food processor the job of making pesto is that much easier. Drop the fresh basil, dried basil, garlic and pine kernels onto the rotating blades. Add the Parmesan cheese and then pour in the olive oil, a little at a time, until the sauce has the consistency of creamy butter. Stir into the cooked pasta immediately before it is served. It is also good with minestrone soup.

M. F. K. Fisher describes in her book, *With Bold Knife and Fork* (Chatto and Windus, 1983) how she soaks dried basil leaves in dry vermouth for an hour or so, then presses them dry before making the pesto. She also suggests using almonds or walnuts instead of pine kernels but to my mind this is stretching the point and although it sounds like a good idea it would be better all round if this permutation were given its own name.

I wonder what the Genovese would make of the following recipe. It is said to have been popular in Ireland during the potato famine. The hot mush, similar to porridge, was made with maize meal. I have included the recipe more out of curiosity than for its culinary merit and I for one will stick to making real pesto.

MAIZE PESTO

Put some marjoram, chopped onion, salt and pepper and some grated cheese in a mortar. Pound well. Stir in boiling water and mix to a paste. Add a little bacon fat or dripping and then pour over a dish of hot mush and greens. Brown and serve immediately.

WALNUT SAUCE

1 tbsp olive oil
100 g (4 oz) ripe tomatoes, chopped
100 g (4 oz) button mushrooms, chopped
2 cloves garlic, chopped
4 black olives, stoned
$\frac{1}{2}$ level tsp mugi miso
225 ml (8 fl oz) tomato juice
50 g (2 oz) walnuts, chopped
3–4 tbsp fresh parsley, finely chopped

Heat the oil in a pan, add the tomatoes, mushrooms and garlic and sauté for 3–4 minutes. Put all the ingredients together, except for the parsley, in a blender or food processor. Process briefly until smooth and creamy. Then pour into a saucepan and simmer for several minutes. Pour over the hot pasta and sprinkle with chopped parsley before serving.

LENTIL BOLOGNESE SAUCE

A delicious vegetarian sauce.

225 g (8 oz) brown lentils
575 ml (1 pint) water
1 bay leaf
olive oil
2 onions, chopped
2 sticks celery, finely chopped
1 clove garlic, peeled and crushed
100 g (4 oz) flat mushrooms, chopped
3 tomatoes, chopped
1–2 tbsp tomato purée
2–3 tsp soya sauce or yeast extract
575 ml (1 pint) bean stock/red wine or water
(or a mixture of all three)
$\frac{1}{2}$ tsp dried mixed herbs
$\frac{1}{2}$ tsp dried oregano
seasoning

Wash the lentils and carefully remove any small stones or pieces of grit. Put them into a pan with the water and bay leaf and bring to the boil. Cover and simmer gently for approximately one hour until they are soft. Check the pan occasionally to make sure that it does not boil dry. If using a pressure cooker, cook at high pressure for 12 minutes. Drain and reserve the stock. Discard the bay leaf.

Heat a tablespoon of oil in a large frying pan, add the onions, celery and garlic and sauté until soft. Add the mushrooms and tomatoes and cook for 4–5 minutes more. Add the tomato purée, soya sauce, the liquid, cooked lentils and herbs. Season to taste. Cover and bring to the boil. Simmer gently for 20–30 minutes until the sauce is thick and richly flavoured.

Serve with a bowl of spaghetti.

TOMATO AND MUSHROOM SAUCE

1 tbsp olive oil
1 large onion, chopped
2 cloves garlic, peeled and crushed
2 carrots, chopped
175 g (6 oz) mushrooms, chopped
675 g (1$\frac{1}{2}$ lb) ripe tomatoes, chopped
150 ml (5 fl oz) red wine
1 tbsp tomato purée
a good pinch of dried basil
a good pinch of dried oregano
1 bay leaf
a scant 1 tbsp parsley, finely chopped
seasoning

Heat the oil in a pan, add the onion, garlic and carrots and lightly sauté, taking care not to let them brown. Add the mushrooms and tomatoes and cook for 2–3 minutes more. Pour over the wine and add the tomato purée, basil, oregano and the bay leaf. Bring to the boil and simmer for 15 minutes or so, until the tomatoes are reduced to a purée.

Remove the bay leaf and pass through a sieve or vegetable mouli or process briefly in a blender or food processor. Return to the pan and stir in the parsley. Heat through, boiling briskly if the sauce is at all watery. Adjust the seasoning to taste. Pour over the cooked pasta and serve immediately.

LASAGNE STUFFED WITH SPINACH, COTTAGE CHEESE AND WALNUTS

FOR THE FILLING:
450 g (1 lb) spinach
100 g (4 oz) natural cottage cheese
50 g (2 oz) chopped walnuts
a knob of butter
50 g (2 oz) button mushrooms, sliced
5 spring onions, trimmed and sliced
pinch of freshly grated nutmeg

REMAINING INGREDIENT:
350 g (12 oz) wholewheat lasagne

Wash the spinach carefully in several changes of water to remove any dirt and grit. Chop off the stalks and place in a large pan. Cover and cook for 10–15 minutes. Drain well, pressing down on the leaves to remove excess water. Chop coarsely. Put the spinach in a mixing bowl and add the cottage cheese and walnuts.

Melt the butter in a small frying pan, add the mushrooms and spring onions and sauté for 4–5 minutes. Stir into the spinach mixture and season with a little nutmeg.

Put the lasagne in a pan of boiling water and simmer gently, uncovered, for 12 minutes until al dente. Drain well and leave to cool.

Place a little of the filling mixture on one end of each piece of lasagne and roll up. When all the sheets of pasta have been stuffed arrange them in the bottom of a buttered ovenproof dish. Cover with greaseproof paper and heat through in a preheated moderate oven.

I usually make a tomato or cheese based sauce to serve with the lasagne. It can either be served separately or poured over the lasagne and heated through in the oven.

PASTA WITH VEGETABLES AND YOGHURT

This serves 2 as a main dish or 4 as a first course.
100 g (4 oz) French beans
2 carrots
$\frac{1}{4}$ cucumber
100 g (4 oz) button mushrooms
olive oil
225 g (8 oz) wholewheat spaghetti
275 ml (10 fl oz) natural yoghurt
1 tbsp unbleached white flour
freshly grated nutmeg

Wash and trim the vegetables. Slice the beans and cut the carrots and cucumber into julienne strips. Roughly chop the mushrooms.

Bring a large pan of water to the boil and add 1 tablespoon olive oil and the pasta. Boil briskly, uncovered, until the pasta is al dente. Meanwhile, steam the beans and carrots until barely tender. Heat a little oil in a frying pan, add the cucumber and mushrooms and sauté for 4–5 minutes. Add the cooked beans and carrots. Mix the yoghurt and flour together before pouring over the vegetables. Bring to the boil, stirring frequently. Simmer until the sauce begins to thicken. Season to taste with nutmeg.

Place the cooked pasta on a serving dish and spoon over the sauce. Serve immediately.

The following are two of the simplest ways of serving pasta. They are both surprisingly good but you really need to use fresh pasta, either shop bought or home-made.

FETTUCINE WITH GARLIC AND OIL

7–8 tbsp olive oil
3 cloves garlic, peeled and crushed
450 g (1 lb) fettucine
seasoning
2 tbsp fresh basil, chopped

Heat the oil in a saucepan, add the garlic and gently sauté until golden coloured. This must be done slowly, over a low heat, so that the garlic does not burn and become bitter.

While watching the garlic bring a large pan of water to the boil. Add the pasta and an additional tablespoon of oil. Boil briskly, uncovered, until the fettucine is tender but firm to the bite. Drain well and put into a serving dish. Pour the garlic sauce over the top and lightly season. Toss and sprinkle the basil over the top. Serve with a green salad and crusty bread. A carafe of red wine would greatly improve the meal.

SPAGHETTINI WITH BUTTER AND PARMESAN

450 g (1 lb) spaghettini
1 tbsp olive oil
75 g (3 oz) butter
Parmesan cheese, grated

Bring a large pan of water to the boil. Add the pasta and the olive oil. Boil briskly, uncovered, until it is tender but firm to the bite. Drain well and toss with the butter. Serve with a bowl of Parmesan cheese.

SPAGHETTI WITH MUSSELS

I get the impression that Italians are fonder of clams than mussels but I am afraid I don't share their enthusiasm. The only clams I have eaten, and they were served to me in an Italian restaurant, were small, rubbery and full of grit. If you know of a better supply, by all means use them in this recipe.

olive oil
1 onion, chopped
1 clove garlic, peeled and crushed
1 red pepper, deseeded and chopped
675 g (1$\frac{1}{2}$ lb) ripe tomatoes, chopped
2–3 tbsp fresh parsley, finely chopped
seasoning
350 g (12 oz) cooked and shelled mussels (for method, see page 156)
450 g (1 lb) spaghetti

Heat a tablespoon or two of oil in a frying pan, add the onion and garlic and sauté until soft and golden. Add the red pepper and the tomatoes and cook gently until the tomatoes are reduced to a virtual purée. If the sauce is too thick add a dash of white wine or water. Stir in the parsley and season. Add the mussels, cover and heat gently.

Bring a large pan of water to the boil and add a tablespoon of olive oil and the pasta. Boil briskly, uncovered, until the pasta is barely tender. Drain well and put into a serving dish. Pour over the hot sauce and serve immediately.

PIZZAS

Pizzas have taken the world by storm and in little over ten years 'pizzeria' (pizza parlours) have become almost as popular and widespread in Britain as they are in their native Italy. In my home town there is a dial-a-pizza service which guarantees the speedy delivery of sizzling hot pizzas to your very door. One reason for the popularity of the pizza is, surely, its convenience. It is really nothing more than a very large, cooked, open sandwich which is as easy to eat with the fingers as it is with a knife and fork.

Originally pizzas must have been quick, rough-and-ready meals for Italian families. It is easy to see how a little dough, left over from a breadmaking session, would be flattened onto a baking tray and topped with a few basic ingredients; perhaps some bright-red Italian plum tomatoes, a few black olives, two or three sardines bought at the market that morning and a sprinkling of sweet basil and oregano.

A good pizza has a light, soft base which is moistened slightly by a thick, rich and aromatic filling; the ingredients for which can be so varied that it is possible to eat a different pizza every week of the year. Some of the best pizzas I have eaten were made at home, for it is really not a very complicated or difficult task. The mouth-watering smell of freshly baked pizza is sufficient reason in itself to cook them. You can also have fun decorating the top with strips of cheese and ham, or a selection of small fish and shellfish, green and black olives, onion rings, or perhaps some brightly coloured peppers.

The type of base used, its shape, size and thickness depends largely on whether the pizza is to be served as a main dish or a snack or whether it is to be followed by other courses. Most pizza bases are made with a yeasted bread dough, but Elizabeth David gives other examples in her book, *Italian Food* (Penguin Books, 1977). For instance, 'a pizza in a private house will usually be made with pastry instead of bread dough as the foundation, and is rather more acceptable to anyone not blessed with the robust stomach of a Neapolitan'.

As with all yeasted mixtures, both bases – the bread dough and the yeasted pastry – are easy enough to make, but need time to prove. They can either be risen relatively quickly in a warm place or more slowly in cooler conditions. I use both methods, depending on what I have planned for the day. There is no reason why the dough should not be covered and left in a coolish place to rise slowly for a few hours while you are away from home.

Some books recommend using a strong bread flour for making pizza bases as the high gluten content makes the dough more pliant and elastic. As I have yet to find a strong wholewheat flour which is organically grown I invariably use a much softer, English flour. The results are nonetheless consistently good. Strong, unbleached white flour can be used but I don't find the results as tasty or as popular as those made with brown flour. Rather than using a lighter white flour when I want to make my pizzas less filling, I simply make 'pizzettes' or tiny pizzas. They can be left open or made into small calzones. A calzone is a pizza resembling a huge Cornish pasty. The familiar round base is folded in half, stuffed and the edges pressed together to seal. It is then baked on its side or deep-fried.

By far the quickest and easiest base to prepare is the scone mix. I had assumed this recipe to be a modern anglicised version of the classic pizza base and was intrigued to find a similar recipe in Elizabeth David's book. Under the heading 'pizza al tegame' (fried pizza) the dough is made with flour, baking powder and water. The Italians fry the base on one side until golden brown before turning it over and spreading on the filling ingredients. The pan is then covered and heated until the cheese melts. This unusual way of cooking a pizza is obviously very quick and invaluable in some parts of Italy where, until recently, domestic ovens were relatively uncommon. You may care to try this method, but I think I'll stick to baking my pizzas, as I always try to use as little fat as possible in my cooking and sometimes even omit the cheese from the top of the pizza itself.

A layer of stringy, chewy Mozzarella cheese has become synonymous with pizzas in Britain, but traditionally the Neapolitan pizza was the only one topped with cheese. The basic filling mixture was one of tomatoes, garlic and black olives while those from the Ligurian area and from Rome consisted simply of onions, olive oil and anchovies.

What you put on the base is a matter of personal choice, but try to resist the temptation to use an assortment of leftovers. A good pizza filling should be prepared and cooked slowly while the dough is being made, so that the flavour has time to develop and the consistency is reduced to that of a thick, creamy sauce. Although I use tinned plum tomatoes in the winter I much prefer using fresh ones, bolstering up their flavour with a little tomato purée. In the summer I buy a quantity of firm, ripe tomatoes when they are cheap, cut them into quarters and freeze them. They prove extremely useful for making pizza fillings and tomato-based sauces, especially at Christmas and late winter when tomatoes are expensive and tasteless. Use straight from the freezer.

BASIC YEASTED DOUGH

MAKES 1 PIZZA
225 g (8 oz) wholewheat flour
pinch of salt (*optional*)
15 g ($\frac{1}{2}$ oz) fresh yeast or 7 g ($\frac{1}{4}$ oz) dried yeast
150–175 ml (5–6 fl oz) warm water ($\frac{1}{2}$ cold/
$\frac{1}{2}$ boiling)
olive oil

Place the flour and salt in a mixing bowl.
Dissolve the yeast in the warm water and stir in
a handful of the flour. Leave in a warm place
for 10 minutes. When frothy stir the yeasted
mixture into the remaining flour. Mix to form
a dough and knead until smooth and elastic.
Cover and leave in a warm place to double in
size.

When the dough is well risen, knock down
and turn out onto a floured board. Roll out to
form a rectangle. Brush with oil. Roll up from
the shortest side until it resembles a swiss roll.
Repeat the rolling and oiling three more times.
Roll out to form a circle measuring 30 cm (12
in) in diameter and 0.75 cm ($\frac{1}{4}$ in) in thickness.
Oil a large baking tray and carefully lift the
pizza base onto it. Pinch the edges to make a
slightly raised rim and brush with oil. The pizza
base is now ready for use.

Spread with the filling and bake in a preheated oven, gas mark 8 (230° C/450° F) for
25–30 minutes.

YEASTED PASTRY DOUGH

MAKES 1 PIZZA
175 g (6 oz) wholewheat flour
pinch of salt (*optional*)
25 g (1 oz) butter, diced
2 tbsp sunflower oil
$\frac{1}{2}$ tsp easy blend dried yeast
1 egg, beaten
a little warm water

Place the flour and salt in a mixing bowl and
rub in the butter and oil using your fingertips.
Add the yeast, the beaten egg and sufficient
warm water to form a fairly soft dough. Cover
and leave in a warm place to double in size.
Turn the dough onto a lightly floured surface
and roll out to a circle about 0.75 cm ($\frac{1}{4}$ in) in
thickness. Oil a baking tray and carefully lift
the pizza base onto it. Pinch the edges to make
a slightly raised rim. The pizza base is now
ready for use.

Spread the filling over the top and bake in a
preheated oven, gas mark 6 (200° C/400° F) for
25 minutes.

QUICK SCONE MIX

MAKES 1 PIZZA
175 g (6 oz) wholewheat self-raising flour
$\frac{1}{2}$ tsp baking powder
15 g ($\frac{1}{2}$ oz) butter
2 tbsp sunflower oil
3–4 tbsp milk

Mix the flour and baking powder together in a
bowl. Rub in the butter and oil, using your
fingertips, and add sufficient milk to form a soft
dough. Knead lightly, turn onto a lightly
floured surface and roll out to a circle about
0.75 cm in thickness. Oil a baking tray and
carefully lift the pizza base onto it. Pinch the
edges to make a slightly raised rim. The pizza
base is now ready for use.

Spread with the filling and bake in a preheated oven, gas mark 5 (190° C/375° F) for 25
minutes.

DELUXE PIZZA FILLING

This is my favourite filling and the one which I give to the family. It is rich and colourful. If the tomatoes are lacking in flavour add a tablespoon or two of tomato purée. The black olives are optional. I always put a few on the top as they are very popular with my friends – I can't abide them. Every year or so I nibble one to see if they have improved but to no avail.

olive oil
1 onion, chopped
1 clove garlic, peeled and crushed
1 green pepper, deseeded and sliced
50 g (2 oz) button mushrooms, sliced
450 g (1 lb) ripe tomatoes, chopped
2–3 tbsp tomato purée, to taste
$\frac{1}{2}$ tsp dried basil
$\frac{1}{2}$ tsp dried oregano
freshly ground black pepper
black olives
100 g (4 oz) Mozzarella cheese, sliced
(*optional*)

Heat the olive oil in a large frying pan, add the onion, garlic and pepper and sauté until they begin to soften. Add the mushrooms and tomatoes and cook gently for several minutes. Stir in the tomato purée, basil and oregano. Season to taste with black pepper. Bring to the boil. Partially cover the pan and reduce the heat. Simmer gently for 15–20 minutes until the mixture thickens. Leave to cool slightly before spooning over the prepared pizza base.

Arrange the olives on top and cover with cheese. Bake in a preheated oven. The temperature of the oven and the cooking time will depend on which type of pizza base you have made.

MUSHROOM AND RED WINE FILLING

1–2 tbsp olive oil
1 onion, chopped
225 g (8 oz) flat mushrooms, chopped
450 g (1 lb) tomatoes, chopped
tomato purée to taste
4 tbsp red wine
$\frac{1}{2}$ tsp dried basil
$\frac{1}{2}$ tsp dried thyme
grated Cheddar cheese

Heat the oil in a large frying pan, add the onion and sauté until soft and golden. Add the mushrooms and tomatoes and cook gently for 6–8 minutes. Stir in the tomato purée. Pour over the wine and season with basil and thyme. Cover and simmer for 15–20 minutes until the sauce is thick and rich. Cool slightly before spreading over the pizza base. Cover with cheese and bake in a preheated oven. The temperature of the oven and the cooking time will depend on which type of pizza you have made.

AUBERGINE FILLING

1–2 tbsp olive oil
1 onion, chopped
1 aubergine, chopped
1 clove garlic, peeled and crushed
450 g (1 lb) ripe tomatoes, chopped
tomato purée to taste
1 tsp dried basil
freshly ground black pepper
100 g (4 oz) Mozzarella cheese, sliced

Heat the oil in a large frying pan, add the onion and sauté until soft and golden. Add the aubergine, garlic and tomatoes and fry for 5–6 minutes, stirring frequently. Cover the pan and reduce the heat. Cook gently until the aubergines are very soft; add a little liquid if the pan boils dry. When the mixture is thick season with tomato purée, basil and black pepper. Spoon over a pizza base, cover with cheese and bake in a preheated oven. The temperature of the oven and the cooking time will depend on which type of pizza base you have made.

NEAPOLITAN PIZZA

The traditional pizza of Naples.

FOR THE BASE:
basic yeasted dough (see page 98)

FOR THE FILLING:
450 g (1 lb) ripe tomatoes, sliced
freshly ground black pepper
a good pinch of dried basil
a good pinch of dried oregano
50 g (2 oz) tin anchovy fillets in oil, drained
but the oil reserved
100–175 g (4–6 oz) Mozzarella cheese, sliced

Make the base as described on page 98. Place the rolled out pizza base on an oiled baking tray and pinch the edges to make a slightly raised rim. Lay the tomatoes over the top and season to taste with black pepper, basil and oregano. Slice the anchovies and place the strips over the tomatoes. Dribble the anchovy oil over the top. Cover with the cheese and bake in a preheated oven, gas mark 8 (230° C/450° F) for 25–30 minutes.

PIZZA MARGHERITA

This is a classic pizza, apparently named after Queen Margherita of Italy, but I first came across it in a small pizzeria known as the 'Pizza Margherita'.

FOR THE BASE:
basic yeasted dough (see page 98)

FOR THE FILLING:
5 tomatoes, thinly sliced
seasoning
1 tbsp fresh oregano, finely chopped or 1 tsp
dried oregano
100–175 g (4–6 oz) Mozzarella cheese, sliced

Make the base as described on page 98. Place the rolled out pizza base on an oiled baking tray and pinch the edges to make a slightly raised rim. Arrange the tomatoes over the top. Season to taste and sprinkle with oregano. Cover with cheese. Place in a preheated oven, gas mark 8 (230° C/450° F) for 25–30 minutes. Serve immediately.

PIZZA À LA MAISON

This pizza is very quick, and is an anglicised version of the Italian 'pizza al tegame' (fried pizza).

FOR THE BASE:
100 g (4 oz) wholewheat self-raising flour
a knob of butter
2 tbsp sunflower oil
water to mix

FOR THE FILLING:
olive oil
1 onion, chopped
225 g (8 oz) ripe tomatoes, chopped
tomato purée to taste
1 tsp dried basil
grated Cheddar cheese

To make the base rub the butter into the flour, using your fingertips, until the mixture resembles breadcrumbs. Add sufficient cold water to form a fairly stiff dough. Knead lightly before turning onto a floured surface. Roll out to a circle about the size of a dinner plate. Keep aside until needed.

Heat a tablespoon of oil in another pan, add the onion and sauté until soft and golden. Add the tomatoes and tomato purée to taste. Stirring well, cook until soft. Stir in the basil and boil briskly until the sauce is reduced and thick.

Meanwhile heat 1–2 tablespoons oil in a frying pan, large enough to take the pizza, and cook the dough for 5–7 minutes. Turn it over and cook the other side. Spread the filling over the pizza base and sprinkle with cheese. Put under a hot grill for a few minutes until the cheese is brown and bubbly. Serve immediately.

PIZZA TRIPOLI

The addition of some chopped, spicy salami adds a little pep to this pizza.

FOR THE BASE:
basic yeasted dough (see page 98)

FOR THE FILLING:
1 tbsp olive oil
1 onion, chopped
1 clove garlic, peeled and crushed
50 g (2 oz) mushrooms, chopped
450 g (1 lb) ripe tomatoes, chopped
tomato purée to taste
50 g (2 oz) salami, chopped
$\frac{1}{2}$ tsp dried basil
$\frac{1}{2}$ tsp dried oregano
freshly ground black pepper
grated cheese (*optional*)

Make the base as described on page 98.

Meanwhile, heat the oil in a large frying pan, add the onion and garlic and sauté for 8–10 minutes. Add the mushrooms and tomatoes and continue cooking until the tomatoes soften. Add the tomato purée if necessary. Cook gently, stirring frequently, until the mixture thickens. Add the salami, herbs and black pepper.

Place the rolled out pizza base on an oiled baking tray and pinch the edges to make a slightly raised rim. Spread the filling over the top and cover with cheese. Bake in a preheated oven, gas mark 8 (230° C/450° F) for 25–30 minutes.

WINTER PIZZA

FOR THE BASE:
basic yeasted dough (see page 98)

FOR THE FILLING:
1 tbsp olive oil
1 large onion, chopped
1 clove garlic, peeled and crushed
50 g (2 oz) button mushrooms, sliced
400 g (14 oz) tin of tomatoes, drained and chopped
$\frac{1}{2}$ tsp dried basil
$\frac{1}{2}$ tsp dried oregano
seasoning
black olives to taste
100 g (4 oz) Bel Paese or Mozzarella cheese, sliced

Make the base as described on page 98. Place the rolled out pizza base on an oiled baking tray and pinch the edges to make a slightly raised rim.

Heat the oil in a frying pan, add the onion and garlic and sauté until soft and golden. Add the mushrooms and tomatoes and simmer gently until the sauce begins to thicken. Stir in the herbs and season to taste.

Spoon the filling over the base and decorate with olives. Lay the cheese on top and bake in a preheated oven, gas mark 8 (230° C/450° F) for 25–30 minutes.

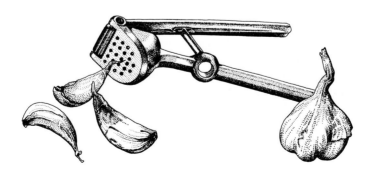

PANCAKES

The eating of pancakes on Shrove Tuesday is common not only in Britain but also in many other Christian countries. It is a symbolic gesture marking the beginning of Lent. Many Christians are forbidden to eat certain foods during Lent, out of respect for the forty days and forty nights Christ spent in the wilderness. All meat has to be eaten by Collop Monday (collop being an old English word for a slice of meat) while the fats, eggs, cream and milk have to be used up the next day. It became the habit to make pancakes with these ingredients and the day itself became known as Pancake Tuesday.

The days preceding Lent were known as Shrovetide as it was customary for people to be shriven (to make their confessions) in preparation for Lent itself. It was also, however, a time of merrymaking and feasts and gave ample opportunity for everyone to use up their stocks of forbidden foods and to relax and enjoy themselves before the rigours of fasting and penitence began. Traditions die hard and although Lent is less strictly observed today Shrove Tuesday is still celebrated with the making, tossing and eating of pancakes.

Pancakes or crêpes can be served as a simple dessert or as a savoury dish, depending on the type of batter used and the fillings or accompaniments. There are endless variations and I enjoy eating them throughout the year as they are economical, filling and quick and easy to make.

I find a light batter, made with unbleached white flour, the best for thin, delicate crêpes, especially those to be eaten as a dessert with a little honey and lemon or a fresh fruit purée. A slightly firmer pancake can be made with a finely ground wholewheat flour and is particularly good stuffed with a savoury filling. Another variety, and one of my favourites, is the buckwheat pancake. Buckwheat flour gives the pancake a delicate nutty flavour which goes particularly well with creamy fillings and sauces.

Brittany is famous for its buckwheat crêpes and in tourist areas many farmers have converted barns into crêperies. The one I visited was furnished with long trestle tables and benches and sold nothing but pancakes and cider. To one side of the main eating area stood the farmer's wife, looking very hot but not in the least flustered. Beside her, on a large rough table, was an enormous bowl of batter into which she dipped a ladle and then poured its contents onto one of two hot griddles. She spread the batter very thinly with a spatula and when one side of the pancake was nicely browned she tossed it onto the other hot plate and started afresh with another ladle full of batter. Then one of the daughters dipped her hands into a glass jar, dolloped some filling into the centre of the crepe, rolled it up and rushed it to the waiting table.

No special culinary equipment or skill is needed to make pancakes. Some cooks recommend leaving the batter to stand for 30 minutes before using but I don't always follow this rule. It is, however, easier to make thin, well-shaped pancakes in a small, thick-bottomed frying pan and it is worth remembering that the first pancake is always the most difficult as it often sticks to the pan. So if at first you don't succeed do try again – as the pan warms to the job the pancakes cook quicker and become easier to toss.

Naturally, the very best pancakes are those tossed straight from the pan onto the waiting plate; however, this isn't very practical when catering for large numbers. It is possible to make pancakes in advance and to keep them stacked in a refrigerator, wrapped in greaseproof paper until needed. They will keep fresh for three to four days and for up to two months if stored in a freezer. To reuse simply brush them over lightly with a little vegetable oil and place in a preheated oven, gas mark 6 (200° C/ 400° F) for 10–15 minutes. There is no need to reheat pancakes in this way if they are to be filled with a savoury stuffing. Drop a spoonful of filling onto the centre of each pancake and roll up, or fold in half twice to form a triangle.

Put them in a lightly buttered ovenproof dish and cover with foil or greaseproof paper. Bake in the oven for 15–20 minutes until heated through.

Stuffed pancakes make an excellent meal and, depending on the filling, can be served for lunch, tea or dinner. I generally serve savoury pancakes with a home-made sauce and side salad. The hot sauce is best poured over them just before serving. Some types of sweet fillings can be heated in the oven but I find fresh fruits, particularly delicate summer ones, are better placed inside crêpes which have already been warmed through and then served with a bowl of cream, yoghurt or a fruit sauce.

Here are some ideas for savoury and sweet fillings:

Savoury Pancakes
- low fat cream cheese with spring onions
- chopped ham and cubes of Gruyère cheese
- mushrooms sautéed in butter and mixed with sour cream or thick set natural yoghurt (stabilise the yoghurt by stirring in a little flour before using. This will stop it curdling when heated)
- grated cheese mixed with mustard, cider vinegar and seasoning and served with a tomato sauce
- cooked, flaked smoked haddock served with a creamy sauce
- tomatoes, onions and peppers sautéed in olive oil and seasoned with basil
- creamed sweetcorn topped with sour cream
- cooked green lentils and onions mixed with parsley and lemon juice
- spinach purée with chopped walnuts and served with a cottage cheese and yoghurt sauce

Sweet Crêpes
- honey and chopped nuts
- spicy apple purée with sultanas
- chopped bananas
- fresh strawberries and low fat cream cheese
- cooked apricots with a fruit purée
- cottage cheese and pineapple flambé
- tangerine segments with a tangy orange sauce
- cashew nut cream
- try flavouring the batter itself with the grated rind and juice of an orange

BASIC BATTER RECIPE

MAKES 10–12 PANCAKES
175 g (6 oz) finely ground wholewheat flour
pinch of salt (*optional*)
2 eggs
200 ml (7 fl oz) water ⎫
225 ml (8 fl oz) milk ⎬ mixed together
1 tbsp oil
oil for cooking

Mix the flour and salt, if you are using it, together in a bowl. Make a well in the centre and add the eggs. Pour in half the liquid and gradually work into the flour. Mix well until smooth. Add the remaining liquid, a little at a time, stirring after each addition. Add the oil and beat the batter vigorously until it is creamy and the surface is covered with bubbles. If using a blender or food processor mix all the ingredients together until smooth.

Heat the oil in a frying pan, shaking it gently round the bottom and the sides. Drain off any excess. Keep the pan fairly hot and pour in some of the batter. Swirl it round to coat the pan thinly but evenly. When the underside of the pancake is patterned brown and the surface has set it is time to turn it over. Experts in the art of pancake tossing say that it is easier if you first tip the pancake a little over the edge furthest away from you, then quickly flip it upwards and towards you so that it turns over and lands neatly in the centre of the pan again. For those of us who haven't quite mastered the art, a fish slice can do the job just as effectively and, in my case, more successfully. The second side of the pancake always cooks quicker than the first and it may be necessary to turn the heat down a little. As you finish each pancake stack them up, interleaved with greaseproof paper, and keep them in a warm place until needed.

BUCKWHEAT BATTER RECIPE

MAKES 8–10 SMALL PANCAKES
50 g (2 oz) unbleached white flour
50 g (2 oz) buckwheat flour
pinch of salt (*optional*)
1 egg
a scant 150 ml (5 fl oz) milk ⎫
a scant 150 ml (5 fl oz) water ⎬ mixed together
oil for cooking

Method as for basic recipe.

DESSERT CRÊPE BATTER RECIPE

MAKES 10 LACY CRÊPES
100 g (4 oz) unbleached white flour
pinch of salt (*optional*)
1 egg
275 ml (10 fl oz) milk
oil for cooking

Method as for basic recipe.

A RICH BATTER

MAKES 8
100 g (4 oz) plain flour (brown or white)
pinch of salt (*optional*)
4 eggs
25 g (1 oz) melted butter
150 ml (5 fl oz) milk

Mix the flour and salt, if you are using it, together in a bowl. Make a well in the centre and break in 2 whole eggs and 2 egg yolks. Pour over the melted butter and stir, gradually drawing in the flour from around the sides of the bowl. Add the milk and beat well. The consistency should be that of single cream — thin down with milk if necessary. Beat the 2 egg whites until stiff and peaked and carefully fold into the mixture. Cook as normal.

PANCAKE PARCELS

FOR THE BATTER:
75 g (3 oz) buckwheat flour
75 g (3 oz) fine wholewheat flour
pinch of salt (optional)
2 eggs
425 ml (15 fl oz) milk
oil for frying

FOR THE FILLING:
450 g (1 lb) leeks, trimmed, cleaned and thinly
sliced
2 tbsp olive oil
25 g (1 oz) wholewheat flour
a scant 150 ml (5 fl oz) dry white wine
150 ml (5 fl oz) water
2 tsp Dijon mustard
3 tbsp fresh parsley, finely chopped

To make the batter mix the flours and salt, if you are using it, in a bowl and make a well in the centre. Add the eggs and half the milk. Stir, using a wooden spoon, and gradually draw in the flour from around the sides of the bowl. Beat well to form a smooth batter and mix in the remaining milk. If using a blender or food processor mix all the ingredients together until smooth. Heat some oil in a 20 cm (8 in) frying pan. Cook as normal. This quantity makes 8–10 pancakes.

Steam the leeks until tender.

Heat the olive oil in a saucepan and stir in the flour. Cook gently for a minute or two, stirring frequently. Remove from the heat and gradually add the wine and water, stirring well after each addition. Return to the stove and slowly bring to the boil, stirring to prevent the sauce becoming lumpy, and cook gently for 4–5 minutes until it begins to thicken. The sauce should be slightly thicker than coating consistency. Stir in the mustard, parsley and cooked leeks.

Place a pancake on the work-top and spread the filling over half of it. Fold the uncovered half of pancake over the filling and then fold in half again to form a triangle. Repeat until each pancake has been stuffed. Arrange them in a buttered shallow ovenproof dish and warm through in a moderate oven for 15–20 minutes until the sauce begins to bubble.

CHRISTMAS PANCAKES

I have seen this recipe in a number of old cookery books. Apparently it was used in winter when eggs were scarce. The snow was thought to lighten the batter. Make a basic batter mix and just before cooking the pancakes go and collect some fresh snow. Quickly stir the snow into the batter and as you cook the pancakes the snow will melt giving them a delicate, lacy appearance.

PANCAKES STUFFED WITH CREAMED LEEKS

MAKES 10–12

FOR THE BATTER:
175 g (6 oz) wholewheat flour
pinch of salt (optional)
2 eggs
425 ml (15 fl oz) milk
oil for frying

FOR THE FILLING:
450 g (1 lb) leeks
1 egg
50 g (2 oz) curd cheese/cottage cheese
1 tsp Dijon mustard
100 g (4 oz) Gruyère cheese, grated

To make the batter mix the flour and salt, if you are using it, together in a bowl. Make a well in the centre and add the eggs. Pour in half the liquid and gradually work into the flour. Mix well until smooth. Add the remaining liquid, a little at a time, stirring after each addition. Add the oil and beat the batter vigorously until it is creamy and the surface is covered with bubbles. If using a blender or food processor mix all the ingredients together until smooth. Cook the pancakes as normal and keep warm until needed.

Trim the leeks, wash carefully and slice thinly. Steam until tender. Place in a blender or food processor with the egg, curd cheese and mustard. Blend until fairly smooth.

Spread a little of the filling over each pancake and roll up. Place in a shallow ovenproof dish lightly rubbed with butter, and sprinkle the grated cheese over the top. Heat through in the oven or under the grill until the filling is warm and the cheese is brown and bubbly.

PALATSCHINKEN (SAVOURY PANCAKE GATEAU)

Makes 8 pancakes and sufficient stuffing to fill a 20 cm (8 in) cake tin, if possible use a cake tin with sprung sides so that when baked the tin can be lifted off and the palatschinken taken to the table on the loose bottom.

The list of ingredients may look rather formidable but don't be daunted, the dish is relatively easy to prepare and well worth the effort. It can be made in advance and heated through just before serving.

FOR THE BATTER:
50 g (2 oz) buckwheat flour
100 g (4 oz) unbleached white flour
pinch of salt (*optional*)
2 eggs
425 ml (15 fl oz) milk
oil for frying

FOR THE FILLING:
2 medium onions
2 medium aubergines
2 tbsp olive oil
1 clove garlic, peeled and crushed
150 ml (5 fl oz) red wine
1 good tbsp tomato purée
a little fresh parsley, finely chopped

FOR THE SAUCE:
1 tbsp olive oil
25 g (1 oz) butter
100 g (4 oz) button mushrooms, finely chopped
40 g (1½ oz) wholewheat flour
275 ml (10 fl oz) water
75 g (3 oz) ground hazelnuts
1 tbsp thick set yoghurt
freshly grated nutmeg
50–75 g (2–3 oz) Gruyère cheese

To make the batter mix the flours and salt, if you are using it, in a bowl and make a well in the centre. Add the eggs and half the milk. Stir, using a wooden spoon, and gradually draw in the flour from around the sides of the bowl. Beat well to form a smooth batter and mix in the remaining milk. If using a blender or food processor mix all the ingredients together until smooth. Heat a little oil in a 20-cm (8-in) frying pan. Cook as normal. This quantity makes approximately 8 pancakes. Stack them, interleaved with greaseproof paper, until needed.

To make the filling dice the vegetables. Heat the olive oil in a large pan, add the onions and garlic and lightly sauté for 5–10 minutes. Add the aubergines and continue to cook over a low heat until they begin to soften. Mix the wine and tomato purée together and pour over the vegetables. Simmer gently until the vegetables are very soft and almost reduced to a purée. The mixture should be fairly thick. (Mash with a fork if necessary.) Season to taste with parsley and set aside to cool.

To make the sauce heat the oil and butter together, add the mushrooms and sauté for 3–4 minutes. Stir in the wholewheat flour and cook for a minute or two more, until the mixture begins to bubble. Remove from the heat and gradually add the water, a little at a time, stirring well after each addition. Only add about three-quarters of the water at this stage. Return to the heat and bring to the boil. Simmer gently, stirring well, until the mixture begins to thicken. Leave to cool for a few minutes before adding the hazelnuts and yoghurt. The sauce should be a little thicker than coating consistency. Adjust the consistency with the remaining water if necessary. Season to taste with nutmeg. Leave to cool.

Lay one pancake in the bottom of the buttered cake tin and spoon over some of the aubergine mixture. Don't be too generous with the filling or sauce otherwise the pancakes start slipping and sliding about when you try to cut the gateau. Lay another pancake on top. Cover with some of the sauce. Repeat the layers until all the pancakes have been used up. Finish with a layer of sauce and grate the cheese over the top.

Bake in a preheated oven, gas mark 6 (200° C/ 400° F) until the pancakes are heated through and the cheese is brown and bubbly.

YEASTED PANCAKES

I have always known this type of pancake as a blini but I noticed that Jane Grigson, in her book *European Cookery* (Michael Joseph, 1983), spells it bliny. Blinis are traditional to Russia and were associated with a pagan festival celebrating the coming of spring. As in Britain, it marked the beginning of a period of religious observance during which certain foods could not be eaten. Although most Russians eat blinis throughout the year they still celebrate Maslenita, the pagan festival, and indulge in a veritable feast of pancakes, eating them with caviar, butter, sour cream, smoked salmon and virtually anything which takes their fancy.

Blinis are always made with a yeasted batter but any type of flour can be used. Wholewheat flour makes a lighter pancake than those made with buckwheat flour but I don't think that they taste quite so good. It is probably a good idea to compromise.

10 g (a scant $\frac{1}{2}$ oz) fresh yeast or
5 g (a scant $\frac{1}{4}$ oz) dried yeast
225 ml (8 fl oz) warm water
150 g (5 oz) unbleached white flour
75 g (3 oz) buckwheat flour
pinch of salt (*optional*)
275 ml (10 fl oz) warm milk
20 g ($\frac{3}{4}$ oz) butter
1 large egg, separated

Cream the yeast in the warm water and stir in a handful of the measured flour. Leave in a warm place for 10–15 minutes. Mix the flours and salt, if you are using it, in a bowl. Make a well in the centre of the flour and gradually stir in the yeast mixture, beating well until smooth. Stand in a warm place until the mixture has doubled in size.

Melt the butter in a pan with the milk and when warm pour into the batter. Add the egg yolk and beat well. Set aside in a warm place for 30 minutes. Beat thoroughly again and leave for a further 30 minutes. Whisk the egg white until stiff and peaked and fold into the batter. Stand for a further 10–15 minutes. Cook as normal, preferably in a small pan.

HUNGARIAN PANCAKES

MAKES 10–12

FOR THE FILLING:
1–2 tbsp olive oil
1 onion, chopped
450 g (1 lb) minced beef
1 green pepper, deseeded and chopped
2 tomatoes, chopped
2 tsp paprika
425 ml (15 fl oz) water
1–2 tbsp soya sauce
150 ml (5 fl oz) natural yoghurt
1 tbsp wholewheat flour
freshly ground black pepper

FOR THE BATTER:
175 g (6 oz) wholewheat flour
pinch of salt (*optional*)
2 eggs
275 ml (10 fl oz) milk }
150 ml (5 fl oz) water } mixed together
1 tbsp sunflower oil
oil for frying

Heat the oil in a pan, add the onion and sauté until soft and golden. Stir in the minced beef and cook for a further 10 minutes or so. Add the pepper and tomatoes and continue to cook for a further 5–7 minutes, stirring frequently. Add the paprika, water and soya sauce. Cover and simmer until the meat is tender. Beat the yoghurt and flour together in a bowl and stir into the pan. Cook uncovered until the sauce is thick and creamy. Season to taste with black pepper.

Meanwhile, make the batter. Place all the ingredients in a blender or food processor and process until smooth. If you haven't a blender mix the flour and salt, if you are using it, together in a bowl. Make a well in the centre and break in the eggs. Pour in half the liquid and, using a wooden spoon, gradually work into the flour. Mix well until smooth. Add the remaining liquid, a little at a time, stirring well after each addition. Add the oil and beat the batter vigorously. Cook as normal and keep the pancakes warm until needed.

Spoon a little of the filling onto each pancake and roll up. Place in serving dish. Serve with a green salad and some granary rolls.

RICE

RICE

Rice is the staple food for nearly half the world's population so it is not surprising to find recipes for Spanish paella, Italian risotto, Middle Eastern pilau and Indian biryani in many of our recipe books. However, for a real appreciation of rice one must look at Japanese and Chinese cooking. The Japanese do not consider that they have eaten unless the meal includes a bowl of rice, and the three main meals of the day are sometimes referred to as 'morning rice', 'afternoon rice' and 'evening rice'. The Chinese too show a similar respect and liking for this grain believing that there is nothing to equal the natural, delicate flavour of perfectly cooked rice.

Rice is a truly exceptional grain in that it grows best in the monsoon regions of Asia where 90 per cent of the world's crop is grown and consumed. It is also cultivated in Italy, Spain, France, North and South America, India, Australia and Africa. Strains have been developed which actually prefer dry conditions. This has proved an important breakthrough, as it has been estimated that 300 gallons of water are needed to produce 1 lb of traditional 'paddy-field' rice.

After the rice is harvested it is threshed and hulled to remove the thick woody husk surrounding the grain. The resultant natural or brown rice is high in nutrients, containing an excellent balance of protein, carbohydrate, fat, vitamins and minerals. Unfortunately, as with wheat, it became fashionable to refine the grain to produce white or polished rice. Eaten originally by the upper classes, white rice was regarded as something of a status symbol and was eagerly adopted by poorer people as the price fell. The loss of nutrients was of little consequence to the wealthy who ate a rich and varied diet but it had a profound effect on the health of the poorer classes who ate approximately $1-1\frac{1}{2}$ lbs of rice a day. (The average Briton now eats $2\frac{1}{2}$ lbs a year.) The result was the emergence of a crippling and often fatal disease known as beri-beri, caused by a dietary deficiency of thiamine (vitamin B_1).

Although we in Britain are unlikely to suffer from beri-beri it still makes good sense to eat brown rice. Not only is it a good source of carbohydrates, protein, B vitamins, calcium and phosphorus but it is also easier to digest, contains more fibre and is more satisfying than white varieties.

There are several thousand varieties, but the basic distinction, in cookery terms, is between long grain and short grain. Long grain varieties become fluffy and separate when cooked and are ideal for savoury dishes such as paella, pilau, plain boiled or fried rice. Short grain rice becomes much stickier and makes admirable puddings, stuffings, rice balls and moulds. However, I must add a word of caution – no two rices cook the same. I once bought the very best quality, organically grown, long grain brown rice from Carolina for a special savoury dish. The result was disastrous. It just so happens that this particular type of rice has a very soft, moist texture when cooked and was totally unsuitable for my purpose. If in doubt ask – it is better to be safe than sorry.

It is not only the type but also the age of the rice which affects the way in which it cooks. Freshly harvested rice cooks more quickly, absorbs less water and is slightly stickier than older rice. In India, the best pilau rices are often left to mature for many years before being used. In Japan, however, a softer, moister rice is preferred, presumably because it is easier to pick up with chopsticks, and freshly harvested rice is regarded as a great delicacy.

There are many schools of thought regarding the best way to prepare rice. Some people wash it, soak it or even dry fry it before cooking. Some cook it with salt, some boil it in an open saucepan while others believe that a final rinsing in cold water gives the best results. I am sure that you too have your own method which I have no wish to contradict. I will, however, give some basic tips about preparing brown rice as this is the only type that I use. Many people prefer its flavour, texture, attractiveness and dietary value, but the transition from white to brown is not always smooth, the two principal areas of complaint being that brown rice either cooks to a mush or remains as hard as little bullets.

I have carried out an experiment in which I cooked two equal quantities of rice in the same amount of water, first in a heavy 'le creuset' type pan and then in a lighter aluminium one. The difference was impressive. The rice simmered in the heavy pan cooked to perfection. It was tender and dry, and each grain was separate and held its shape. On the other hand the rice cooked in the lighter pan took longer to cook, needed more water and did not cook evenly – being soft and soggy at the bottom of the pan and hard and chewy at the top.

As well as using a good heavy pan I suggest that you also measure the rice into a mug or cup and cook it in approximately twice as much water. Of all the many different ways of cooking brown rice I find this one the simplest and most reliable. The rice will be perfectly cooked when all the water has been absorbed and the pan is dry. Generally 1 mugful of brown rice weighs 225 g (8 oz) and will be sufficient for 3–4 people. If you like to season rice with salt always add it after the rice has cooked, for the osmotic effect of salt lengthens the cooking time and stops the rice softening.

BOILED BROWN RICE

1 cup of long grain brown rice
a scant 2 cups of water
seasoning

Place the rice in a heavy pan. Add the water and bring to the boil. Cover and simmer gently for 35–40 minutes. Do not stir the rice once it has begun to cook as this breaks the soft bran layer causing the rice to become sticky. At the end of the cooking period push the handle of a fork or spoon into the middle of the pan and part the rice a little. If all the water has been absorbed and the pan is dry test a grain or two. The rice should be tender but still have a slight resistance to the bite. Replace the lid as quickly as possible and remove from the heat. Leave to stand for 5–10 minutes. Season to taste.

Short grained varieties should be cooked in full, as opposed to scant, cups of water and will take about 5–10 minutes longer.

PRESSURE-COOKED BROWN RICE

1 cup of long grain brown rice
2 cups of water
seasoning

Place the rice in a pressure cooker with the water. Cover and bring to full pressure. Reduce the heat and cook for 20 minutes. Remove from the stove and allow to come down from pressure gradually. Stir well, replace the lid and leave to stand for 5 minutes. Season to taste.

RICE WITH MUSHROOMS AND SPRING ONIONS

1–2 tbsp olive oil
bunch of spring onions, trimmed and sliced
100 g (4 oz) button mushrooms, quartered
350 g (12 oz) long grain brown rice
a scant 850 ml (1½ pints) chicken stock
seasoning

Heat the oil in a heavy pan, add the spring onions and mushrooms and sauté for 4–5 minutes. Add the brown rice and cook for several minutes, stirring frequently, until the rice becomes slightly translucent. Pour over the stock and cover with a lid. Simmer, without stirring, for 35–40 minutes. When all the water has been absorbed and the rice is dry and tender remove from the heat and leave covered for 5–10 minutes. Season to taste before serving.

RICE SALAD WITH HERBS

225 g (8 oz) long grain brown rice
a scant 575 ml (1 pint) water
juice of 1 lemon
4–5 tbsp olive oil
seasoning
2 tbsp fresh parsley, finely chopped
2 tbsp fresh chives, finely chopped
1 tbsp fresh mint, finely chopped

Place the rice in a heavy pan with the water and the juice of half the lemon. Bring to the boil and cover with a lid. Simmer gently, without stirring, for 35–40 minutes until all the water has been absorbed and the rice is dry and tender. Remove from the heat. Mix the remaining lemon juice and olive oil together and stir into the rice while it is still hot. Season to taste. Replace the lid and leave to cool. Gently stir in the herbs before serving.

PERSIAN RICE

75 g (3 oz) blanched almonds, halved
3 tbsp olive oil
2 large onions, finely chopped
350 g (12 oz) long grain brown rice
75 g (3 oz) currants or black Afghan raisins
4–5 tbsp fresh parsley, finely chopped
juice of 1 lemon
a scant 850 ml (1½ pints) water
seasoning

Dry fry the almonds in a heavy frying pan over a moderate heat, shaking the pan frequently, until they begin to brown. Tip out of the pan and keep aside until needed. Heat the oil in a heavy pan, add the onions and sauté until soft and golden brown. Stir in the rice and continue to cook until it begins to look slightly translucent. Add the remaining ingredients including the almonds and cover with a lid. Simmer, without stirring, for 35–40 minutes until all the water has been absorbed and the rice is tender and dry. Season to taste and toss lightly before serving.

FRENCH BEANS WITH BROWN RICE AND HAM

I serve this dish with crisp bread rolls as a first course dish or as a light meal for 2 people.

450 g (1 lb) French beans, trimmed
100 g (4 oz) long grain brown rice, cooked
225 g (8 oz) thinly-sliced York ham
juice of 1 lemon
1–2 tbsp fresh parsley, finely chopped
seasoning

Slice the beans and steam or boil until barely tender. Drain. Place in a pan with the cooked rice. Cut the ham into strips and add the other ingredients. Cook slowly, stirring frequently, until all the lemon juice has been absorbed and the rice is hot. Season to taste before serving.

TOMATO AND PEANUT RICE

olive oil
1 large onion, chopped
2 cloves garlic, peeled and crushed
2.5 cm (1 in) fresh root ginger, peeled and
grated
450 g (1 lb) tomatoes, chopped
350 g (12 oz) long grain brown rice
50 g (2 oz) creamed coconut
a good pinch cayenne pepper
a scant 725 ml ($1\frac{1}{4}$ pints) water
225 g (8 oz) peanuts
seasoning

Heat a tablespoon of oil in a heavy pan, add the onion and sauté for 8–10 minutes until soft. Add the garlic and ginger and cook for a minute or two more, before stirring in the tomatoes and rice. When the tomatoes have softened add the creamed coconut, cayenne pepper and water. Cover and bring to the boil.

Meanwhile, dry fry the peanuts in a heavy frying pan over a moderate heat. Shake the pan frequently and turn out onto a clean tea cloth when the nuts are nicely browned. Rub with the cloth to remove their skins. Pick out the cleaned peanuts and stir into the rice. Replace the lid and continue to simmer, without stirring, until all the water has been absorbed and the rice is tender. Total cooking time for the rice is about 35 minutes. Season to taste.

YELLOW RICE WITH PEPPERS

350 g (12 oz) long grain brown rice
2 red peppers, deseeded and sliced
2 good pinches of saffron strands
a scant 850 ml ($1\frac{1}{2}$ pints) water
seasoning

Place the rice in a heavy pan and add the peppers, saffron and water. Bring to the boil and cover with a lid. Simmer gently, without stirring, for 35–40 minutes until all the water has been absorbed and the rice is dry and tender. Remove from the heat and leave covered for a further 5–10 minutes. Season to taste before serving.

GINGERED PEANUT AND RICE LOAF

175 g (6 oz) peanuts
225 g (8 oz) long or short grain brown rice,
cooked
2 tbsp crunchy peanut butter
1 green pepper, deseeded and finely chopped
1 leek, finely chopped
2.5 cm (1 in) fresh root ginger, peeled and
grated
2 large eggs, beaten
1–2 tsp soya sauce

Dry fry the peanuts in a heavy frying pan over a moderate heat, shaking the pan frequently, until they are lightly browned. Cool slightly before grinding coarsely – I use my blender, dropping the nuts onto the rotating blades. Place all the ingredients in a bowl and mix together well.

Line a 450 g (1 lb) loaf tin with greaseproof paper and brush with oil. Spoon in the mixture and press down lightly with the fingertips. Bake in a preheated oven, gas mark 5 (190° C/ 375° F) for 25–30 minutes. Serve warm or cold.

APRICOT AND ALMOND PILAFF

25 g (1 oz) butter
2 mild onions, chopped
75 g (3 oz) cashew nuts
100 g (4 oz) button mushrooms, sliced
350 g (12 oz) long grain brown rice
50 g (2 oz) dried apricots, soaked overnight or
simmered in water until they soften
a scant 850 ml ($1\frac{1}{2}$ pints) water or chicken
stock
seasoning

Melt the butter in a heavy pan, add the onions and sauté until soft and golden. Add the cashews and fry gently, turning occasionally, until they too are lightly browned. Add the mushrooms and rice and cook for a minute or two more. Drain and chop the apricots and stir them into the rice before pouring over the water or stock. Cover with a tight-fitting lid and simmer, without stirring, for 35–40 minutes until the water has been absorbed and the rice is dry and tender. Season to taste before serving.

SEAFOOD DELIGHT

This dish can be made in advance and heated through at the last moment.

350 g (12 oz) long grain brown rice
a scant 850 ml (1½ pints) water
2–3 tbsp olive oil
1 onion, sliced
1 clove garlic, peeled and crushed
1 green pepper, deseeded and chopped
3 tomatoes, chopped
100 g (4 oz) garden peas, shelled
100 g (4 oz) peeled prawns
100 g (4 oz) cooked and shelled mussels
(for method, see page 156)
50 g (2 oz) pine kernels
freshly ground black pepper
75 g (3 oz) Gruyère cheese, grated
25 g (1 oz) Parmesan cheese, grated

Put the rice in a heavy pan and pour over the water. Cover with a tight-fitting lid and bring to the boil. Cook gently, without stirring, for 35–40 minutes until the rice is dry and tender. Remove from the heat but leave covered until needed.

Heat the oil in a pan, add the onion and garlic and sauté until soft and golden. Add the green pepper, tomatoes and peas and cook gently for 5–8 minutes. Stir in the prawns, mussels and pine kernels and heat through. By this time there should be 3–4 tablespoons of stock in the bottom of the pan. Stir in the cooked rice and season to taste with black pepper. Spoon into a shallow ovenproof dish and sprinkle the cheeses on top. Place in a preheated hot oven or under a hot grill until the cheese browns and bubbles. Serve with crusty bread and a green salad.

PAELLA

There are hundreds of different recipes for paella. Some include squid, some artichokes while others use firm, spicy sausages called chorizos. Basically a simple paella should be made with a mixture of pork, chicken, fish and rice, lightly flavoured with saffron and tomatoes. It is traditionally cooked in a heavy, shallow pan known as a paellera. It is now possible to buy such pans in kitchen shops but a large frying pan will do the job just as well, though you may have to spoon the paella into a more attractive dish when taking it to the table.

SERVES 8
450 g (1 lb) pork fillet
1 kg (2–2¼ lb) chicken
olive oil
2 onions, chopped
2 cloves garlic, peeled and crushed
275 g (10 oz) long grain brown rice
2 tomatoes, chopped
a good pinch of saffron strands
725 ml (1¼ pints) chicken stock
225 g (8 oz) mussels, cooked in their shells
(for method, see page 156)
seasoning

Put the pork and chicken into a roasting tin and brush with a little olive oil. Place in a preheated oven, gas mark 5 (190° C/375° F) for 50–60 minutes, removing each piece of meat as soon as tender. When cool enough to handle cut the pork into bite-sized pieces and joint the chicken.

Meanwhile, heat 1–2 tablespoons of olive oil in a large heavy pan, add the onions and garlic and sauté until soft. Add the rice and stir-fry for 1–2 minutes. Add the tomatoes, saffron and chicken stock. Cover the pan and bring to the boil. Simmer for 35 minutes until the rice is tender and dry. Stir in the pieces of pork and chicken and the mussels. Season to taste. Spoon into a large shallow ovenproof dish and cover with foil. Return to the oven and cook for a further 15–20 minutes until heated through.

RISOTTOS

In the past, along with many older and wiser cooks, I have been guilty of describing almost any savoury rice dish as a risotto. An authentic risotto, however, should be a creamy mixture of tender but firm grains, neither too dry nor too runny. The other dishes I so carefully prepare, taking every precaution to ensure that the rice stays dry and individually grained, would best be described as pilaus or pilafs. Elizabeth David describes, in her excellent book *Mediterranean Food* (Penguin Books, 1965) the difference as follows, '[in a risotto] one must be able to taste each grain of rice although it is not separated as in a pilaff'.

To make a good risotto you must ignore everything I have previously told you about cooking rice. The method involved is fairly straightforward but very time-consuming. A risotto can never be left to look after itself. It needs to be coaxed, cajoled and constantly stirred from the minute it begins to cook right until it is rushed to the table. Strictly speaking one should use a round grained Arborio rice from Italy but I find that the long grain brown rice found in many wholefood shops, most of which comes from Italy, is perfectly adequate. I do, however, try to avoid the slightly chubbier long grained rice from Carolina in the United States, as it has a tendency to cook to a mush.

RISOTTO BIANCO

Basic risotto recipe and method.

olive oil
butter
1 small onion, finely chopped
275 g (10 oz) long grain brown rice
1.5 litres ($2\frac{1}{2}$ pints) chicken stock
seasoning

Heat together a tablespoon of oil and a good knob of butter in a large heavy pan. Add the onion and sauté until it begins to soften and become golden brown. Add the rice and stir well for 3–4 minutes until well coated in the fat.

Meanwhile, heat the stock and keep it simmering gently. Pour approximately 150 ml (5 fl oz) of the stock over the rice. Stir frequently to ensure even cooking and to stop the rice sticking to the bottom of the pan. Each time the rice dries out cover with a little more liquid. Don't cook the rice on too high a flame as the water will evaporate too quickly and the rice will not have time to soften. On the other hand if it cooks too slowly it becomes horribly sticky and gluey. I keep the pan on a moderate heat, letting the stock simmer and bubble without actually breaking into a brisk boil.

Brown rice takes longer to cook than white varieties and I don't find it necessary to stir the risotto all the time it is cooking. A good stir each time you add more stock is usually sufficient, providing that you don't let the pan boil dry. However, after 30–35 minutes it becomes necessary to give the risotto your undivided attention. Reduce the amount of stock you are adding at any one time to about 60 ml (4 tablespoons). Continue stirring and adding stock until the rice becomes tender but resistant to the bite. I use a wooden fork in preference to the clumsier wooden spoon which can easily crush the soft grains of rice.

The exact quantity of liquid absorbed by the rice will vary each time you make a risotto. Much depends on the height of the flame, the thickness of the pan and last but not least the quirks of the rice itself. Learn to be your own judge in this matter so that you use just enough liquid for the cooked rice to become creamy without turning sticky. Never be tempted to speed up the process by adding too much liquid to the pan at any one time, particularly in the final stages. A risotto is not boiled rice. Just add a little stock as and when needed and be patient. Season to taste before serving.

Strictly speaking, once a risotto is made it must be served immediately and should, under no circumstances, be reheated. This is one practical reason why even the best restaurants rarely serve an authentic risotto. Many chefs cheat by making a rice pilau and then finishing it off 'à la risotto' just before it is taken to the table.

In Italy risottos are never served with another meat, fish or chicken dish but as a course or dish in their own right. Even a simple risotto bianco is served with Parmesan cheese and a green salad as a light main dish or starter. The list of ingredients which can be added to a risotto is virtually endless. Here are some of my favourite variations.

RISOTTO WITH COURGETTES

4 courgettes
olive oil
butter
1 small onion, finely chopped
1 clove garlic, peeled and crushed
275 g (10 oz) long grain brown rice
1.2 litres (2 pints) chicken stock
seasoning
Parmesan cheese, grated

Trim the courgettes and cut into fairly thick slices.

Heat a tablespoon of oil and a knob of butter in a large pan, add the onion and garlic and sauté until soft and golden brown. Add the courgettes and fry on both sides. Stir in the rice and cook for a minute or two more. Heat the stock and keep it simmering gently. Pour over about 275 ml (10 fl oz) hot stock. Stir the contents of the pan carefully and then cover and bring to the boil. Reduce the heat and simmer gently until all the liquid has been absorbed. Carefully stir in a further 275 ml (10 fl oz) stock and cook until that too has been absorbed. Continue to simmer the rice, adding stock when necessary. When the rice is tender season to taste and sprinkle with Parmesan cheese.

I also like the very plain risotto, known in Italy as risotto alla parmigiana. The rice is simply flavoured with good stock and Parmesan cheese. The success of the dish rests on the quality of the stock and on the cheese. If possible buy a chunk of Parmesan and either grate it yourself at home, or ask them to do it for you in the shop. Most delicatessen and Continental stores sell Parmesan by the block. Go to one with a high turnover.

PARMESAN RISOTTO (Risotto alla Parmigiana)

25 g (1 oz) butter
1 shallot, finely chopped
275 g (10 oz) long grain brown rice
$1\frac{1}{4}$ litres (2 pints) chicken stock
4 tbsp Parmesan cheese, grated

Melt the butter in a large heavy pan, add the shallot and sauté until it softens. Add the rice and stir-fry for 2–3 minutes. Heat the stock and keep it simmering gently. Add 150 ml (5 fl oz) hot stock. Stir the contents of the pan carefully and then cover and bring to the boil. Reduce the heat and simmer gently until all the liquid has been absorbed. Continue to simmer the rice, adding 150 ml (5 fl oz) stock as the rice dries out. Stir often to prevent the rice sticking.

When the rice is almost ready add the grated Parmesan cheese. Mix well. Serve as soon as the rice is tender.

PRAWN AND GREEN PEA RISOTTO

olive oil
1 onion, chopped
275 g (10 oz) long grain brown rice
150 ml (5 fl oz) dry white wine
850 ml (1½ pints) fish stock
225 g (8 oz) green peas
225 g (8 oz) peeled prawns
seasoning

Heat 1–2 tablespoons of oil in a pan, add the onion and sauté until soft. Stir in the rice and cook for a minute or two more until well coated in oil. Pour over the wine and simmer briskly until it has all been absorbed. Heat the stock and keep it simmering gently. Add 150 ml (5 fl oz) hot stock and the green peas, stirring the contents of the pan carefully so as not to squash the peas. Cover and bring to the boil. Reduce the heat and simmer gently until all the liquid has been absorbed by the rice. Carefully stir in a further 150 ml (5 fl oz) stock and cook until that too has been absorbed. Continue to simmer the rice, adding stock when necessary. When the rice is tender gently stir in the prawns. Season to taste.

Spoon the risotto into an ovenproof dish and place in a preheated oven, gas mark 6 (200° C/ 400° F) for 15–20 minutes. Turn the risotto occasionally while it is in the oven to prevent the top becoming hard and crunchy.

RISOTTO CROQUETTES

An excellent recipe for using up leftover risotto. Take a good tablespoon of cooked rice and press it flat in the palm of one hand. Place a chunk of cheese, preferably Mozzarella, in the centre and cover with another dollop of rice. Form into a small ball, completely enclosing the cheese. Arrange on a greased baking tray and bake in a preheated oven, gas mark 6 (200° C/ 400° F) for 20–25 minutes until firm to handle. Serve hot or cold.

MUSHROOM RISOTTO

2 tbsp olive oil
350 g (12 oz) button mushrooms, roughly chopped
1 clove garlic, peeled and crushed
275 g (10 oz) long grain brown rice
150 ml (5 fl oz) dry white wine
850 ml (1½ pints) chicken stock
freshly grated nutmeg
2 tbsp Parmesan cheese, grated

Heat the olive oil in a heavy pan, add the mushrooms and garlic and sauté for 4–5 minutes. Stir in the rice and continue to sauté for a further 2–3 minutes until it becomes slightly translucent. Pour over the wine and simmer until it has almost evaporated. Heat the stock and keep it simmering gently. Add 150 ml (5 fl oz) of hot stock. Season with a little nutmeg. Stir well and cook until the pan is almost dry. Continue adding small amounts of stock to the risotto as it dries out, remembering to stir the rice frequently.

Add the last 150 ml (5 fl oz) stock, a little at a time, stirring all the time to prevent the risotto sticking to the bottom of the pan. When the rice is tender stir in the Parmesan and season to taste with a little more nutmeg. Serve immediately.

RISOTTO BURGERS

Another use for leftover rice. Shape into burgers and coat in fine soft wholewheat breadcrumbs. Fry gently in oil until crisp and golden, turning just once to avoid breaking the burgers. They can be cooked in the oven, as in the recipe for risotto croquettes.

BREADMAKING

BREADMAKING

I bake all my own bread and, for me, bread-making is one of the most enjoyable and satisfying forms of cooking. Having produced my fair share of 'building bricks' the appearance and smell of three well-risen, freshly baked loaves never fails to give me a feeling of pleasure and amazement.

Although I derive a lot of satisfaction from donning my 'master baker's hat', there are times when it is inconvenient, and it would be nice to be able to pop round the corner to the supermarket or baker's for a loaf. Unfortunately there are very few shops that sell what I would call good bread. White bread sales still account for 80–85 per cent of all bread sold.

In order to produce white bread the flour is bleached, usually with chlorine dioxide. The processing not only whitens and matures the flour but also destroys many nutrients, particularly vitamin E. Other additives are permitted by law, and many large bakeries claim that they are essential if they are to produce a 'good' loaf, in other words one that rises well, is light in texture, uniform in shape and keeps its fresh appearance for several days. In Britain the permitted additives include:

1 bleaching agent
2 improving agents
4 preservatives
5 anti-oxidants
4 emulsifiers
1 colouring agent
4 nutrients

The list of additives in American bread is even longer and it has been reported that one loaf was found to contain 93 extra ingredients.

The growing demand for a more wholesome loaf has resulted in manufacturers producing many different types of brown bread, reputed to be 'better' and 'healthier', but I remain sceptical about such claims. From reading the labels it is evident that many of these brown loaves contain just as many additives as white ones. In fact, some are made from bleached white flour with small amounts of bran, wheatgerm and caramel added for extra texture and colour.

The inferior nutritional value of white flour has been recognised since the 1940s and during the War a 'national loaf' using wheatmeal flour was introduced to help safeguard the nation's health during the period of food rationing. After the reintroduction of white bread it was considered necessary to add five nutrients (vitamins B_1, B_2, niacin, iron and calcium) to the flour to help make up its nutritional deficiencies. This step was little more than a gesture, for out of the 24 nutrients contained in the whole wheat grain only a few survive the refining process and even then the quality is severely reduced.

The difference between the vitamin and mineral content of wholewheat flour and refined varieties remains impressive, even taking into account the added nutrients in white flour.

nutrient	% loss in white flour
thiamine (vitamin B_1)	77.1
riboflavin (vitamin B_2)	80.0
niacin	80.8
vitamin B_6	71.8
pantothenic acid	50.0
vitamin E	86.3
calcium	60.0
phosphorus	70.9
magnesium	84.7
potassium	77.0
sodium	78.3
chromium	40.0
manganese	85.8
iron	75.6
cobalt	88.5
copper	67.9
zinc	77.7
selenium	15.9

Faced with these facts (and of course the fact that home-made bread tastes so good) there is little wonder that more people are baking their own bread.

Breadmaking is a simple process but it is not

without pitfalls. One important decision to make is which type of wheat flour to use as there are a number to choose from:

100% wholewheat flour – the whole grain is milled. Nothing is added and nothing removed.

85–81% flour – 15–19% of the bran and wheatgerm are extracted. It is sometimes called wheatmeal flour although this name may also be applied to what is nothing more than bleached white flour with added bran and colouring.

70–76% flour – all the bran and wheatgerm are removed to make a white flour. It is possible to buy this flour without added bleach or chemicals, sold as unbleached white flour. It is no more nutritious than ordinary white flour but it is possibly less harmful to our health.

The best bread flour is made from Canadian hard wheat. It has a high gluten content and makes a light, well-risen loaf. However, I prefer to use British flours even though they are lower in gluten and produce a slightly denser loaf. The principal advantage of British flour is that many small farmers produce organic grain. That is to say it has not been sprayed with any chemical insecticides and pesticides which can adversely affect the nutritional quality of the grain and may also be detrimental to our health. I also use a stoneground flour. Most flours are milled between high-speed metal rollers which generate so much heat that valuable vitamins are destroyed. There are a number of organically grown, stoneground 100 per cent wholewheat flours available in the shops. I would suggest that you buy one that has been finely milled. Coarse flour may look more wholesome but it is much more difficult to handle.

One difficulty experienced by many bread-makers is crumbly loaves which are difficult to slice. It is a complaint made against shop-bought bread as well as home-made loaves. In most cases the bread in question has been made with a British flour. I haven't experienced the problem and can only hazard a guess as to its cause. It may be a result of proving the dough too quickly, proving it for too long, using too much fat or using flour that is too fresh. Professional bakers, buying direct from local millers, often leave the flour to mature for a short time before using it.

Other common problems are:

1. Bread failing to rise – yeast can be killed by using hot water or proving it in too hot a place. Very cold conditions will inactivate the yeast.
2. The crust coming away from the loaf – the dough may not have been kneaded sufficiently or may have been proved too quickly.
3. Dry heavy bread – mixture too dry or overcooking.
4. Bread uncooked in the middle – dough too wet or insufficient cooking.
5. Bread that rises and then collapses – over proving.
6. Bread that has a flat pitted crust – dough too wet.

Yeasts

Before I give any recipes perhaps I ought to describe the different types of yeast available. When making bread it is important to use baker's yeast; brewer's yeast or wine yeast simply will not do. Baker's yeast can be bought fresh, looking rather like putty, or as dry active yeast granules. Always check whether the dried yeast is an easy blend variety – this will be

stated on the packet. These yeasts require no pre-mixing with water; you just sprinkle the granules into the flour, with the fat and salt, and then mix in the warm liquid and knead. They are very useful as they save both time and washing up, and they give good results too. Ordinary dried yeast needs to be activated before being mixed with the flour, as does fresh yeast. I mix them with about 275 ml (10 fl oz) of measured warm water and a handful of measured flour and leave the mixture in a warm place for 10–20 minutes until it is frothy. It is not necessary to use sugar, flour works just as well.

I prefer using fresh yeast and have almost convinced myself that the results are better. Luckily my local grocer stocks fresh yeast for it is perishable and is best used soon after purchase. It will keep in a refrigerator for up to two weeks but must be discarded as soon as it begins to discolour. It does freeze. I also have a few packets of dried yeast in the cupboard for emergencies. They last much longer, the packets often being date stamped a year ahead. When baking use twice as much fresh yeast as dried and don't be tempted to use more than stated in the recipe. Additional yeast speeds up the rising and proving stages but it has a detrimental effect on the flavour and keeping qualities of the finished loaf. Generally speaking you will need to use less easy blend dried yeast than other dried varieties; always read the directions on each sachet of dried yeast before using it.

BASIC BREAD RECIPE

MAKES 3 LARGE LOAVES
50 g (2 oz) fresh yeast
or 25 g (1 oz) dried yeast
850 ml (1½ pints) warm water
(½ cold/½ boiling)
1½ kg (3 lb) flour
2 tsp salt (*optional*)
1 tbsp sunflower oil

Cream the yeast, 275 ml (10 fl oz) of the warm water and 100 g (4 oz) of the flour together in a small bowl. Leave for 10 minutes in a warm place until the mixture begins to froth. Mix the remaining flour, salt and oil together in a large bowl and stir in the rest of the warm water and the yeast mixture. Mix to form a dough. Turn onto a floured surface and knead briefly until smooth and elastic. Return to the bowl and cover with a polythene bag. Leave in a warm place to double in size. Turn onto a lightly floured board and knead again. Cut into three and roll into shape. Place in 3 oiled bread tins, cover, and leave in a warm place to double in size. Bake in a preheated oven, gas mark 6 (200° C/400° F) for 40 minutes.

Test the bread by tipping it out of the tins and tapping the base of each loaf with the knuckles. When the bread sounds hollow it will be cooked. To stop the crust becoming tough and leathery I brush each loaf with a mixture of milk and water as soon as they are out of the oven and standing on wire racks. Then cover with a clean tea cloth and throw over a thicker kitchen towel. Leave covered until the bread has cooled.

Sometimes, when I am in a hurry, I miss out the first rising stage and simply put the kneaded dough straight into oiled tins. It is then left to prove and is baked in the usual way. Although this bread doesn't have such a good texture as normal bread it is still quite acceptable and is a godsend when time is at a premium.

An even quicker method of making bread was given to me by a member of the Burley-in-Wharfedale Women's Institute. Using the basic recipe prepare the dough in the usual way. After the first kneading cut into shape and place in oiled bread tins. Put the dough into a cold oven and set the temperature control to gas mark 6 (200° C/400° F). As the oven heats up the dough will rise. By the time the temperature reaches the preset level the yeast is killed and bread begins to bake. Remove from the oven after 35 minutes, checking first that the bread is done. It is important that your oven is slow in heating up, otherwise the yeast is killed before the dough has had time to rise.

CORN BREAD WITH HERBS

This is one of my favourite breads, the light sweet-tasting corn meal sets off the flavour of the herbs. Corn meal or maize meal is a delicately coloured flour available from most wholefood shops and delicatessen. It is, as the name suggests, milled from maize and is popular in the United States where it is used to make a variety of golden-coloured breads and pancakes. Corn meal contains little, if any, gluten and when used on its own produces a heavy, flat bread. It is best mixed with another flour. I generally use a wholewheat flour but, for an even lighter loaf use half corn meal and half unbleached white flour.

Cornflour is not the same product as corn meal. To make cornflour the germ and bran are first removed from the grain. The starchy residue is then washed and the pure starch separated out and dried. The fine white powder which remains is known as cornflour and is used principally as a thickening agent.

MAKES 1 LOAF
20 g ($\frac{3}{4}$ oz) fresh yeast
or 1 tsp dried yeast
225 g (8 oz) wholewheat flour
275 ml (10 fl oz) warm water
($\frac{1}{2}$ cold/$\frac{1}{2}$ boiling)
225 g (8 oz) corn meal
2 tsp mixed dried herbs
salt to taste
1 tbsp sunflower oil

Cream the yeast with a handful of the measured flour and 150 ml (5 fl oz) of the warm water in a small bowl. Leave in a warm place until the mixture begins to froth. Mix the flours together in a larger bowl and stir in the mixed herbs and salt.

Pour the yeasted mixture into the larger bowl with the remaining warm water and the oil. Mix to form a dough and turn onto a lightly floured surface. Knead until the dough is smooth and slightly elastic. Return to the bowl, cover and leave in a warm place to double in size. Turn onto a floured surface, punch the dough down and knead again. Put into an oiled bread tin or roll into shape. Cover again and leave in a warm place to prove. When well-risen bake in a preheated oven, gas mark 6 (200° C/400° F) for 35–40 minutes.

GRANARY BREAD

MAKES 3 LOAVES
50 g (2 oz) fresh yeast
or 25 g (1 oz) dried yeast
425 ml (15 fl oz) warm water
($\frac{1}{2}$ cold/$\frac{1}{2}$ boiling)
675 g (1$\frac{1}{2}$ lb) wholewheat flour
675 g (1$\frac{1}{2}$ lb) granary flour
salt to taste
1 tbsp sunflower oil
425 ml (15 fl oz) warm milk
($\frac{1}{2}$ cold/$\frac{1}{2}$ boiling)
additional granary flour for dusting

Cream the yeast in a small bowl with a little of the warmed water and a handful of the measured flour. Leave in a warm place for 15–20 minutes until bubbly and frothy. Mix the remaining flours, salt and oil together in a large bowl and stir in the yeast mixture, the rest of the warm water and the milk. Knead on a floured surface until smooth and elastic. Return to the bowl, cover and leave in a warm place until the dough has doubled in size. Turn onto a lightly floured surface, knead again and cut into three. Roll each in granary flour and lay in 3 oiled bread tins. Cover and set aside to prove. Bake in a preheated oven, gas mark 6 (200° C/400° F) for 40 minutes.

PLAITED CHEESE LOAVES

MAKES 2 LOAVES
25 g (1 oz) fresh yeast
or 15 g ($\frac{1}{2}$ oz) dried yeast
150 ml (5 fl oz) warm water
($\frac{1}{2}$ cold/$\frac{1}{2}$ boiling)
675 g (1$\frac{1}{2}$ lb) wholewheat flour
2 tsp cayenne pepper
salt to taste
freshly ground black pepper
2 tbsp sunflower oil
150 ml (5 fl oz) warm milk
($\frac{1}{2}$ cold/$\frac{1}{2}$ boiling)
175 g (6 oz) grated mature Cheddar cheese
1 egg, beaten
additional oil to glaze

Cream the yeast in a small bowl with the warm water and a handful of the measured flour. Leave in a warm place until frothy. Put the remaining flour in a large bowl and season with cayenne, salt and black pepper. Rub in the oil.

Pour the yeast mixture into the larger bowl with the warm milk. Add most of the grated cheese, keeping a little back, and the egg and mix well. Add more warm water if necessary. Knead on a floured surface until smooth and elastic. Return to the bowl, cover and leave in a warm place to double in size. Turn onto a lightly floured surface, knead the dough again and divide into two. Cut each piece into three strips and roll them out like sausages, approximately 30 cm (12 in) long. Plait them and squeeze the ends together to hold the plait firm. Arrange the two plaits on an oiled baking tray and brush with oil. Sprinkle with the remaining cheese. Prove again and when doubled in size bake in a preheated oven, gas mark 6 (200° C/400° F) for 35 minutes. Test that they are done before cooling on a wire rack.

COTTAGE MILK LOAVES

I am not especially fond of white bread, finding it rather boring in comparison to the nutty taste of wholewheat bread. Milk loaves are, however, the exception for they taste deliciously sweet and have a lovely light moist texture.

MAKES 2 LOAVES
25 g (1 oz) fresh yeast
or 15 g ($\frac{1}{2}$ oz) dried yeast
675 g (1$\frac{1}{2}$ lb) unbleached white flour
425 ml (15 fl oz) warm milk
($\frac{1}{2}$ cold/$\frac{1}{2}$ boiling)
2 tbsp sunflower oil
1 egg

In a small bowl cream the yeast with a handful of the measured flour and half the warm milk. Leave in a warm place until the mixture begins to froth and bubble. Put the remaining flour into a large bowl.

Pour the yeast mixture into the larger bowl and add the remaining warm milk, the oil and half the beaten egg. Add a pinch of salt to taste. Mix together well and turn onto a lightly floured surface. Knead until the dough is smooth and elastic. Return to the bowl, cover and keep warm until it doubles in size. Knead again on the floured surface and cut the dough in half. Take each slab of dough and cut again, making one piece larger than the other.

To shape the bread knead each piece of dough into a round and then flatten gently with the palm of your hand. Tuck the edges underneath, towards the centre, so it ends up shaped like a pin cushion. Place the two larger rounds on an oiled baking tray, rounded side up and sit the smaller rounds on top. Make a hole through the middle of each loaf with the handle of a wooden spoon dipped in flour. Leave in a warm place to prove. When well risen brush with the remaining beaten egg, mixed with some milk if necessary, and bake in a preheated oven, gas mark 6 (200° C/400° F) for 25–30 minutes.

RYE BREAD WITH CARAWAY

Rye bread has a distinctive flavour but it is a difficult bread to make because rye flour contains very little gluten and the results can be on the heavy side. I find it best to mix the rye with equal amounts of wholewheat flour. For an extra tangy loaf try substituting buttermilk or yoghurt for some of the water.

MAKES 2 LOAVES
25 g (1 oz) fresh yeast
or 15 g ($\frac{1}{2}$ oz) dried yeast
425 ml (15 fl oz) warm water
($\frac{1}{2}$ cold/$\frac{1}{2}$ boiling)
350 g (12 oz) rye flour
350 g (12 oz) wholewheat flour
salt to taste
1 tbsp sunflower oil
1 tbsp caraway seeds
additional caraway seeds

Cream the yeast in a small bowl with a handful of the measured flour and half the measured warm water. Leave in a warm place until the mixture begins to froth. Mix the remaining flours together in a large bowl. Stir in the salt, oil and caraway seeds. Add the yeast mixture and the remaining warm water. Turn onto a lightly floured surface and knead until smooth and elastic. Return to the bowl, cover and keep warm until the dough has doubled in size. Knead again on the floured surface and cut the dough in half. Shape into cobs. Sprinkle the work-top with caraway seeds and lightly press the rounded cobs down onto them. This helps the seeds to stick to the dough, for all too often, the seeds I lovingly sprinkle over my loaves fall off as soon as they are tipped upside down.

Working round each cob, tuck the bottom edge underneath before placing the bread, rounded side up, on an oiled baking tray. This will stop the dough from spreading as it rises and will ensure that the loaf retains its cob-like appearance. Leave to prove and when nicely risen bake in a preheated oven, gas mark 6 (200° C/400° F) for 30–40 minutes.

SOURDOUGH BREAD

Before yeast was discovered as a raising agent it was common practice to leave a small amount of unleavened bread dough in a warm place for a few days to ferment. Then, this slightly sour tasting mixture was worked into the next batch of unleavened dough making it rise much more than it would otherwise have done. Generally a small piece of dough was kept back from each baking session to be used as a starter the next time bread was made. This type of bread became known as sourdough.

To make the starter mix 3 tablespoons of wholewheat flour with 3–4 tablespoons of water. Pour the thick batter into a jam jar, leaving an air space at the top. Cover loosely and stand in a warm place for 4–6 days, shaking the jar occasionally. When the mixture begins to ferment and bubble it is ready for use.

MAKES 3 LOAVES
1 jam jar of starter
900 g (2 lb) wholewheat flour
salt to taste
2 tbsp sunflower oil
425 ml (15 fl oz) warm water
($\frac{1}{2}$ cold/$\frac{1}{2}$ boiling)

Place the starter, half the flour, salt, oil and warm water in a bowl and beat well. Cover and leave in a warm place overnight. In the morning remove $\frac{1}{2}$ a jam jar full of batter and reserve for the next breadmaking day. Then add the remaining flour, turn onto a lightly floured surface and knead to form a firm dough. Divide into two and roll into shape. Place in oiled tins and make a deep slash through the top of each loaf, with a sharp knife. Leave in a warm place to prove, which may take up to 2 hours. When well risen, bake in a preheated oven, gas mark 6 (200° C/400° F) for 35 minutes.

WHOLEWHEAT SPLITS

MAKES 9 SQUARES
450 g (1 lb) wholewheat flour
1 tbsp sunflower oil
1 tsp salt (*optional*)
20 g ($\frac{3}{4}$ oz) fresh yeast
or 1 tsp dried yeast
150 ml (5 fl oz) warm water
($\frac{1}{2}$ cold/$\frac{1}{2}$ boiling)
150 ml (5 fl oz) warm milk
($\frac{1}{2}$ cold/$\frac{1}{2}$ boiling)
additional milk

Put the flour in a bowl and add the oil and salt. Make a well in the centre of the flour and crumble in the yeast. Pour over the warm water and milk and stir gently with a fork but do not introduce too much flour into the well. Leave the mixture in a warm place until the liquid froths. Mix the contents of the bowl together and knead, on a floured board, to form a dough. Return to the bowl and leave in a warm place to double in size.

Turn out onto a lightly floured board and knead again. Roll out to form an oblong 2.5 cm (1 in) thick. Place on an oiled baking tray and leave to rise again. When well risen, bake in a preheated oven, gas mark 5 (190° C/375° F) for 15–20 minutes. Brush with milk and cover with a cloth. While still warm cut into squares, split and butter. Serve immediately.

IRISH SODA BREAD

This is one of the easiest breads to make and it always turns out beautifully. It is best eaten warm, straight from the oven, although it does keep in the freezer. I generally make it along with some home-made soup and eat them together on the same day.

MAKES 2 LOAVES
450 g (1 lb) wholewheat flour
salt to taste
1 tsp bicarbonate of soda
1 tsp cream of tartar
2 tbsp sunflower oil
275 ml (10 fl oz) buttermilk
or equal parts yoghurt and milk

Mix all the dry ingredients together in a bowl. Rub in the oil. Heat the buttermilk or yoghurt and milk until warm and stir into the mixture. Work with the hands to form a fairly soft smooth dough. Try not to add extra flour, at least in the early stages when the dough should be fairly sticky. Cut into two pieces and shape into rounds. Place on a lightly floured baking tray and, with a sharp knife, make a deep cross on the top of each. Cut right down to, but not through, the bottom of each loaf. This is important as it helps the bread to rise and cook through in the centre. Bake in a preheated oven, gas mark 6 (200° C/400° F) for 25–30 minutes.

CORNISH SAFFRON BREAD

Saffron has a wonderful and distinctive flavour of its own but the main reason for adding it to bread dough must be on account of its rich honeyed colour. Saffron bread can be eaten at any meal but it is especially good with fish dishes.

It is strange how fashions change. At one time saffron was so common in Britain, grown principally around Saffron Walden and in the Duchy of Cornwall, that Lord Bacon wrote in his *History of Life and Death*, 'the English are rendered sprightly by a liberal use of saffron in sweetmeats and broths'. One could argue that saffron has priced itself out of the market for it is expensive today, but presumably it is also a question of supply and demand. Perhaps if we could, simultaneously, revive an interest in the traditional growing areas and stimulate demand the price would fall, and once again it could be added liberally to breads, cakes, purées, soups and sauces.

MAKES 1 LOAF
1 packet of whole saffron strands
275 ml (10 fl oz) warm water
($\frac{1}{2}$ cold/$\frac{1}{2}$ boiling)
20 g ($\frac{3}{4}$ oz) fresh yeast
or 1 tsp dried yeast
450 g (1 lb) unbleached white flour
salt to taste
1 tbsp sunflower oil
1 egg, beaten
milk to glaze

Soak the saffron in half the warm water. Cream the yeast with the remaining water and a handful of measured flour and leave in a warm place until frothy. Put the remaining flour in a bowl and stir in the salt and oil.

After 15 minutes or so the colour should have been leached from the saffron into the water and the liquid can be strained to remove the strands. Pour over the flour and stir in the frothy yeast mixture and beaten egg. Mix well. Turn onto a lightly floured surface and knead to form a smooth bread dough. Return to the bowl, cover and leave in a warm place to rise.

Knead again on the floured surface and shape as desired. Bake in a preheated oven, gas mark 6 (200° C/400° F) until done. Bread rolls will cook in about 15 minutes and loaves in about 35 minutes.

ROSEMARY AND ONION BAPS

MAKES 6 BAPS
125 ml (4 fl oz) warm milk
($\frac{1}{2}$ cold/$\frac{1}{2}$ boiling)
125 ml (4 fl oz) warm water
($\frac{1}{2}$ cold/$\frac{1}{2}$ boiling)
1 tbsp sunflower oil
7 g ($\frac{1}{4}$ oz) dried yeast
275 g (10 oz) wholewheat flour
1 small onion, finely chopped
1 tbsp fresh rosemary, finely chopped
1 tsp salt (*optional*)

Mix the warm milk and water, the oil, yeast and a handful of flour together in a small bowl and leave in a warm place until bubbly and frothy.

Put the remaining flour in a bowl and stir in the onion, rosemary and seasoning. Pour over the yeasted mixture and mix to form a dough. Turn onto a lightly floured surface and knead until smooth and elastic. Return to the bowl and leave in a warm place to double in size. Knead again on the floured surface and cut the dough into 6 pieces. Shape into rolls, tucking the bottom edge under each shaped roll to prevent them spreading when put to prove. Prove in a warm place until well risen. Bake in a preheated oven, gas mark 6 (200° C/400° F) for 15–20 minutes.

Brush with milk and cover with a clean cloth. Leave to cool on a wire rack.

SESAME ROLLS

These rolls are soft and light textured and are ideal for dinner parties and sandwiches. They require only one rising and can be made fairly quickly. They are best eaten on the day of baking unless kept in a freezer. Bread freezes very well but I find, particularly with wholewheat varieties, that loaves and, more especially, breadcakes begin to dry out after a couple of weeks.

MAKES 8 ROLLS
15 g ($\frac{1}{2}$ oz) fresh yeast
or 7 g ($\frac{1}{4}$ oz) dried yeast
200 ml (7 fl oz) warm milk
($\frac{1}{2}$ cold/$\frac{1}{2}$ boiling)
350 g (12 oz) wholewheat flour
salt to taste
1 tbsp sunflower oil
1 egg, beaten
milk to glaze
sesame seeds

Cream the yeast, the warm milk and a handful of the measured flour together in a small bowl. Leave in a warm place to froth.

Put the remaining flour in a large bowl and add salt to taste. Rub in the oil. Pour over the frothy yeast mixture and the beaten egg. Mix to form a soft dough, turn onto a lightly floured surface and knead until smooth and elastic. Divide the dough into 8 and shape into rolls. Tuck the edges underneath to stop them losing their shape. Brush with milk. Sprinkle the sesame seeds over the work-top and lightly press each roll onto them. Place on an oiled baking tray and leave in a warm place to rise. When doubled in size bake in a preheated oven, gas mark 6 (200° C/400° F) for 20 minutes.

Brush with a little more milk and stand on a wire rack. Cover with a clean cloth and leave to cool.

FIBRE
IN THE DIET

FIBRE IN THE DIET

Since the publication of the 'F Plan', dietary fibre has become a household word and sales of bran must have reached record levels. Although widely thought of as a slimming aid or cranky health food, dietary fibre is essential for everyone, regardless of size or weight. Research has shown that lack of fibre in the diet can cause constipation, haemorrhoids and diverticulitis and may be a contributory factor in heart disease, mature onset diabetes and obesity.

The incidence of these physical disorders has increased to such an extent in recent years that the Health Education Council has stated that 'all in all fibre is the single most important form of food likely to be lacking in your everyday diet'. It has been estimated that an average diet contains a quarter of the dietary fibre that it did a hundred years ago.

In the past people ate many high fibre foods, including unrefined cereals (brown bread, pot barley, oatmeal, porridge etc), pulses (beans and peas), fresh vegetables, fruit and nuts. By comparison a modern diet consists largely of animal products (meat, eggs and dairy foods), fats, sugar and refined cereals (white bread, cornflakes, fancy cakes etc) which, as shown in the following table, contain very little fibre.

A typical diet:

Breakfast	Fibre Content
cornflakes	very low in fibre
sugar	zero/very low in fibre
milk	zero fibre
white toasted bread	very low in fibre
butter	zero fibre
marmalade	very low in fibre
1 boiled egg	zero fibre
tea/coffee	zero fibre

Lunch	
ham on white bread roll	very low in fibre
soft drink	zero fibre
fruit pie with white pastry	very low in fibre

Evening meal	
beef, potatoes and frozen peas	low to moderate fibre
ice cream	zero fibre
wafers	very low fibre
coffee	zero fibre

Many people, aware of the health implications of a low fibre diet, are adding bran to their food. Although bran is an excellent source of fibre it is not a pleasant or appetising product and can spoil the taste and texture of other foods if used without discretion. I prefer to incorporate fibre into my diet in a more palatable way, by eating foods which naturally contain high levels of fibre and which can be made into delicious, mouthwatering dishes. To develop your own high fibre diet follow these simple guidelines:

1. One of the easiest ways of eating more fibre is to use a 100 per cent wholewheat flour in your baking. It can be used to make pastry, pasta, pancakes, Yorkshire puddings, sauces, cakes and biscuits as well as bread.

2. Eat more unrefined starchy carbohydrates such as wholewheat flour, wholewheat pasta, brown rice and potatoes. Cut down on cakes and biscuits which contain little fibre and a lot of sugar. Not only will this improve the fibre content of your diet but it may also help your waistline. Wholewheat bread and potatoes are not fattening in themselves but will pile on the pounds if eaten with lots of butter or cooked in fat.

3. Eat more fresh vegetables and salads.

4. Eat plenty of fresh fruit. Even soft fruits such as peaches, plums, melons and oranges contain fibre.

5. Eat a high fibre breakfast cereal.

6. Use meat sparingly. Try adding some beans, peas and lentils to casseroles, stews, burgers etc.

MUESLI

100 g (4 oz) porridge oats
100 g (4 oz) oat flakes
50 g (2 oz) barley flakes
50 g (2 oz) rye flakes
50 g (2 oz) wheat flakes
50 g (2 oz) raisins
50 g (2 oz) sultanas
50 g (2 oz) hazelnuts, chopped
50 g (2 oz) sunflower seeds

Mix all the ingredients together in a bowl. Serve with fresh fruit, fruit juice, milk or yoghurt.

Wholewheat Berries

Wholewheat berries can be bought in most wholefood shops. They are much cheaper than brown rice but lack refinement. Nonetheless they are popular, particularly with macrobiotics, and are certainly worth trying. Their robust, nutty flavour is very pleasant but even when cooked wholewheat berries need a lot of chewing.

WHOLEWHEAT PILAFF

225 g (8 oz) wholewheat berries
850 ml (1$\frac{1}{2}$ pints) water
2 tbsp sunflower oil
1 onion, chopped
2 carrots, thinly sliced
100 g (4 oz) button mushrooms, sliced
2–3 tsp soya sauce
1 bunch of watercress, trimmed and chopped

Put the wholewheat berries in a pan and dry fry them over a fairly high flame, shaking the pan frequently, until they are lightly browned. Remove from the pan and cool before returning to the pan, and pouring over the water. Bring to the boil, cover and simmer for 1$\frac{1}{2}$ hours until they have softened. Drain well.

Heat the oil in a large frying pan or wok, add the onion and carrots and sauté for 8–10 minutes. Stir in the mushrooms and cook for a minute or two more. Add the wholewheat berries and the soya sauce. Mix well and heat through. Add the chopped watercress and cook until it wilts. Serve immediately.

FRUMENTY

A hearty and nutritious breakfast food eaten in the north of England since the time of the Roman invasion. Traditionally the wholewheat was cooked overnight in a very slow oven with milk and spices. Eggs were beaten into the mixture just before it was served. My version of frumenty is lighter, fruitier and takes less time to prepare. It can be eaten piping hot on cold winter mornings or refreshingly chilled during the summer months.

225 g (8 oz) wholewheat berries
850 ml (1$\frac{1}{2}$ pints) water
675 g (1$\frac{1}{2}$ lb) cooking apples, cored
275 ml (10 fl oz) natural unsweetened apple juice
100 g (4 oz) sultanas
$\frac{1}{2}$ tsp ground cinnamon
$\frac{1}{2}$ tsp ground nutmeg

Put the wholewheat berries into a pan and dry fry them over a fairly high flame, shaking the pan frequently, until they begin to darken in colour and smell deliciously nutty. Remove from the pan. Cool before returning to the pan and pouring over the water. Bring to the boil. Cover and simmer for 1$\frac{1}{2}$ hours until they begin to soften. Drain well.

Slice the apples and put into another pan with the remaining ingredients. Simmer gently for 5–10 minutes until the apples soften. Stir the cooked wholewheat into the apple mixture and serve.

CREAMY MUSHROOM RICE

A delicious dish that tastes as good as a proper risotto but is much simpler to make.

2 tbsp olive oil
15 g ($\frac{1}{2}$ oz) butter
225 g (8 oz) button mushrooms, halved if necessary
1 clove garlic, peeled and crushed
225 g (8 oz) long grain brown rice
500 ml (18 fl oz) water
3 tbsp dry white wine
freshly ground black pepper
200 ml (7 fl oz) sour cream
3 tbsp Parmesan cheese, grated
1 tbsp fresh chives, chopped

Heat the oil and butter together in a heavy pan, add the mushrooms and garlic and lightly sauté. Add the brown rice and stir well. Pour over the water and wine and bring to the boil. Cover and simmer gently for 35–40 minutes until the pan is dry and the rice tender. Remove from the heat but leave covered for a further 5–10 minutes.

Season with black pepper and stir in the sour cream and Parmesan cheese. Garnish with chives before serving.

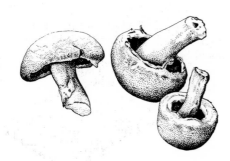

LENTIL MOUSSAKA

FOR THE FILLING:
225 g (8 oz) brown lentils
575 ml (1 pint) water
2 tbsp olive oil
2 onions, sliced
2 cloves garlic, peeled and crushed
100 g (4 oz) mushrooms, sliced
1 large ripe tomato, chopped
2–3 tbsp tomato purée
1 level tsp ground cinnamon
2–3 tsp soya sauce
2 tbsp fresh parsley, finely chopped
seasoning
2 large aubergines
wholewheat flour
additional olive oil

FOR THE SAUCE:
2 tbsp olive oil
25 g (1 oz) unbleached white flour
275 ml (10 fl oz) milk
1 egg yolk
75 g (3 oz) Cheddar cheese, grated
25 g (1 oz) Parmesan cheese, grated
a little freshly grated nutmeg

Wash the lentils and carefully pick them over, removing any small stones and pieces of grit. Put into a pan with the water, cover and bring to the boil. Simmer for 50–60 minutes until tender, making sure the pan does not boil dry. If using a pressure cooker cook for 12 minutes. Drain and discard the stock.

Heat the oil in a large frying pan, add the onions and garlic and sauté for 8–10 minutes. Add the mushrooms and tomatoes and cook until the tomatoes soften. Stir in the tomato purée, ground cinnamon, soya sauce, parsley and cooked lentils. Season well.

Wash, trim and slice the aubergines and dust with flour. Heat some of the additional oil in a frying pan, add the aubergines and sauté until golden brown on both sides. Use as little oil as possible, as the aubergines soak it up like blotting paper. Drain on absorbent paper when ready.

Place alternate layers of lentil mixture and aubergines in an oiled ovenproof dish, finishing with a layer of aubergines.

To make the sauce heat the oil in a pan and stir in the unbleached white flour. Remove from the heat and gradually add the milk. Return to the heat and bring to the boil, stirring frequently. When it has thickened cool slightly before stirring in the egg yolk and cheese. Season with nutmeg and pour over the aubergines.

Bake in a preheated oven, gas mark 6 (200° C/400° F) for 25–30 minutes. Serve with a green salad and some fresh bread.

COTTAGE PIE

This is a delicious vegetarian version of shepherd's pie. Brown lentils look similar to mince when cooked but they do not taste the same. You could also use half minced meat and half lentils.

225 g (8 oz) brown lentils
575 ml (1 pint) water
1 bay leaf
1–2 tbsp sunflower oil
2 onions, chopped
2 carrots, thinly sliced
2 tsp yeast extract
2 tsp tomato purée
150 ml (5 fl oz) bean stock
1–2 tbsp fresh rosemary, chopped
a pinch of ground nutmeg
seasoning
350 g (12 oz) potatoes, cooked and mashed

Wash the lentils and carefully pick them over, removing any small stones or pieces of grit that may be lurking in their midst. Put into a pan with the water and bay leaf. Cover and bring to the boil. Simmer for 50–60 minutes until soft. Make sure that the pan does not boil dry. If using a pressure cooker cook for 12 minutes. Drain and reserve the stock. Discard the bay leaf.

Heat the oil in a frying pan, add the onions and carrots and sauté for 10 minutes until they begin to soften. Mix the yeast extract, tomato purée and bean stock together and pour into the pan. Stir in the cooked lentils and the rosemary. Add a pinch of nutmeg and adjust the seasoning to taste.

Spoon the mixture into a casserole dish and lay the mashed potatoes over the top. Bake in a preheated oven, gas mark 5 (190° C/375° F) for 35–40 minutes.

MIXED VEGETABLE AND PINE KERNEL CASSEROLE

Millet may be another ingredient which is new to you. It is a pleasant, highly nutritious grain and the staple food of many Africans, Asians and Indians. I use millet quite often, in a wide variety of dishes, because it is easy to digest, has a nice nutty taste and cooks very quickly.

To bring out its full flavour and to reduce the cooking time I dry fry the grain before simmering it in water. Simply tip the millet into an old pan and put it over a fairly hot flame. Shake the pan frequently and cook until the millet becomes a little darker in colour. Tip from the pan as soon as it is ready to prevent it burning. When it has cooled slightly, return to the heat and simmer in two and a half times its volume of water for 15–20 minutes until light and fluffy. Drain if necessary.

50 g (2 oz) millet, cooked
1 large aubergine
2–3 tbsp olive oil
1 large onion, sliced
1 clove garlic, peeled and crushed
225 g (8 oz) tomatoes, sliced
50 g (2 oz) pine kernels, lightly roasted
2 tbsp fresh lemon oregano
or use dried oregano and a dash of lemon juice
150 ml (5 fl oz) water
1 tbsp tomato purée
seasoning

Cook the millet as described above and set aside until needed. Wash and trim the aubergine. Cut into slices 0.75 cm ($\frac{1}{4}$ in) thick. Heat the oil in a frying pan, add the aubergines and sauté lightly until they begin to brown. Drain on absorbent paper when ready. Add the onion and garlic to the remaining oil in the pan and soften.

Arrange half the aubergine in the bottom of a casserole dish. Next add half the tomatoes, followed by some onions, pine kernels and a sprinkling of lemon oregano. Repeat the layers.

Mix the water and tomato purée together and season. Pour over the casserole. Spoon the cooked millet over the top and bake in a preheated oven, gas mark 4 (180° C/350° F) for 40–45 minutes.

LEEK AND MUSTARD QUICHE

FOR THE PASTRY:
225 g (8 oz) wholewheat flour
50 g (2 oz) butter, diced
4 tbsp sunflower oil
8 tsp cold water
2 tsp Dijon mustard

FOR THE FILLING:
450 g (1 lb) leeks
50 g (2 oz) Gruyère cheese, grated
2 large eggs
150 ml (5 fl oz) milk
freshly ground black pepper

To make the pastry put the flour in a bowl and rub the butter and oil into the flour, using your fingertips, until the mixture resembles breadcrumbs. Add the cold water and mix to form a dough. Roll out on a lightly floured board and line a 25 cm (10 in) flan ring. Press down lightly but firmly with the fingertips and prick the pastry with a fork. Blind bake in a preheated oven, gas mark 6 (200° C/400° F) for 10–12 minutes. Brush with the mustard and leave to cool.

Wash, trim and slice the leeks. Steam until barely tender. Place in the blind baked pastry case and cover with three-quarters of the cheese. Beat the eggs and milk together and season with black pepper. Pour over the leeks and sprinkle with the remaining cheese. Return to the oven and bake for a further 20–25 minutes.

SPICY GREEN PEA PILAU

This recipe was given to me by an Indian colleague.

1 tbsp sunflower oil
1 onion, chopped
1 clove garlic, peeled and crushed
1 green pepper, deseeded and sliced
2 tsp cumin seeds
2 tsp coriander seeds, crushed
2.5 cm (1 in) fresh root ginger,
peeled and grated
100 g (4 oz) button mushrooms, halved
2 tomatoes, chopped
450 g (1 lb) garden peas, cooked
225 g (8 oz) long grain brown rice, cooked

Heat the oil in a pan, add the onion and garlic and sauté until soft and golden. Add the green pepper and cook for a few minutes more. Stir in the spices and root ginger and stir-fry for 1–2 minutes. Add the mushrooms and tomatoes. Cook until the tomatoes begin to soften; then stir in the cooked peas and rice. Heat through and serve.

ALMOND AND CASHEW NUT ROAST

A slightly extravagant nut roast but well worth the extra expense. It has a fine flavour and makes an excellent lunch or buffet dish, served hot or cold. It freezes and is useful to have in stock at Christmas when you might be called on to make a meal at short notice.

25 g (1 oz) butter
1 onion, chopped finely
2 tomatoes, chopped finely
100 g (4 oz) mushrooms, finely chopped
1 tbsp wholewheat flour
275 ml (10 fl oz) vegetable stock or water
2–3 tsp soya sauce
2 tsp mixed dried herbs
100 g (4 oz) ground almonds
100 g (4 oz) lightly roasted cashew nuts,
coarsely ground
225 g (8 oz) fresh wholewheat breadcrumbs
2 eggs, beaten
freshly ground black pepper

Melt the butter in a large pan, add the onion and sauté until soft and golden. Add the tomatoes and mushrooms and cook for 3–4 minutes more. Stir in the flour, stock or water, soya sauce and mixed herbs. Cook for a minute or two more before adding the remaining ingredients. Season to taste with black pepper.

Line a 900 g (2 lb) loaf tin with greaseproof paper and brush with oil. Spoon in the mixture and press down lightly. Cover with greaseproof paper or foil and bake in a preheated oven, gas mark 5 (190° C/375° F) for 45 minutes. Remove the paper covering and bake for a further 10–15 minutes until lightly browned. Leave to cool in the tin for 5 minutes or so before turning out onto a serving dish.

CELERY BREAD

MAKES 1 LOAF
450 g (1 lb) wholewheat flour
15 g ($\frac{1}{2}$ oz) fresh yeast
or 7 g ($\frac{1}{4}$ oz) dried yeast
a scant 275 ml (10 fl oz) warm water
($\frac{1}{2}$ cold/$\frac{1}{2}$ boiling)
1 tbsp sunflower oil
2 sticks celery, finely chopped
1 tbsp celery seeds
1–2 tbsp soya sauce

Mix a handful of the measured flour, the yeast and warm water together in a small bowl until fairly smooth. Leave in a warm place until frothy.

Heat the oil in a pan, add the chopped celery and sauté until soft. Then put it into another bowl with the celery seeds and soya sauce and stir in the rest of the flour. Pour in the yeast mixture and mix to form a dough. Turn onto a lightly floured surface and knead until smooth and elastic. Return to the bowl and leave in a warm place to double in size.

Knead again on a floured surface and roll into shape. Place in an oiled bread tin and leave to prove. Bake in a preheated oven, gas mark 6 (200° C/400° F) for 40 minutes. Tip the bread out of the tin and tap it on the bottom to test if it is cooked. Place on a cooling rack and brush with milk. Cover with a clean cloth and leave to cool.

HERB BREAD

MAKES 1 LOAF
450 g (1 lb) wholewheat flour
pinch of salt (*optional*)
15 g ($\frac{1}{2}$ oz) fresh yeast
or 7 g ($\frac{1}{4}$ oz) dried yeast
275 ml (10 fl oz) warm water ($\frac{1}{2}$ cold / $\frac{1}{2}$ boiling)
2 tbsp fresh marjoram or 2 tsp dried
1 tbsp fresh rosemary or 1 tsp dried
1 tbsp fresh sage or 1 tsp dried

FOR THE GARNISH:
blue poppy seeds

Mix a handful of the measured flour, the yeast and water together in a small bowl until fairly smooth. Leave in a warm place until frothy. Put all the remaining ingredients in another bowl, stir in the frothed yeast mixture and mix to form a bread dough. Turn onto a lightly floured surface and knead until smooth and elastic. Return to the bowl, cover and leave in a warm place to double in size.

Knead again on a floured surface and roll into shape. Sprinkle the poppy seeds on a clean work-top and press the dough down onto them. Drop the bread into an oiled loaf tin and leave in a warm place to prove. When well risen, bake in a preheated oven, gas mark 6 (200° C/400° F) for 40 minutes. Tip the bread out of the tin and tap it on the bottom to test if it is cooked. Place on a cooling rack and brush with a little milk or water. Cover with a cloth and leave to cool.

FOOD
FOR OUTDOORS

FOOD FOR OUTDOORS

Some of my best memories of summer are associated with eating out of doors, either in friends' gardens or in the countryside. Such meals are often arranged on the spur of the moment, when the combination of warm weather and sunshine forces one to take an impromptu holiday. In fact this is the best way to organise them, for the weather, here in Britain at least, is so unpredictable that any attempt to plan ahead inevitably results in a wet day and disappointment.

Picnics

Picnics do not need to be lavish affairs, and a quick trip to the local shops can provide you with an excellent variety of appetising foods. Many main course dishes can be made in advance and kept in the fridge or freezer until needed. Salads need only be washed and dried before setting off for if the dressing is added too soon the greens become limp and unappetising by the time they are served. Take the dressing, ready made, in a screw top jar and toss with the salad greens just before eating.

The perfect picnic site is a matter of personal choice but I like those situated beside water – except when the midges are out and about. A small, fast running stream is not only attractive to look at and listen to but it can be used to cool the wine and fruit juices and to wash up the dirty dishes.

Wicker hampers are the most attractive way of carrying one's chattels to the picnic site but they aren't the most practical as the food generally gets tipped about as it is being carried. A large open basket or plain cardboard box are much more functional.

MINCED BEEF LOAF

This meat loaf is firm and substantial. It is best eaten cold and looks rather like pâté de campagne when sliced. It tastes very good too.

450 g (1 lb) chuck steak
100 g (4 oz) lean bacon
3 large slices of wholewheat bread
$\frac{1}{4}$ level tsp dried mixed herbs
1 level tbsp fresh parsley, chopped
50 g (2 oz) mushrooms, finely chopped
1 egg, beaten
seasoning

Trim the meat and bacon and mince with the bread or process in a food processor. Place in a bowl and mix together with the herbs, mushrooms and egg. Season to taste. Press the mixture into a 450 g (1 lb) loaf tin and cover with a piece of foil. Bake in a preheated oven, gas mark 5 (190° C/375° F) for $1\frac{1}{4}$ hours. Leave to cool in the tin.

RICE AND CHEESE SQUARES

MAKES 10
1 tbsp sunflower oil
1 onion, finely chopped
225 g (8 oz) long grain brown rice, cooked
175 g (6 oz) Cheddar cheese, grated
2–3 tbsp fresh parsley, finely chopped
freshly ground black pepper

Heat the oil in a frying pan, add the onion and sauté until soft and golden. Add it to the remainder of the ingredients in a bowl and mix well. Press together until the mixture is quite sticky. Press into the bottom of an oiled baking tin, so that it is about 2.5 cm (1 in) thick. Bake in a preheated oven, gas mark 6 (200° C/400° F) for 25–30 minutes. Cut into squares but leave in the tin to cool.

PISSALADIÈRE

Pissaladière consists of a bread dough base spread with a mixture of onions, tomatoes, anchovies and black olives. It is a close relative of the Italian pizza, the principal difference being that it is made without a cheese topping.

FOR THE BASE:
225 g (8 oz) wholewheat flour
15 g ($\frac{1}{2}$ oz) fresh yeast or
7 g ($\frac{1}{4}$ oz) dried yeast
150 ml (5 fl oz) warm water
($\frac{1}{2}$ cold/$\frac{1}{2}$ boiling)
sunflower oil

FOR THE FILLING:
4 tbsp olive oil
900 g (2 lb) onions, sliced
2 cloves garlic, peeled and crushed
225 g (8 oz) ripe tomatoes, chopped
10 anchovy fillets
stoned black olives
freshly ground black pepper

Mix a handful of the measured flour, the yeast and warm water together in a small bowl until fairly smooth. Leave in a warm place until frothy. Put the flour into a large bowl and pour in the yeast mixture. Mix to form a dough, turn onto a highly floured surface and knead until soft. Return to the bowl, cover and leave in a warm place to double in size.

Meanwhile, heat the olive oil in a large frying pan, add the onions and garlic and sauté for 10–15 minutes until soft and golden. Add the tomatoes and cook for a further 15 minutes.

Knock down the well-risen dough and knead again on a floured surface. Roll out to a circle of about 0.75 cm ($\frac{1}{4}$ in) in thickness and lift onto an oiled baking tray. Brush with sunflower oil. Spoon the filling mixture over the top and cover with a lattice of anchovy fillets. Arrange the olives on top. Bake in a preheated oven, gas mark 6 (200° C/400° F) for 35 minutes.

SAVOURY RICE BALLS

MAKES 8
100 g (4 oz) millet, cooked
175 g (6 oz) long grain brown rice, cooked
2 carrots, finely grated
2–3 tbsp fresh parsley, finely chopped
5–6 spring onions, finely chopped
3–4 tsp soya sauce

To cook the millet put into an old pan over a high heat. Dry fry, shaking the pan frequently, until the grains begin to pop and brown. Remove from the pan immediately and leave to cool for 5 minutes. Return to the pan, cover with 350 ml (12 fl oz) water and simmer for 15–20 minutes until soft and fluffy. Drain if necessary.

Add the millet to the remainder of the ingredients in a bowl, mix well and season to taste. Squeeze the mixture between the fingers until it becomes sticky and then shape into balls, dipping your hands in cold water if they become too sticky. Place on an oiled baking tray and bake in a preheated oven, gas mark 5 (190° C/375° F) for 25–30 minutes until they feel firm.

VEGETARIAN SCOTCH EGGS

MAKES 4
olive oil
2 onions, finely chopped
1 large carrot, finely grated
100 g (4 oz) soft wholewheat breadcrumbs
50 g (2 oz) roasted sunflower seeds, ground
1 tsp Dijon mustard
1 tbsp tomato purée
1 level tsp mixed dried herbs
1 egg, beaten
seasoning
4 hard-boiled eggs, shelled

Heat 1–2 tablespoons of oil in a frying pan, add the onions and sauté until soft and golden. Remove from the heat and mix in the remaining ingredients except for the hard-boiled eggs. Season to taste.

Divide the mixture into four and lightly press it round each egg. Place on an oiled baking tray and bake in a preheated oven, gas mark 6 (200° C/400° F) for 20–25 minutes.

MIDDLE EASTERN SPINACH PASTRIES

FOR THE PASTRY:
200 g (7 oz) strong wholewheat flour
$\frac{1}{4}$ tsp cream of tartar
150 g (5 oz) hard butter
6–7 tbsp cold water

FOR THE FILLING:
900 g (2 lb) fresh spinach
100 g (4 oz) curd cheese
100 g (4 oz) Gruyère cheese
freshly grated nutmeg

FOR THE GLAZING:
1 beaten egg
Parmesan cheese, grated

Mix the flour and cream of tartar together in a bowl. Rub in 25 g (1 oz) of the butter using your fingertips. Add the water and, with a fork, mix to form a soft dough. Turn onto a lightly floured board and knead lightly until smooth and pliant. Wrap in polythene and put in a cool place to rest for 30 minutes.

Meanwhile, sprinkle the remainder of the butter with a little flour, and with a rolling pin, beat out to form a neat oblong about 1.25 cm ($\frac{1}{2}$ in) thick. Roll out the rested dough to an oblong a little larger than the butter shape and long enough for the two ends of the dough to fold over the butter and slightly overlap. Place the butter in the centre and fold the pastry over to cover it completely. Press the edges together to seal. Give the dough a half turn to bring the open ends to the top and bottom. With the rolling pin press the dough gently, from the centre to the top and bottom, and then quickly and lightly roll out the dough to form an oblong three times as long as it is wide. (Don't roll out too thinly or the layers of dough and butter will merge.) Mark the pastry into thirds without cutting through the dough, and fold the bottom third over the centre and the top third down over both. Seal the edges and give the pastry a half turn. Repeat the rolling, folding and turning once more then wrap in polythene and chill for 30 minutes.

After two further rolls, folds and turns the pastry must rest again. Roll, fold and turn twice more. The pastry is now ready for use.

To make the filling wash the spinach carefully and trim off the stalks. Shred finely and place in a large pan. Cook gently until soft and limp. There should be no need to add any water, but shake the pan occasionally to prevent the spinach from sticking to the bottom. Drain well, pressing down on the leaves to get rid of any excess liquid. Leave to cool. Then stir in the curd cheese and grated Gruyère. Season with nutmeg.

Cut the dough into two pieces and roll out to form two rectangles measuring 18.5 x 25 cm (7 x 10 in). Cut each into six. Place 2 tsp of filling in the middle of each pastry square and dampen the edges with water. Fold to form a triangle and press the edges together to seal. Brush with beaten egg but without allowing the glaze to run down the sides as this will stop the pastry rising evenly. Sprinkle with Parmesan cheese.

Bake in a preheated oven, gas mark 8 (230° C/450° F) for 20–25 minutes.

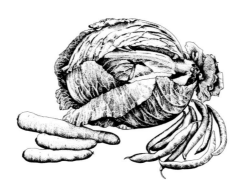

STUFFED VINE LEAVES

3 tbsp olive oil
1 large onion, finely chopped
100 g (4 oz) long grain brown rice
50 g (2 oz) pine kernels
25 g (1 oz) raisins
275 ml (10 fl oz) water
seasoning
3 tbsp fresh parsley, finely chopped
1 tbsp lemon juice
24 vine leaves

Heat the olive oil in a large heavy pan, add the onion and sauté until soft and golden brown. Add the rice, pine kernels and raisins and stir well. Cook for a minute or two before pouring over 175 ml (6 fl oz) of the water. Bring to the boil. Cover and simmer gently until all the water has been absorbed. This will take about 10–15 minutes. Season to taste. Stir in the parsley and lemon juice. Leave to cool.

To prepare the vine leaves soak them for a minute or two in a large bowl of water. Gently separate them and lay on a wire rack to drain. I use packeted vine leaves which are easily obtained from delicatessen. If using fresh leaves they need to be blanched and then drained.

When the stuffing mixture has cooled place a heaped tablespoon in the centre of each leaf. Roll up into a cigar shape, tucking in the ends. Put a layer of unused leaves in the bottom of a pan and arrange the stuffed vine leaves on top. Pour over the remaining water and cover with a plate (to serve as a weight). Cover with a lid and bring to boil. Simmer gently for 30–40 minutes until the water has been absorbed. Leave to cool in the pan.

VEGETABLE PASTIES

MAKES 6–7
450 g (1 lb) wholewheat shortcrust pastry
(for method, see page 12)
3 potatoes, scrubbed
3 carrots
1 onion, chopped
1 tbsp sunflower oil
100 g (4 oz) garden peas, shelled
1 tbsp fresh rosemary, chopped
1 tbsp fresh lemon thyme, chopped
seasoning
2 eggs, beaten

FOR THE GLAZING:
1 beaten egg

Wash, trim and dice the potatoes and carrots. Put in a pan, cover with water and cook until barely tender. Add the peas 5–10 minutes before the end of cooking. Drain.

Heat the oil in a pan, add the onion and sauté until soft. Remove from the heat and stir in the cooked vegetables and herbs. Season to taste. Add the beaten eggs and leave aside until needed.

Make the pastry. Roll it out on a lightly-floured surface and cut into 6–7 rounds 15 cm (6 in) in diameter. Spoon some of the filling into the centre of each pastry circle and fold in half. Dampen the edges with water and press together to seal. Crimp the sealed edges, brush with beaten egg and place on an oiled baking tray. Bake in a preheated oven, gas mark 6 (200° C/400° F) for 25 minutes.

SOYA PÂTÉ

This is quite a remarkable dish. The ingredients are so basic that it is hard to imagine what the finished dish will be like. The simplicity of the method does not help either but there is no need to worry. The resultant pâté is delicious. It keeps well in both fridge and freezer.

100 g (4 oz) butter
a scant 100 g (4 oz) soya flour
1 tsp yeast extract

Melt the butter in a small pan and add the sieved flour. Add the yeast extract and stir well. Spoon into a small pot and leave in a cool place to firm up.

COULIBIAC

100 g (4 oz) couscous
300 ml (11 fl oz) boiling water
1 bunch of spring onions, chopped
100 g (4 oz) button mushrooms, sliced
100 g (4 oz) frozen peas
$\frac{1}{4}$ cucumber, cut into julienne strips
1 tbsp Dijon mustard
1 tbsp white wine vinegar
1 tbsp fresh parsley, chopped
1 tbsp fresh chives, chopped
2 tsp fresh mint, chopped
1 tsp fresh thyme, chopped
1 tsp fresh lemon oregano, chopped
seasoning
4 hard-boiled eggs
450 g (1 lb) wholewheat shortcrust pastry
(for method, see page 12)

FOR THE GLAZING:
milk

Put the couscous in a small bowl with the boiling water. Leave to stand for 15–20 minutes. Drain and mix in the remaining ingredients except for the eggs and pastry. Season to taste. Shell the eggs and cut into slices.

Make the pastry and cut it in half. On a lightly floured surface roll out both pieces into rectangles measuring 22.5 x 32.5 cm (9 x 13 in). Place one sheet on a greased baking tray and spoon over the filling, leaving a 2.5 cm (1 in) margin around the edge. Arrange the eggs on top. Cover with the remaining pastry. Dampen the edges with water and press together to seal. Trim away any surplus pastry. Brush with milk and bake in a preheated oven, gas mark 6 (200° C/400° F) for 25–30 minutes.

DEEP MUSHROOM PIE

olive oil
4 shallots, finely chopped
1 clove garlic, peeled and crushed
450 g (1 lb) button mushrooms, whole or halved
1 tbsp fresh parsley, finely chopped
2 tbsp dry white wine
225 ml (8 fl oz) natural yoghurt
2 egg yolks
a good pinch of paprika
freshly grated nutmeg
175 g (6 oz) wholewheat shortcrust pastry
(for method, see page 35)

FOR THE GLAZING:
milk

Heat 1–2 tablespoons of oil in a frying pan and add the shallots and garlic. Fry until they soften, stirring frequently. Stir in the mushrooms and cook for a minute or two more. Stir in the parsley and then, using a slotted spoon, transfer the vegetables into a pie dish. Pour the wine into the pan and bring to the boil. Pour over the mushrooms.

Beat the yoghurt and egg yolks together and season with paprika and nutmeg. Pour into the pie dish.

Make the pastry and roll it out on a lightly floured surface to a circle large enough to cover the pie. Cover with the pastry top. Brush the pastry with milk and bake in a preheated oven, gas mark 6 (200° C/400° F) for 25 minutes.

Barbecues

Barbecuing is an old and relatively primitive form of cooking. In the beginning it was simply a question of grilling food over an open fire but these days it has become big business and the range of 'essential' equipment and gadgets on sale is enormous. If organising a large party or lavish outdoor dinner I can appreciate the value of a sophisticated barbecue but for informal occasions I much prefer more basic pieces of equipment. A small charcoal container and a cooking rack are generally adequate for my needs. They are easy to assemble and make cooking in either the garden or out in the countryside relatively straight forward and pleasurable. Skewers and double-sided grills with long handles are useful, making the handling of hot food so much easier.

Fish and meat are the most popular foods for a barbecue and they are usually served with rolls, salads and any number of sauces. Sauces are not essential but they do tend to counteract the dryness which can be a feature of barbecued foods.

BARBECUED GAMMON

4–6 slices of gammon

FOR THE MARINADE:
2 tbsp soya sauce
2 tbsp peanut oil
a scant 1 tbsp honey
1.25 cm ($\frac{1}{2}$ in) fresh root ginger,
peeled and grated

Trim the gammon and place in a bowl or dish. Put the remaining ingredients in a small pan and heat gently until well mixed. Pour over the gammon and leave in a cool place for 1–2 hours. Lift the gammon from the dish and cook gently, basting occasionally with the marinade.

DEVILLED CHICKEN

SERVES 4
4 pieces of chicken
3 tbsp olive oil
1 tbsp white wine vinegar
1 tbsp Dijon mustard
1 tbsp fresh thyme, finely chopped
seasoning

Mix the oil, vinegar, mustard and thyme together and brush over the chicken. Season to taste. Cook the chicken slowly, basting occasionally with the oil mixture, for 30–40 minutes.

SKEWERED BEEF WITH MUSHROOMS AND OLIVES

675 g ($1\frac{1}{2}$ lb) rump steak
225 g (8 oz) button mushrooms
10 stoned black olives
olive oil
1 clove garlic, peeled and crushed
a good pinch of cayenne pepper

Trim the meat and cut into chunks. Wipe the mushrooms. Thread the meat, mushrooms and olives alternately onto skewers. Mix together 3–4 tablespoons of olive oil with the garlic and paprika. Brush the skewers with a little of the baste. Cook, basting occasionally with the oil mixture.

BARBECUED BURGERS

450 g (1 lb) minced beef
1 small onion, chopped
1 tbsp fresh sage, finely chopped
2–3 tsp soya sauce
seasoning

Mix all the ingredients together in a bowl. Turn the mixture onto a clean work-top and divide into four. Using a spatula or knife, lightly shape each portion of meat into a flat round, about 2.5 cm (1 in) thick. Cook over a medium heat for 10–12 minutes, turning once.

BARBECUED LAMB WITH ROSEMARY AND COURGETTES

675 g (1½ lb) lean lamb, chops or steaks
olive oil
2 tbsp fresh rosemary, finely chopped
2 courgettes
seasoning

Trim the meat and cut into chunks. Brush with oil and roll in the chopped rosemary. Slice the courgettes and blanch for 1–2 minutes in boiling water. Thread the ingredients alternately on to skewers. Season and cook until the lamb is tender.

BARBECUED LAMB CHOPS

4–6 lamb chops
4–5 tbsp olive oil
2–3 tbsp lemon juice
1 small onion or shallot, finely chopped
1 tbsp fresh parsley, finely chopped
a good pinch paprika
seasoning

Trim the chops and place in a shallow dish. Mix the remaining ingredients together and pour over the lamb. Leave in a cool place for 2–3 hours. Lift the lamb from the marinade and cook gently, basting occasionally with the remaining marinade.

BARBECUED SHELLFISH

8 large peeled prawns
175 g (6 oz) cooked and shelled mussels
(for method, see page 156)
175 g (6 oz) scallops
100 g (4 oz) bacon

FOR THE MARINADE:
4–5 tbsp olive oil
2 tbsp lemon juice
seasoning

Put the prawns, mussels and scallops in a bowl. Mix the marinade ingredients together and pour over the fish. Leave in a cool place for 2–3 hours. Trim the bacon and cut each slice in half. Wrap a piece around each scallop. Thread the fish alternately on skewers. Brush with the remaining marinade and cook gently, basting occasionally.

GRILLED RED MULLET

4–6 red mullet
50 g (2 oz) butter
1 tbsp lemon juice
freshly ground black pepper

Trim, gut and scale the fish. Melt the butter in a small pan and stir in the lemon juice and black pepper. Brush over the fish. Cook gently, basting occasionally with the melted butter.

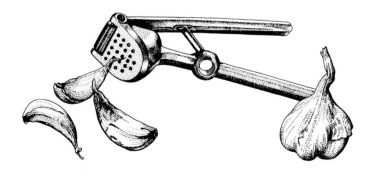

THE HEALTHY GOURMET

THE HEALTHY GOURMET

There is little doubt that the British are becoming more health conscious and are trying to eat less fat (especially animal fat), salt and sugar while increasing their consumption of dietary fibre. Unfortunately wholesome foods have the reputation of being brown, bland, stodgy and boring and are seldom considered suitable for serving on special occasions. All too often good food, in the traditional sense of the word, is associated with fussy, over-rich dishes containing lashings of cream, butter and cheese in the style of haute cuisine and cordon bleu. This style of cooking seems outdated today, belonging to an age when there was no shortage of time, money or help in the kitchen and also before the health risks of over-indulging in rich foods were appreciated.

I had hoped that the development of 'nouvelle cuisine' and 'cuisine minceur', a few years ago, would herald a new, healthier way of eating but neither seem to have achieved any great nor lasting success. It is hardly surprising for the recipes remain just as convoluted, time-consuming and expensive as the original haute cuisine ones and take little account of the needs or constraints of the modern cook. Recipes ought to cater for our hectic lifestyles and our desire for health and fitness. Standards don't have to be lowered, nor do traditional dishes have to be discarded. Good food should be both enjoyable and healthy.

It is not difficult to prepare meals for the modern gourmet, provided that as much thought and attention are given to the ingredients as to the recipe itself. By substituting brown flour for white, brown rice for white rice, cold pressed oils for chemically treated ones, yoghurt for cream, butter for margarine, fresh vegetables for frozen or tinned ones and herbs and other natural seasonings for synthetic products, there is no reason why almost every conceivable type of dish cannot be made a little healthier and why we shouldn't carry on enjoying our favourite meals.

Cooking for dinner parties need not be very different from preparing normal family meals. It is both unnecessary and unwise to succumb to the temptation of trying to impress guests with a succession of exotic dishes – a surfeit of different dishes is quite needless and large quantities of rich food make everyone only tired and lethargic. A light first course and dessert, with a more substantial main course, are more than adequate. If you choose dishes that you yourself enjoy preparing and eating I am sure that your guests will enjoy them too. No one likes to see the cook and hostess looking hot, flustered and unhappy.

Healthy gourmet food need be neither cranky nor pretentious. With the minimum of effort and an eye for presentation, dishes can be made to look good, taste delicious and should actually make you feel good too.

COOKING FOR A VEGETARIAN

MENU 1

egg and herb pâté with toasted fingers
tarte au champignons
side salads
new potatoes
fresh fruit bowl

TARTE AU CHAMPIGNONS (Mushroom Tart)

FOR THE PASTRY:
175 g (6 oz) wholewheat flour
50 g (2 oz) unbleached white flour
50 g (2 oz) butter, diced
4 tbsp sunflower oil
2 tbsp fresh parsley, chopped
1 sprig of fresh thyme, chopped
a little fresh basil, chopped
1 tsp Dijon mustard
1 egg, beaten

FOR THE FILLING:
3 tbsp olive oil
1 large onion, finely chopped
225 g (8 oz) button mushrooms, finely chopped
50 g (2 oz) wholewheat flour
pinch of freshly grated nutmeg
275 ml (10 fl oz) milk
4 tbsp natural yoghurt
2 egg yolks
freshly ground black pepper

To make the pastry mix the flours together in a bowl. Rub in the butter and oil, using your fingertips, until the mixture resembles bread-crumbs. Stir in the herbs, mustard and egg. Knead lightly to form a pastry dough. Turn onto a lightly-floured board, roll out and line a 25 cm (10 in) flan ring. Prick the pastry base lightly with a fork and blind bake in a pre-heated oven, gas mark 6 (200° C/400° F) for 10 minutes.

To make the filling heat the oil in a large frying pan, add the onion and sauté until soft and golden. Add the mushrooms and cook for a further 5 minutes. Stir in the flour and cook for a minute or two more. Remove from the heat and gradually add the milk, stirring well after each addition. Return to the stove and heat through until it begins to thicken. Remove from the heat. Season with a little nutmeg and black pepper. Mix the yoghurt and egg yolks together and stir most of it into the filling mixture – leave a tablespoon or two aside with which to glaze the top of the tart. Spoon the mixture into the pastry case and brush with the remaining yoghurt and egg mixture. Bake in a preheated oven, gas mark 6 (200° C/400° F) for 25–30 minutes. Serve warm.

MENU 2

hummus and pitta bread
braised vegetables with herbs
rice balls
cheese board

BRAISED VEGETABLES WITH HERBS

1–2 tbsp olive oil
2 mild onions, sliced
2 cloves garlic, peeled and crushed
4 carrots, sliced
4 courgettes, sliced
450 g (1 lb) peas, shelled
1 aubergine, chopped
3 tbsp dry white wine
1 tbsp fresh oregano, chopped
1 tbsp fresh marjoram, chopped
1 tbsp fresh lemon thyme, chopped
seasoning

Heat the oil in a large pan, add the onions and garlic and sauté for 10 minutes. Add the carrots and cook for a further 5 minutes. Stir in the courgettes, peas and aubergine and cook for 5 minutes more. Add the remaining ingredients and cover with a tight-fitting lid. Cook over a low heat until all the vegetables are tender.

MENU 3

tomato and orange soup
mushroom risotto
green salad
apricot and banana whip

TOMATO AND ORANGE SOUP

675 g (1½ lb) tomatoes
2 onions
3 sticks celery
2 large oranges
2 tbsp sunflower oil
25 g (1 oz) butter
150 ml (5 fl oz) dry white wine
575 ml (1 pint) water
a pinch of ground ginger
seasoning
2 tbsp fresh chives, finely chopped

Wash, trim and chop the vegetables. Grate the orange skins and reserve the grated zest. Heat together the oil and butter in a pan, add the onions and sauté for 10 minutes. Add the tomatoes and celery, the juice squeezed from the oranges and the white wine. Cover and cook gently for 25 minutes.

Remove the lid and add the water. Purée the soup by passing it through a vegetable mouli or process it briefly in a food processor or blender until smooth. Pass it through a sieve to strain. Return to the pan. Add a little ground ginger and season to taste. Heat through and sprinkle with the grated orange zest and chopped chives before serving.

MENU 4

gazpacho
brazil nut and chick pea en croûte
mixed vegetables
potatoes en papillote
moulded cheese cake with fresh fruit purée

This menu would be ideal for the Christmas festivities. Many of the dishes can be made in advance and kept either in the freezer or refrigerator. (The soup and main dish can be frozen, the sweet should be kept in a cool place. The vegetables are best prepared the day they are to be eaten.)

GAZPACHO

¼ cucumber, chopped
½ green pepper, deseeded and chopped
½ small onion, chopped
350 ml (12 fl oz) tomato juice
75 ml (3 fl oz) water
1 tbsp tomato purée
seasoning

Using a food processor or blender, add all the ingredients a little at a time, and process until fairly smooth. Pass through a coarse sieve or colander. Season to taste.

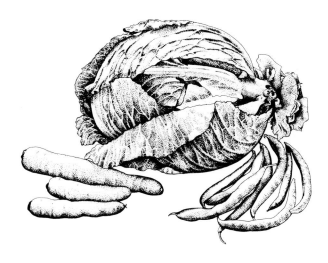

BRAZIL NUT AND CHICK PEA EN CROÛTE

FOR THE FILLING:
1 tbsp olive oil
1 large onion, finely chopped
225 g (8 oz) mushrooms, finely chopped
100 g (4 oz) chick peas, cooked and coarsely mashed
225 g (8 oz) brazil nuts, ground
175 g (6 oz) soft wholewheat breadcrumbs
2 tbsp red wine
2–3 tsp yeast extract
$1\frac{1}{2}$ tsp mixed dried herbs
$\frac{1}{2}$ tsp dried oregano
freshly ground black pepper

FOR THE PASTRY:
450 g (1 lb) wholewheat flour
175 g (6 oz) butter, diced
4 tbsp sunflower oil
5 tbsp cold water

To cook the chick peas soak overnight in plenty of water. Drain and put into a pan or pressure cooker with 1.1 litres (2 pints) of fresh water. Cover, bring to the boil and simmer until tender. Check the pan regularly to make sure the contents don't boil dry. If simmered this will take $2-2\frac{1}{4}$ hours or 20–25 minutes in a pressure cooker. Drain again.

To make the filling heat the olive oil in a large frying pan, add the onion and sauté for 10 minutes until soft and golden. Add the mushrooms and cook until their juices begin to run. Add the remaining filling ingredients and season to taste.

To make the pastry put the flour in a bowl and rub in the butter and oil until the mixture resembles breadcrumbs. Add the water and mix to form a pastry dough. Turn onto a lightly floured surface and roll out three-quarters of the pastry and use it to line a 900 g (2 lb) loaf tin. Spoon in the filling. Roll out the remaining pastry to a rectangle large enough to cover the pie. Dampen the pastry rim and cover the pie with the pastry top. Press the edges together to seal. To achieve an attractive finish brush with beaten egg.

Bake in a preheated oven, gas mark 6 (200° C/400° F) for 25–30 minutes. Leave to cool for 5–10 minutes in the tin before serving. Serve hot or cold.

MENU 5

cauliflower soup
granary bread
nutty moussaka
mixed salads
raspberry snow

CAULIFLOWER SOUP

1 cauliflower
1 small leek
1 small onion
2 tbsp sunflower oil
25 g (1 oz) butter
50 g (2 oz) unbleached white flour
425 ml (15 fl oz) milk
425 ml (15 fl oz) water
4–5 tbsp fresh parsley, finely chopped
seasoning
75 g (3 oz) white Stilton cheese, grated

Wash and trim the cauliflower. Break into small pieces and blanch in boiling water. Heat the oil and butter together in a pan, clean and slice the leek and onion and add them to the pan. Sauté for 8–10 minutes. Stir in the flour and cook until it begins to bubble. Remove from the heat and gradually pour in the milk and water, stirring well after each addition. Return to the heat and bring to the boil, stirring frequently. Add the cauliflower and cook until tender. Purée the soup by passing it through a sieve or vegetable mouli, or by processing it briefly in a food processor or blender.

Return the purée to the pan and add the parsley. Season to taste. Heat through and ladle into serving bowls. Sprinkle with grated cheese.

NUTTY MOUSSAKA

50 g (2 oz) bulgur
200 ml (7 fl oz) boiling water
2 aubergines
olive oil
1 onion, sliced
1 clove garlic, peeled and crushed
100 g (4 oz) mushrooms, chopped
100 g (4 oz) walnuts, chopped
100 g (4 oz) ground hazelnuts
2–3 tsp soya sauce
2 tbsp fresh parsley, finely chopped
1 tbsp fresh thyme, finely chopped
2 tbsp tomato purée
3–4 tbsp water or red wine
seasoning

FOR THE TOPPING:
425 ml (15 fl oz) natural yoghurt
2 eggs
grated cheese (*optional*)

Place the bulgur in a small bowl and pour over the boiling water. Leave to stand for 15–20 minutes. Drain well.

Slice the aubergines fairly thinly. Brush a heavy cast iron frying pan with olive oil and place over a high heat. When hot cook the aubergines until lightly browned on both sides. There should be no need to add further oil; the aubergines simply absorb it like blotting paper. Drain on absorbent paper.

Heat a little more oil in another pan, add the onion and garlic and sauté for 6–7 minutes. Add the mushrooms and cook until the juices begin to run. Stir in the bulgur, walnuts, ground hazelnuts, soya sauce, parsley, thyme and tomato purée. Moisten with water or red wine. Season to taste.

Beat the yoghurt and eggs together.

Place alternate layers of aubergines and the nut mixture in an ovenproof dish, finishing with a layer of aubergines. Sprinkle with cheese if you are using it. Pour over the yoghurt mixture and bake in a preheated oven, gas mark 6 (200° C/400° F) for 25–30 minutes until the topping is firm to the touch and lightly browned.

MENU 6

mushroom pâté
sesame rolls
coulibiac
salads
apricot sorbet

MUSHROOM PÂTÉ

200 g (7 oz) soft wholewheat breadcrumbs
150 ml (5 fl oz) hot water
50 g (2 oz) butter
1 onion, finely chopped
450 g (1 lb) button mushrooms, finely chopped
100 g (4 oz) coarsely ground walnuts
juice of $\frac{1}{2}$ lemon
25 g (1 oz) fresh yeast
1 clove garlic, peeled and crushed
freshly grated nutmeg
seasoning

Soak the breadcrumbs in the hot water for 10–15 minutes. Melt the butter in a pan, add the onions and fry until soft, without allowing them to brown. Add the mushrooms and cook for a further 3–4 minutes. Squeeze any surplus water from the breadcrumbs before mixing with the vegetables. Add the walnuts and lemon juice and if necessary cook over a gentle heat until the mixture is dry. Stir in the remaining ingredients and season to taste. Spoon into a dish and place in the refrigerator until firm.

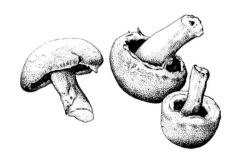

MENU 7

crudités
chestnut pâté pie
Brussels sprouts
potatoes cooked with rosemary
sugar-free Christmas pudding

Another Christmas menu and one which will be the envy of the meat-eating guests.

CHESTNUT PÂTÉ PIE

I am reluctant to use tinned foods as they generally contain unspecified amounts of salt, sugar and other less familiar additives, but there is an exception to every rule and fortunately tinned chestnut purée is relatively free from additives. According to the label of one popular brand it contains nothing more than chestnuts and water. Be sure to buy the savoury variety as some chestnut purées contain large quantities of sugar and are used for making desserts such as marrons glacés and chestnut gateau.

FOR THE PASTRY:
350 g (12 oz) wholewheat flour
100 g (4 oz) butter, diced
4 tbsp sunflower oil
4 tbsp cold water

FOR THE FILLING:
1 onion
1 clove garlic, peeled and crushed
2 sticks celery
100 g (4 oz) mushrooms
2 tbsp sunflower oil
400 g (14 oz) chestnut purée
1 tbsp lemon juice
$\frac{1}{2}$ tsp dried marjoram
1 egg
seasoning

FOR THE GLAZING:
1 egg, beaten

To make the pastry place the flour in a bowl and rub in the butter and oil until the mixture resembles breadcrumbs. Add the cold water and knead to form a dough. Turn onto a lightly-floured surface, roll out three-quarters of the dough and use it to line an oiled 900 g (2 lb) loaf tin. Put the pastry case in the refrigerator while making the filling.

To make the filling wash, trim and finely chop the vegetables. Heat the oil in a large pan, add the onion, garlic and celery and sauté until soft and golden. Add the mushrooms and cook for a further 3–4 minutes. Mash the chestnut purée with a fork until smooth and stir in the vegetables. Add the remaining ingredients and season to taste. Spoon into the lined loaf tin.

Roll out the remaining pastry to a rectangle large enough to cover the pie. Dampen the pastry rim and cover the pie with the pastry top. Press the edges together to seal. Brush with a little beaten egg and bake in a preheated oven, gas mark 4 (180° C/350° F) for 1 hour.

SUGAR-FREE CHRISTMAS PUDDING

This is a fine pre-war recipe which has no added sugar. Strict vegetarians may object to the suet.

100 g (4 oz) mixed candied peel, finely chopped
grated zest and juice of 1 lemon
225 g (8 oz) shredded suet
50 g (2 oz) flour
225 g (8 oz) soft wholewheat breadcrumbs
225 g (8 oz) sultanas
225 g (8 oz) seedless raisins
100 g (4 oz) currants
50 g (2 oz) blanched almonds, chopped
$\frac{1}{2}$ a nutmeg, grated
15 g ($\frac{1}{2}$ oz) ground cinnamon
15 g ($\frac{1}{2}$ oz) ground mixed spice
150 ml (5 fl oz) milk
4 eggs, beaten
a good port-wine glassful of Jamaica rum
(*optional*)

Put the mixed peel in a large bowl and add the grated zest of the lemon. Stir in the suet, flour, breadcrumbs, dried fruit, nuts and spices. Mix the milk and eggs together and gradually stir into the mixture. Next add the juice of the lemon and rum. If you are not using spirits, then add extra milk. After all the family have stirred the pudding and made their wishes, cover and leave for 1–2 hours. Spoon into a well-buttered pudding basin, cover with a piece of greaseproof paper and a pudding cloth or lid. Steam for 5 hours. The longer the pudding is cooked the darker and richer it becomes.

MENU 8

marinated carrot salad
flageolet beans au gratin
granary bread
blackberry and apple pie

MARINATED CARROT SALAD

675 g (1½ lb) carrots, coarsely grated
75 g (3 oz) raisins
125 ml (4 fl oz) natural thick set yoghurt
juice of 1 orange

Put the carrots and raisins in a mixing bowl. Mix the yoghurt and orange juice together and pour over the carrots and raisins. Stir well. Leave for several hours. Pile into a serving bowl.

FLAGEOLET BEANS AU GRATIN

SERVES 4
100 g (4 oz) flageolet beans, soaked overnight and then drained
275 ml (10 fl oz) water
2 leeks, sliced
1–2 tbsp olive oil
225 g (8 oz) mushrooms, halved if necessary
1 tbsp fresh parsley, finely chopped
1 tbsp lemon juice
seasoning
225 g (8 oz) buckwheat spaghetti

FOR THE SAUCE:
25 g (1 oz) butter
25 g (1 oz) unbleached white flour
275 ml (10 fl oz) milk
150 ml (5 fl oz) sour cream or natural yoghurt
freshly grated nutmeg

Put the beans in a pan, cover with the water and bring to the boil. Cover and simmer for approximately 1¼ hours. Make sure that the pan doesn't boil dry. It will take 15 minutes in a pressure cooker. Drain.

Steam the leeks. Meanwhile, heat the oil in a pan, add the mushrooms and sauté for 4–5 minutes. Remove from the heat and add the leeks, parsley, lemon juice, and cooked beans. Season to taste.

Cook the pasta, uncovered, in a large pan of boiling water to which you have added 1 tablespoon of olive oil. When almost soft, drain and spoon into the bottom of an ovenproof casserole. Place the cooked vegetables and bean mixture over the top.

To make the sauce melt the butter in a pan and stir in the flour. When the mixture begins to bubble remove from the heat and gradually add the milk, stirring well after each addition. Return to the heat and stir until the sauce begins to thicken. Cool slightly before stirring in the yoghurt or cream and season with nutmeg. Pour into the dish and bake in a pre-heated oven, gas mark 6 (200° C/400° F) for 15–20 minutes until heated through. If the pasta and vegetables are kept warm while the sauce is being made it can just be browned under a hot grill before serving.

MENU 9

vegetable soup with Parmesan
wholewheat croûtons
savoury rice mould
midsummer casserole
khoshaf

VEGETABLE SOUP WITH PARMESAN

675 g (1½ lb) potatoes, peeled and chopped
1 onion, chopped
1 carrot, chopped
1 stick celery, chopped
a scant 725 ml (1¼ pints) milk
1–2 tbsp Parmesan cheese, grated
seasoning

FOR THE GARNISH:
fresh parsley or chives, chopped

Place the vegetables in a pan and add just enough water to cover. Bring to the boil and simmer gently until tender. Drain but reserve the cooking stock. Either process the vegetables and the remainder of the ingredients in a food processor or blender until smooth or pass through a sieve or vegetable mouli. Return to the pan and gradually add the cooking stock until the desired consistency is reached. Stir well and season to taste. Sprinkle with parsley or chives before serving.

SAVOURY RICE MOULD

1 tbsp olive oil
1 onion, finely chopped
1 clove garlic, peeled and crushed
1 stick celery, finely chopped
2 ripe tomatoes, chopped
1 small green pepper, deseeded and finely chopped
225 g (8 oz) long grain brown rice
a good pinch of saffron strands
150 ml (5 fl oz) dry white wine
a scant 425 ml (15 fl oz) water
25 g (1 oz) toasted pine kernels

Heat the oil in a heavy pan, add the onion, garlic and celery and sauté for 8–10 minutes. Add the tomatoes and green pepper and cook for 2–3 minutes more. Stir in the brown rice and continue to sauté for 3–4 minutes, stirring frequently until the rice has begun to look translucent. Sprinkle the saffron over the top and pour in the wine and water. Bring to the boil. Cover and simmer, without stirring, over a gentle heat for 35–40 minutes until the rice is tender and dry.

Sprinkle the pine kernels in the bottom of a lightly oiled ring mould and spoon over the cooked rice. Press down gently but firmly and place in a preheated oven, gas mark 5 (190° C/375° F) for 15–20 minutes. Cool slightly before turning out onto a serving dish. (If the dish is to be served cold firm up in the refrigerator rather than baking it in the oven.)

MIDSUMMER CASSEROLE

olive oil
1 onion, chopped
1 clove garlic, peeled and crushed
450 g (1 lb) courgettes, sliced
450 g (1 lb) tomatoes, chopped
2 tbsp tomato purée
3–4 potatoes, chopped
450 g (1 lb) French beans, sliced
1 tbsp fresh basil, chopped
1 tbsp fresh oregano, chopped
pinch of mixed dried herbs
seasoning
275 ml (10 fl oz) water
or ½ water/½ dry white wine

Heat 1–2 tablespoons of oil in a large pan, add the onion and garlic and sauté for 8–10 minutes. Then add the courgettes and stir fry for 2–3 minutes. Next add the tomatoes and cook until they begin to soften. Put in the other ingredients and bring to the boil. Cover and simmer gently until the vegetables are tender. Adjust the seasoning to taste. Serve.

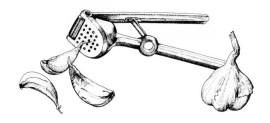

FRENCH CUISINE

FRENCH CUISINE

French cuisine is reputed to be the best in the world although there are signs of change, particularly in tourist areas where pizza parlours and cafés selling 'frites' with everything are becoming increasingly common. On the whole, however, the French have a high regard for food and it plays a special part in their daily lives. In rural areas, at least, lunch is the most important meal of the day and everything grinds to a halt between 12.00 and 2.00 p.m. Even the roads become noticeably quieter and one feels decidedly British to be out and about at such a time. It is quite definitely a case of mad dogs and Englishmen go out in the midday sun.

I too adopt the habit of eating my main meal at lunch-time either in hotels and restaurants or picnicking al fresco when visiting France. One of the pleasures of the holiday is stopping off at small towns and having a leisurely coffee and croissant on the terrace of a café before spending half an hour or so wandering around the shops and market stalls buying bits and pieces for lunch. My picnics consist of local pâtés, hams and cheeses, huge tomato-flavoured tomatoes, young sweet carrots bought in bundles with their leaves still on, big fat prunes so soft and succulent that they can be eaten straight from the packet, fresh peaches and cherries and thick slices of deliciously buttery pastries and cakes. Sometimes I buy slices of quiche, pizza or pissaladière but more often than not I settle for a loaf of freshly baked bread. In most French towns it is now possible to find a baker selling wholewheat or rye bread, both of which I prefer to the traditional baguette. Crusty French bread makes a good light accompaniment to a main meal but isn't very substantial or filling when eaten as a sandwich or with salady things.

Most restaurants offer a choice of menus as well as a selection of wines and it is not difficult to find something to suit everyone's taste and pocket. Not caring for rich, heavy food I prefer to eat in the more modest restaurants, particularly in 'les routiers' and 'les logis'.

(Unfortunately I have yet to come across a cuisine nouvelle restaurant on my travels.) In general the food prepared in these small restaurants is unassuming but good, cooked in the main by the women of the family who have learnt their skills not in top-class restaurant kitchens but in their own homes. They cater for local people rather than tourists and at the stroke of 12 the dining rooms begin to fill up with farm workers, car mechanics, office workers, family groups and even the local gendarme. The atmosphere is always relaxed and friendly, becoming noisier and more animated as the meal goes on. It is rather like eating with a large French family.

Sometimes there is little choice and everyone is offered the same menu. It all depends on what Madame has been able to buy at the market that morning. One of the best meals I have eaten consisted of a delicious creamy green pea soup, a huge platter of langoustines, a dish of tomatoes and grated carrot tossed in a vinaigrette dressing, and an excellent lamb stew with potatoes. The sweets are, in the main, very simple. The choice is usually between ice cream, fresh fruit and cheese. Ice cream seems to be universally popular but even the burliest of workmen could not resist the dainty bowls of ripe cherries offered at one restaurant.

The simplicity and freshness of such meals is the key to the success and greatness of French cuisine. Of course the cooking of the old-style chefs, in the fashion of haute cuisine, has played an important part but it has had little influence outside top-class restaurants and the would-be international jet-set. The majority of Frenchmen, old and young, rich and poor, have an underlying respect and admiration for food. They do not try to emulate the professional chef or patissier, who has had years of training and is assisted by a battery of kitchen staff and equipment, but prepare food in a way more suited to their own lifestyles. This does not mean to say their meals are thrown together willy-nilly but that they avoid all unnecessary fuss and frills.

The French are, however, just as particular as any top chef about the ingredients they use and choose only the best, preparing them in such a way that their freshness and flavour can be savoured in the final dish. The great French chef Escoffier gave an excellent piece of advice when he wrote 'faites simple' but even this would be wasted on someone who doesn't appreciate and enjoy the simple pleasures of eating good food.

COUNTRY SOUP

2 potatoes, chopped
2 leeks, chopped
2 onions, chopped
2 carrots, chopped
2 tomatoes, chopped
1 clove garlic, peeled and crushed
seasoning
1 tbsp single cream or yoghurt

Put the vegetables in a large pan and barely cover with water. Bring to the boil and simmer for 45 minutes. Purée the mixture by passing it through a sieve or vegetable mouli or process it briefly in a food processor or blender. Return to the pan and adjust the consistency and seasoning to taste. Stir in the cream or yoghurt and heat through.

FARMHOUSE SOUP
WITH BACON

50 g (2 oz) flageolet beans,
soaked overnight and then drained
50 g (2 oz) haricot beans,
soaked overnight and then drained
3 carrots, roughly chopped
3 potatoes, roughly chopped
3 sticks celery, sliced
3 leeks, sliced
2 cloves garlic, peeled and chopped
225 g (8 oz) green (unsmoked) bacon, trimmed
and chopped
2 tsp Dijon mustard
2 tbsp fresh parsley, chopped
freshly ground black pepper

Put all the ingredients in a large pan or pressure cooker and barely cover with water. Bring to the boil, cover and simmer for 60 minutes. If using a pressure cooker cook for 12 minutes. Be sure to add more water to the pan if it looks like boiling dry – this will not be necessary when using a pressure cooker. Adjust the seasoning to taste before serving.

CELERY SOUP

1 head celery, chopped
1 large onion, chopped
225 g (8 oz) potatoes, peeled and chopped
575 ml (1 pint) vegetable stock or water
275 ml (10 fl oz) milk
juice of $\frac{1}{2}$ lemon
seasoning

Put the celery, onion, potatoes and stock or water in a large pan. Bring to the boil, cover and simmer for 25–30 minutes until the vegetables are tender. Purée the mixture by passing it through a sieve or vegetable mouli or process it briefly in a food processor or blender. Return to the pan and stir in the milk. Add the lemon juice and season to taste. Heat through and serve.

CREAM OF RUNNER BEAN SOUP

This is a delicious soup and an excellent way of using up a surfeit of beans from the garden. It freezes very well too.

50 g (2 oz) haricot beans, soaked overnight in water and then drained
1 stick celery, sliced
575 ml (1 pint) chicken stock
450 g (1 lb) runner beans, sliced
275 ml (10 fl oz) milk
juice of $\frac{1}{2}$ lemon
seasoning

Put the haricot beans in a large pan with the celery and stock. Bring to the boil, cover and simmer for 60 minutes until tender or cook in a pressure cooker for 12–15 minutes. Add the runner beans and continue to cook until they too are tender. Pour in the milk and pass the soup through a vegetable mouli or sieve or process it in a food processor or blender until it is smooth and creamy.

Return to the pan and add the lemon juice. Season to taste. Heat through before serving.

MARINATED BEANS

This vegetable dish can be eaten hot or cold.

675 g ($1\frac{1}{2}$ lb) runner beans
4 tbsp olive oil
3 large ripe tomatoes, finely chopped
4 shallots, finely chopped
4 tbsp fresh parsley, chopped
5 coriander seeds, crushed
seasoning

Slice the beans and put into a pan with the other ingredients. Barely cover with water and bring to the boil. Simmer for 20–25 minutes. Remove the beans with a slotted spoon and boil the remaining stock. Reduce by two-thirds and then pour over the beans.

SORREL OMELETTE

Sorrel is an extremely popular herb on the Continent. It resembles spinach both in appearance and flavour. According to one of my old reference books, 'greensauce' made from sorrel, vinegar and sugar was a common accompaniment to meat and poultry until the eighteenth century here in England. I now have a large clump of sorrel growing in my herb garden and use it often in salads and soups and to make this delicious omelette. It has a sharp, refreshing taste.

SERVES 2
a handful of sorrel
a little butter
4 eggs, beaten

Trim the stalks from the sorrel and wash carefully. Chop and throw into a pan with a knob of butter. Cook gently until soft. Meanwhile, melt another knob of butter in a small frying pan or omelette pan. Pour in the beaten egg and cook over a moderate heat, tipping the pan and lifting the edges of the omelette as the eggs begin to set so that the liquid can run underneath. When the omelette is speckled brown underneath but is still slightly runny on top spoon over the cooked sorrel. Fold the omelette in half and serve immediately.

LEEKS IN WALNUT VINAIGRETTE

Walnut oil is perhaps my favourite oil, though it is not nearly so versatile as olive oil. It is a mellow, richly-flavoured oil which tastes distinctly nutty. It comes into its own when used as a salad dressing.

8 thin leeks
4 tbsp walnut oil
2 tbsp lemon juice
seasoning
1 tbsp fresh chives, chopped

Trim and clean the leeks and cut them into lengths of about 10 cm (4 in). Steam or lightly boil until barely tender. Meanwhile, mix the oil, lemon juice and seasoning together. As soon as the leeks are tender place in a serving dish and pour over the vinaigrette. Sprinkle the chives on top. Leave to cool, turning the leeks occasionally.

A potato salad can be made in the same way, but remember to use waxy potatoes and dress them while hot.

SEAFOOD À LA FRANÇAISE

A rich fish stew.

450 g (1 lb) mussels
150 ml (5 fl oz) water
3 tbsp olive oil
2 onions, sliced
2 cloves garlic, peeled and crushed
4 large tomatoes, chopped
150 ml (5 fl oz) dry white wine
1 bay leaf
seasoning
450 g (1 lb) cod fillets, skinned, boned and chopped
100 g (4 oz) peeled prawns
1 tbsp fresh parsley, chopped

Scrub the mussels thoroughly, pulling off their 'beards' and discarding any that are open. Rinse them in several changes of water to rid them of all sand. Put them in a large pan with half of the measured water. Cover and cook over a high flame for 5 minutes, shaking the pan occasionally. When most of the mussels have opened remove from the heat. Discard any that remain shut. Remove the top shell from each mussel. Reserve the cooking stock, strain well and keep aside with the mussels.

Heat the oil in a large frying pan, add the onions and sauté until soft. Add the garlic, tomatoes, the remaining water, the wine, bay leaf and season to taste. Simmer for 15 minutes. Add the cod and cook for a further 5 minutes. Add the mussels, their cooking stock and the prawns. Simmer gently for 4–5 minutes. Sprinkle with fresh parsley and serve immediately with crusty bread.

MOULES MARINIÈRE

This really is an excellent dish and surprisingly quick and easy to prepare.

2.5 kg (5 lb) mussels
1 onion, chopped
2 cloves garlic, peeled and crushed
275 ml (10 fl oz) dry white wine
3 tbsp fresh parsley, finely chopped
freshly ground black pepper

Scrub the mussels thoroughly, removing their 'beards' and discarding any that are open. Rinse them in several changes of water to rid them of all sand. Put into a large pan with the chopped onion, garlic and wine. Bring to the boil and cover with a tight-fitting lid. Cook fiercely, giving one or two good shakes to the pan and after 3–4 minutes check to see if the mussels have begun to open. Remove from the heat when most have opened and discard any that do not open of their own accord.

Tip the contents of the pan into a large colander placed over a bowl to collect the stock. Remove the top shell of each mussel. Strain the stock through muslin and return to a clean pan. Bring to the boil and throw in the mussels, still attached to one half of their shell. Cook for 1–2 minutes before placing them in individual serving bowls. Strain the stock a second time and pour over the mussels. Sprinkle with parsley and black pepper and serve with crusty bread.

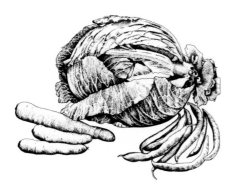

BOEUF BOURGUIGNON

The classic stew.

olive oil
675 g (1½ lb) chuck beef,
trimmed and roughly chopped
2 onions, chopped
1 clove garlic, peeled and crushed
1 carrot, chopped
5 shallots
1 sprig of fresh thyme
1 sprig of fresh parsley
1 bay leaf
½ bottle of Burgundy
100 g (4 oz) mushrooms
seasoning

Heat 2–3 tablespoons of oil in a large heavy pan, add the meat and brown it on all sides. Remove it with a slotted spoon and add the onions and garlic to the pan. Sauté until soft and golden. Return the meat to the pan with the carrot, shallots and herbs. Pour over the wine and cover with a tight-fitting lid. Simmer gently for 2–2½ hours until the meat is tender. Half an hour before you estimate the meat will be ready add the mushrooms. Season to taste.

Some people remove the vegetables and herbs before serving but I generally leave them in.

CHICKEN WITH BASIL

FOR THE STUFFING:
3 tbsp olive oil
3 shallots, finely chopped
2 slices of wholewheat bread, crusts removed
and broken into crumbs
2 tbsp fresh basil, finely chopped

REMAINING INGREDIENT:
1¼ kg (2½–3 lb) chicken

Heat 1 tablespoon of the oil in a small pan, add the shallots and sauté until soft and golden. Remove from the heat and mix together with the bread and the basil. Stuff the filling into the body cavity of the bird. Place on a baking tray and brush with the remaining oil. Bake in a preheated oven, gas mark 6 (200° C/400° F) for 45 minutes or so until tender. Baste well during cooking.

NORMANDY CHICKEN

$1\frac{1}{4}$ kg ($2\frac{1}{2}$–3 lb) chicken
50 g (2 oz) wholewheat flour
50 g (2 oz) butter
2 cooking apples, peeled, cored and sliced
1 bay leaf
275 ml (10 fl oz) dry cider
2 tbsp olive oil
275 ml (10 fl oz) milk
seasoning
freshly grated nutmeg

Joint the chicken and dust the pieces with half the flour. Melt the butter in a casserole-type pan, add the chicken pieces and brown them on all sides. Remove the chicken with a slotted spoon and keep warm. Add the apples and sauté for several minutes before returning the chicken to the pan. Toss in the bay leaf and pour over the cider. Cover and simmer for 20–25 minutes until the chicken is tender.

Heat the oil in a small pan and stir in the remaining flour. Cook for a minute or two until it begins to bubble. Remove from the heat and gradually stir in the milk. Return to the stove and heat through, stirring frequently, until the sauce begins to thicken. Lift the chicken pieces and the apple from the pan and keep aside. Slowly stir the sauce into the pan juices and mix together well. Season with black pepper and nutmeg. Remove the bay leaf. Return the chicken and apples to the pan and heat through before serving.

CASSOULET

A traditional French stew that is both delicious and filling. It can be made the day before it is needed provided that it is reheated thoroughly.

225 g (8 oz) haricot beans, soaked overnight and then drained
850 ml ($1\frac{1}{2}$ pints) water
450 g (1 lb) pork, shoulder or leg
100 g (4 oz) bacon
olive oil
1 onion, chopped
1 clove garlic, peeled and crushed
1 sprig of fresh parsley
1 sprig of fresh sage
1 sprig of fresh thyme
175 g (6 oz) garlic sausage, sliced
4–6 small pieces of chicken
seasoning

Put the beans into a pan and cover with the water. Cover, bring to the boil and simmer for about 60 minutes until tender. If using a pressure cooker the beans need only be soaked for 6 hours and cooked for 12 minutes. Drain and reserve the bean stock.

Trim and chop the pork and bacon. Heat 1–2 tablespoons of oil in a large pan, add the onion and garlic and brown. Add the pork, bacon and herbs. Cover with a tight-fitting lid and cook gently for 45–50 minutes, stirring occasionally. Add the chicken, the cooked beans, garlic sausage and 425 ml (15 fl oz) bean stock. Season to taste and cover again. Cook for a further 50–60 minutes. Add further bean stock if necessary.

Serve with potatoes and a green vegetable or salad.

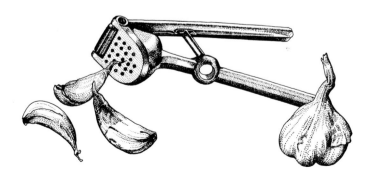

LAMB STEW WITH SUMMER VEGETABLES

olive oil
2 onions, chopped
675 g (1½ lb) middle neck of lamb
350 g (12 oz) small new carrots
450 g (1 lb) small new potatoes
450 g (1 lb) garden peas, shelled
1 tbsp fresh parsley, finely chopped
1 tsp fresh mint, finely chopped
seasoning

Heat 1–2 tablespoons of olive oil in a pan, add the onions and gently sauté. Trim the meat from the bone and cut into chunks. Add the meat to the pan and brown on all sides. Add the bones, having first trimmed off as much of the fat as possible, and barely cover with water. Cover and simmer for 55–60 minutes. Then remove the bones.

Meanwhile, prepare the vegetables, leaving them whole. Add the carrots and potatoes to the stew and cook for 10–15 minutes before adding the peas and herbs. It may be necessary to add more water but try and keep it to the minimum. Cook until the vegetables are tender and season to taste before serving.

BRAISED LETTUCE WITH HAM AND TOMATOES

olive oil
3 shallots or 1 small onion, chopped finely
100 g (4 oz) ham, roughly chopped
225 g (8 oz) tomatoes, chopped
2 medium lettuces, shredded

Heat a tablespoon or two of oil in a large, heavy-bottomed pan, add the shallots and ham and lightly sauté for a minute or two. Add the tomatoes and cook for a further 10 minutes. Put in as much lettuce as the pan will hold and heat it gently, stirring occasionally, until it has reduced in volume. Add more lettuce and cook in the same way. Repeat until all the lettuce has been added. Then cover with a tight-fitting lid and cook gently for 10–15 minutes. Toss well before serving.

BRAISED GREEN PEAS WITH BUTTER (PETIT POIS À LA FRANÇAISE)

This is one of the classic ways of preparing young sweet peas of early summer. It is also the first dish I ate which contained cooked lettuce and much to my surprise I found it nicer than when eaten raw in salads.

1 crisp lettuce heart
450 g (1 lb) small, tender green peas
4 shallots, sliced
6 sprigs of fresh parsley, tied together
25 g (1 oz) unsalted butter
2 tbsp cold water
seasoning

Cut the lettuce heart in quarters and bind each segment with soft string. Place all the ingredients in a pan and bring to the boil. Toss lightly before covering. Simmer gently for 20 minutes, stirring occasionally, until the vegetables are tender. If necessary cook over a fierce heat, shaking the pan, to drive off any excess water.

Remove the parsley and cut the string from the lettuce. Season and toss before serving.

BLANQUETTE DE POMMES DE TERRE AUX POIREAUX (WHITE POTATO AND LEEK STEW)

A really delicious vegetable dish which I have unashamedly taken from Anne Willan's excellent book, *French Regional Cooking* (Hutchinson, 1981).

50 g (2 oz) butter
450 g (1 lb) leeks, washed, trimmed and sliced
1 tbsp flour
625 ml (23 fl oz) milk
1 kg (2 lb) potatoes, scrubbed and thinly sliced
1 sprig of fresh thyme
1 sprig of fresh marjoram
1 bay leaf
freshly ground black pepper
freshly grated nutmeg

In a large heavy pan melt the butter. Add the leeks and cook gently and slowly until soft. Although a blanquette should, strictly speaking, be white I like to cook the leeks until they just begin to turn a delicate golden brown colour.

Sprinkle with flour and cook gently for a minute or two, stirring frequently. Gradually stir in the milk and then bring to the boil. Add the remaining ingredients and season to taste with black pepper and nutmeg. Cover and cook over a very low heat, stirring frequently, for 45 minutes or until the potatoes are tender.

Discard the herbs and adjust the seasoning to taste. Spoon the stew into a shallow dish and, if you like, place under a hot grill to brown before serving.

POMMES DE TERRE RISSOLÉES (GOLDEN POTATOES)

Pommes frites are just as popular at roadside cafés in France as they are in England but many smaller French restaurants, particularly those in Brittany, serve pommes de terre rissolées. They are aptly named, being fried in butter until they look like little golden balls, crisp on the outside and beautifully soft inside. I can't imagine cooking them at home as I don't like frying potatoes and would certainly be reluctant to do so in butter, but I shall look forward to eating them again next time I visit Brittany.

675 g (1$\frac{1}{2}$ lb) small new potatoes
50 g (2 oz) butter

Wash the potatoes well and cook them in a pan of boiling water until they are just tender. Drain well and rinse under cold running water. Remove their skins carefully.

Melt the butter in a frying pan and when foaming add the potatoes and cook, stirring frequently, until they are golden brown and slightly crisp. Serve.

SPANISH COOKERY

SPANISH COOKERY

Spain is a country I would very much like to revisit. I first went there as a wide-eyed schoolgirl and still cling to nostalgic memories of cool dark monastic cloisters lining sunny quadrangles planted with orange trees; of evenings too hot for sleeping and full of the sound of castenets and of La Mancha, the high dusty plain, home of Don Quixote's windmills.

My second visit, some ten years later, was a much more down-to-earth affair, for although I had time on my hands I had very little money. In spite of the austerity of the trip I spent some of my last pesetas in a small white-washed restaurant overlooking the Mediterranean with the lights of Gibraltar twinkling in the distance. The meal was plain — some kind of tortilla or omelette, hunks of bread and rough red wine. It was delicious, far better than anything I had eaten in the tourist bars around Malaga.

Spain is like any other country in this respect. There are three broad styles of cooking within its borders. First are the hotels which, with the exception of a few regional dishes, serve the same food in almost every corner of the world. This includes the grand hotels that cook haute cuisine and the more modest establishments whose menus read 'chips with everything'. Next are small restaurants, frequented by locals and rarely discovered by the tourist. They can produce some excellent dishes made with local recipes, local ingredients and local charm. Finally there are the truly indigenous meals cooked at home, which are seldom found in any recipe book and which only a few lucky 'foreigners' get a chance to sample.

One general misconception about Spanish food, which must be dispelled from the start, is that it is excessively greasy. Greasy cooking is bad cooking anywhere and there is no reason why Spanish food should be any worse in this respect than that of any other country. Certainly they use large quantities of olive oil but this usually takes the place of animal fats such as butter. I, for one, like the taste of a good olive oil and find that it complements and enhances the flavour of a wide variety of foods. If a recipe seems to be overgenerous in its use of oil, whether it be French, Indian or Spanish, simply cut down on the amount according to taste. Obviously this is difficult when making pastries or cakes but very little Spanish food is baked in the oven. Most oil is used for sautée-ing or frying and can easily be reduced in quantity, particularly when heated in a well seasoned pan.

Spain is a big country and has a wide range of regional delicacies. There are countless varieties of chorizo (sausage) spiced and coloured with garlic and paprika (they can be bought in many delicatessen); many different hams; grapes and raisins from Malaga; olives, rice, almonds, pomegranates and figs from Andalusia in the South; the bitter Seville orange (which I am told is rarely seen in the local shops for the Spanish do not share our passion for marmalade) and cheeses from La Mancha. Fish, chicken and eggs seem to be preferred to meat although there are many excellent recipes for game birds, particularly pheasant and partridge, and for rabbit and hare.

Although it would be wrong to make too many generalisations about Spanish cooking it does share a number of features with other Mediterranean cuisines. For instance, the habit of eating tapas or entremesas (hors d'oeuvres) with drinks before a meal. This is similar to the Greek habit of providing (free of charge) little dishes of appetising titbits at bars in the early evening. The idea is to whet one's palate for the good things to come but whether they stimulate the appetite for alcohol or food is open to conjecture. Fresh fruit is also as likely as not to be served after the meal for the Spanish seldom make desserts. Many restaurants, however, do include ices on their menus. As in France the nearest thing they have to the English pudding is a range of beautiful but expensive sweet pastries which are bought from a local bakery on very special occasions.

FISH SOUP

A lovely soup, one which looks as good as it tastes.

1–2 tbsp olive oil
2 tomatoes, sliced
1 onion, finely chopped
1 clove garlic, peeled and crushed
1 red pepper, deseeded and chopped
850 ml (1½ pints) fish stock
50 g (2 oz) soft breadcrumbs
450 g (1 lb) white fish, skinned,
boned and chopped
seasoning

Heat the oil in a large pan, add the tomatoes, onion, garlic and pepper and sauté for 5–6 minutes. Pour over half the stock and add the breadcrumbs. Purée the mixture by passing it through a sieve or vegetable mouli or process it briefly in a food processor or blender. Return to the pan and adjust the consistency as desired with the remaining stock. Add the fish and gently cook until tender. Season to taste.

ALMOND SOUP

1 tbsp olive oil
3 cloves garlic, peeled and crushed
1 red pepper, deseeded and chopped
1 sprig of fresh parsley, chopped
a good pinch of saffron strands
725–850 ml (1¼–1½ pints) water
2 slices of wholewheat bread, crusts removed
100 g (4 oz) blanched almonds,
roasted and chopped
seasoning

Heat the oil in a pan, add the garlic and sauté gently, taking care not to let it burn. Add the red pepper, parsley, saffron and half the water. Bring to the boil and simmer gently for 10 minutes. Break the bread into crumbs and place in a food processor or blender with the remaining ingredients. Process until fairly smooth. Pass through a sieve and return to the pan. Add more water until the desired consistency is reached. Season to taste. Heat through before serving.

CHICK PEA SOUP

1–2 tbsp olive oil
4 tomatoes, chopped
2 onions, sliced
2 cloves garlic, peeled and crushed
225 g (8 oz) chick peas, soaked overnight
and then drained
850 ml (1½ pints) water
1 tbsp fresh parsley, chopped
1 bay leaf
1 tsp paprika
1 tsp allspice
1 tbsp medium curry powder

FOR THE GARNISH:
fresh parsley, chopped
wholewheat croûtons

Heat the olive oil in a large pan, add the tomatoes, onions and garlic and sauté for 5–10 minutes. Add all the remaining ingredients and bring to the boil. Simmer for 1½–2 hours until the chick peas are soft, checking the contents of the pan occasionally to make sure they do not boil dry, or pressure cook for 20–25 minutes. Remove the bay leaf.

Pass three-quarters of the soup through a sieve or vegetable mouli or process briefly in a blender or food processor until smooth. Stir into the unblended soup in the pan and adjust the seasoning if necessary. Heat through. Garnish with parsley and croûtons before serving.

WHITE GAZPACHO

30 almonds, blanched and chopped
4 cloves garlic, peeled and left whole
1 tbsp olive oil
1 tbsp lemon juice
50 g (2 oz) soft breadcrumbs
575 ml (1 pint) water
450 g (1 lb) small seedless white grapes
ice cubes

Pound the almonds, garlic and olive oil together in a pestle and mortar or process them briefly in a food processor or blender. Mix in the lemon juice and breadcrumbs. Gradually add the water until the mixture is smooth. Push through a sieve before pouring into a soup tureen. Add the grapes and half a dozen ice cubes. Leave in a cool place for one hour before serving.

SOPA DE AJO (GARLIC SOUP)

There are many versions of this traditional Spanish soup. This recipe is more sophisticated than most. It does not like being kept waiting nor will it reheat.

850 ml (1½ pints) chicken stock
a good pinch of saffron strands
3–4 tbsp olive oil
7–8 cloves garlic, peeled and left whole
2 slices of bread, crusts removed
freshly ground black pepper
2 eggs, beaten

Put the stock and saffron in a pan and bring to the boil. Remove from the heat and leave to infuse for 15 minutes.

Heat the oil in a pan and add the whole cloves of garlic. Fry gently until they are golden brown. Meanwhile, slice the bread into small cubes and brown them in the pan along with the garlic.

Strain the stock before pouring it into the pan containing the garlic and croûtons. Bring to the boil and simmer for 5 minutes. Season to taste with black pepper. Remove from the heat and gradually stir into a soup tureen containing the 2 beaten eggs. Serve immediately.

EGGS À LA FLAMENCO

olive oil
1 large onion, chopped
2 cloves garlic, peeled and crushed
2 red peppers, deseeded and chopped
6 small tomatoes, chopped
225 g (8 oz) French beans, sliced and cooked
225 g (8 oz) peas, cooked
175–225 g (6–8 oz) chorizos, thinly sliced
seasoning
6 eggs

Heat 1–2 tablespoons of oil in a frying pan and add the onion, garlic and peppers. Sauté for 5–7 minutes. Add the remaining ingredients and cook for a further 5 minutes until the tomatoes soften. Season to taste. Break the eggs over the top and cook gently until they set. They can either be cooked over a flame or baked in a preheated moderate oven for 15 minutes.

BASQUE OMELETTE

SERVES 2
1 tbsp olive oil
2 red peppers, deseeded and chopped
2 tomatoes, chopped
seasoning
4 eggs

Heat the oil in a frying pan, add the peppers and tomatoes and lightly sauté until they begin to soften. Season to taste. Beat the eggs together and pour over the mixture. Cook over a fairly low heat and as the egg sets at the edge of the pan, draw the mixture back gently with a fork to allow some of the mixture on the surface to run underneath. Cook until set. Spanish omelettes are cooked more than our own and they are often cooked on both sides. They are eaten hot or cold.

SHELLFISH WITH SAFFRON RICE

SERVES 6
450 g (1 lb) squid
2 tbsp olive oil
2 onions, chopped
1 clove garlic, peeled and crushed
1 red pepper, deseeded and sliced
450 g (1 lb) long grain brown rice
225 g (8 oz) tomatoes, chopped
350 ml (12 fl oz) water
150 ml (5 fl oz) dry white wine
a good pinch of saffron strands
seasoning
225 g (8 oz) peeled prawns
225 g (8 oz) mussels, shelled and cooked
fresh parsley, finely chopped

Squid can be prepared for cooking in no more time than it takes to gut any other fish. Although I must admit it is not one of my favourite pastimes I have perfected a simple method which is quick, straightforward and relatively clean. First locate the tentacles, the sac-like body with its two fins and the narrow head between the tentacles and the body. Then cut off the individual tentacles just below where they are attached to the head. Place aside. Lightly take hold of the head in one hand and the body in the other. Pull the two sections gently apart. The viscera, including the ink-sac, will come away with the head and can be discarded. The sac-like body will be empty except for the quill and a little mucous membrane. Locate the end of the transparent quill, grasp it by the tip and gently pull it free from the body and discard. Rinse the body under cold running water and carefully pull away the membrane with the fingers.

Some squid are sold still shrouded in their veil-like translucent skin, irregularly mottled with blue-grey patches. It covers the body and is easily peeled away. Also remove the skin from the two fins before pulling them from the body. They come away quite easily and should be placed with the tentacles. Rinse the body and pat dry. The cleaned squid, consisting of tentacles, two triangular fins and sac-like body is now ready for use. Cut the body into rings, 1.25 cm (1 in) wide.

Heat the oil in a large pan, add the onions and garlic and sauté until soft. Add the red pepper and cook for a minute or two more. Stir in the rice, tomatoes, water, wine, saffron and the squid. Season to taste. Bring to the boil. Cover and simmer, without stirring, for 35 minutes until all the liquid has been absorbed and the rice is tender.

Spoon the rice into an ovenproof dish and lay the prawns and mussels on the top. Bake in a preheated oven, gas mark 7 (220° C/425° F) for 10 minutes until heated through. Sprinkle with parsley before serving.

ARROZ CON MEJILLONES (RICE WITH MUSSELS)

3–4 cloves garlic, peeled
2 tbsp fresh parsley, finely chopped
a good pinch of saffron strands
2 tbsp olive oil
450 g (1 lb) long grain brown rice
1 litre (1¾ pints) water or fish stock
450 g (1 lb) mussels, cleaned, cooked
and shelled (for method, see page 156)

TO GARNISH:
fresh parsley, chopped
black olives

Pound the garlic, parsley and saffron together in a mortar. Heat the oil in a heavy pan and add the garlic purée. Fry lightly for a minute or two without browning. Stir in the rice and mix together thoroughly to ensure that it is evenly coated in oil. Pour over the water or stock. (I always rinse out the mortar with the liquid before tipping it into the pan.) Bring to the boil. Cover and simmer gently, without stirring, until almost all the water has been absorbed. Place the mussels on top of the rice, replace the lid and continue cooking until the rice is dry and tender.

Remove from the heat and carefully stir the rice with a rice paddle or wooden fork. Replace the lid and leave aside for 5–10 minutes for the rice to dry out. Cover with a cloth to retain the heat if the pan isn't a heavy Le Creuset type or place in a warm oven. Sprinkle with parsley or black olives before serving.

CHICKEN WITH GARLIC

$1\frac{1}{4}$ kg ($2\frac{1}{2}$–3 lb) roasting chicken
2–3 tbsp olive oil
a knob of butter
10–15 cloves garlic, peeled and left whole
freshly ground black pepper

Joint the bird. In a large heavy pan or flame-proof casserole heat together the oil and butter. Add the chicken pieces and fry until they begin to brown. Add the whole cloves of garlic and cover the pan with a tight-fitting lid. Cook over a very gentle heat for 25–30 minutes, basting and turning the chicken frequently, until the meat is tender. Remove the garlic from the buttery stock and adjust the seasoning before serving.

BEEF CASSEROLE

2–3 tbsp olive oil
1 onion, chopped
1 clove garlic, peeled and crushed
675 g ($1\frac{1}{2}$ lb) chuck steak
350 ml (12 fl oz) dry white wine
150 ml (5 fl oz) wine vinegar
1 tsp mixed dried herbs
1 tsp paprika
$\frac{1}{2}$ tsp cayenne pepper
3 tomatoes, chopped
350 ml (12 fl oz) stock or
water and 2 tbsp soya sauce
450 g (1 lb) small new potatoes, scrubbed
seasoning

Heat the oil in a large pan, add the onion and garlic and sauté until soft and golden. Trim the meat of excess fat, cut into chunks and add to the pan. Sauté until it is brown on all sides. Add the wine, wine vinegar, herbs and spices and simmer gently for 5–10 minutes. Stir in the tomatoes and stock and bring to the boil. Cover and simmer for $1\frac{1}{2}$ hours. Add the potatoes and cook until they are tender. Season to taste and serve.

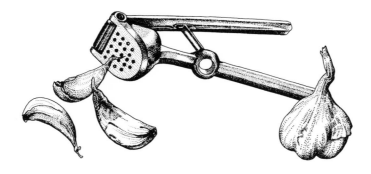

INDIAN COOKERY

INDIAN COOKERY

It is rather presumptuous of an English cook to write about Indian cookery and I hasten to point out that I am no great authority on the subject. But I do enjoy preparing and eating spicy foods and have learnt a great deal from a student of mine who was delighted to reverse our roles and to teach me how to cook.

I can remember, with some embarrassment, my early attempts at making curries in my student days. The curry powder and vegetables all came out of tins and success was measured purely and simply in terms of hotness. I naïvely believed that the experience of eating a curry had to be one of intense pain as well as pleasure. Thankfully I have progressed beyond this stage and have learnt to appreciate that Indian food is not synonymous with the curry and that word is used by the British to describe all kinds of dishes, including the simple dhal, fried koftas of minced beef or puréed vegetables, tandoori or oven-baked dishes, biryani rice dishes flavoured and coloured with turmeric and rich stews cooked with spiced yoghurt.

Naturally it is essential to use the correct ingredients when preparing Indian dishes. Fresh parsley cannot replace fresh coriander, nor can ground ginger be as authentic as fresh root ginger, and commercial curry powders are no substitute for the individual spices. Buy spices in small quantities and keep them in a cool, dark place for they soon lose their flavour. Whenever possible buy whole spices and grind them at home, as and when needed. The most useful spices to keep in the kitchen are: fresh coriander (keep it in the fridge or freezer) and coriander seeds; fresh and dried chillis (remove the white seeds to obtain maximum flavour and minimum heat); fresh and dried ginger; cumin seeds; black mustard seeds; turmeric; garam masala (add at the end of cooking otherwise it becomes bitter); saffron; cardamom seeds; and cinnamon sticks. The last two spices are cooked whole and removed from the pot before serving or left on the side of the plate by the diner.

Whether you are ordering a meal in a restaurant or cooking one at home it should be balanced, not simply in terms of food value but also from the point of view of texture, flavour and colour. When invited to dinner by an Indian family I was served a delicious, dryish vegetable curry (home-made with no name and no recipe), chapati, rice and a thin mulligatawny soup and a pickle. All the dishes arrived on the table at the same time and were eaten in any order, according to personal taste.

Before eating the meal I was invited behind the scenes and was shown how to make chapati. Chapati are unleavened bread made from very finely ground wholewheat flour often sold as chapati flour or ata in Indian shops. They are cooked on a tarva, a slightly concave, circular, cast iron griddle that is preheated before the chapati are cooked on it. This preheating helps to keep the chapati soft and pliant. If you haven't got such a pan try using a cast iron frying pan.

The actual cooking is comparatively easy compared with the task of rolling out a succession of beautifully thin and circular chapati. The secret is to use the specially-designed rolling pin which is an essential piece of equipment in every Indian kitchen. It looks a little like a chair rung, being thicker in the middle than at the ends, and is much thinner than a conventional western rolling pin. It is used in the normal fashion but by applying pressure to one side it is possible to make the chapati dough rotate round the floured board. This ensures that the finished item is of an even thickness, size and shape. Many Indian women spend up to an hour everyday making chapati for their families. It is a joy to watch them and to see the pile of perfectly-shaped chapati rise beneath the cloth covering.

CHAPATI

MAKES 12
250 g (9 oz) chapati flour
1 tbsp sunflower oil
150 ml (5 fl oz) warm water (approx)

Put the flour in a bowl and rub in the oil. Gradually add the water and knead to form a soft dough. Chapati dough should be quite soft; the amount of water used will vary with the type of flour. Place the tarva or frying pan on a medium heat for 10 minutes. Divide the dough into 12 small balls and roll out on a floured board until each is about 15 cm (6 in) in diameter. Put the chapati into a preheated tarva or cast iron frying pan. Cook the chapati on one side until it begins to be speckled brown, turn over and cook on the other side for half a minute. Lift the pan from the heat and pick up the chapati. Throw it on top of a low flame. It will puff up. Omit this stage if you do not use a gas hob. Remove from the heat and cover with a clean cloth to keep warm while the other chapati are being prepared. For a richer chapati rub both sides with butter before stacking.

LAMB CURRY

675 g (1½ lb) best end of neck of lamb
2–3 tbsp groundnut oil
2 onions, chopped
2–3 cloves garlic, peeled and crushed
1.25 cm (½ in) fresh root ginger,
peeled and grated
1 green chilli, finely chopped
1½ tsp ground cumin
1 tsp ground coriander
1 tsp ground paprika
1 tsp black mustard seeds
1 tsp fenugreek
½ tsp fennel seeds
a good pinch ground cinnamon
juice of 1 lemon
seasoning
3 tbsp sour cream or yoghurt
fresh coriander, finely chopped

Trim the meat and cut into chunks.
   Heat the oil in a pan, add the onions, garlic, ginger and chilli and sauté for 10 minutes. Add the spices and fry, stirring constantly, for a further 3–4 minutes. Stir in the meat and cook until browned on all sides. Add the lemon juice

and a little water. Season to taste and cover. Bring to the boil and simmer gently for 1½ hours. Remove from the heat and stir in the sour cream or yoghurt. Return to the stove and heat through without boiling. Serve with a garnish of coriander leaves.

LAMB WITH ALMONDS

If you don't have a mincer ask your butcher to mince the lamb. He should be happy to oblige, particularly if given a couple of hours' notice. Try and get meat from a leg of lamb; it is less fatty than other cuts.

2–3 tbsp sunflower oil
2 onions, chopped
2.5 cm (1 in) fresh root ginger, peeled and
grated
2 cloves garlic, peeled and crushed
1 tbsp turmeric
1 tbsp ground coriander
1 tsp ground cumin
1 tsp cayenne pepper
50 g (2 oz) blanched almonds
675 g (1½ lb) minced lamb
2 tomatoes, chopped
1 aubergine, chopped
seasoning
2 tbsp fresh coriander, finely chopped

Heat the oil in a large pan, add the onions and cook until soft and golden. Add the ginger, garlic and spices and stir for 2–3 minutes more, stirring often. Add the almonds and fry lightly until they begin to brown. Next add the lamb and cook until that too is browned. Add the tomatoes and aubergines and a spoonful or two of water. Cover the pan and simmer for 30 minutes until the meat is tender, stirring occasionally. Season to taste and sprinkle with the coriander before serving.

BEEF CURRY

2–3 tbsp sunflower oil or ghee
2 onions, chopped
2 green chillies, finely chopped
3 cloves garlic, peeled and crushed
2 tbsp ground coriander
1 tsp ground cumin
1 tsp ground cinnamon
1 tsp ground cloves
1 tsp fenugreek
$\frac{1}{2}$ tsp ground ginger
675 g ($1\frac{1}{2}$ lb) braising steak
seasoned flour
3 tbsp red wine vinegar
575 ml (1 pint) beef stock
1 bay leaf
1 tbsp garam masala

Heat the oil in a large pan, add the onions, chillies and garlic and sauté until soft. Stir in the spices and cook for a minute or two more. Trim the meat, cut into chunks and dust with seasoned flour. Add to the pan and cook until it is lightly browned on all sides. Pour over the vinegar and stock and add the bay leaf. Bring to the boil, cover and simmer gently for $1\frac{1}{2}$–2 hours until the meat is tender. Adjust the seasoning to taste. Stir in the garam masala before serving and remove the bay leaf.

CHICKEN CURRY

2–3 tbsp sunflower oil
2 onions, chopped
1 clove garlic, peeled and crushed
1 green chilli, finely chopped
2 tbsp ground coriander
1 tsp cumin seeds
1 tsp cardamom seeds, crushed
1 tsp turmeric
$\frac{1}{2}$ tsp fenugreek
$1\frac{1}{2}$ kg (3 lb) chicken, jointed
50 g (2 oz) creamed coconut
350 ml (12 fl oz) water
seasoning

Heat the oil in a large heavy pan, add the onions and sauté until soft and golden. Stir in the garlic, chilli and spices and fry for several minutes, stirring frequently. Add the chicken joints and cook until well browned on all sides. Add the remaining ingredients and bring to the boil. Cover and simmer for 45–55 minutes until the chicken is tender. Season to taste.

SUNITA'S VEGETABLE CURRY

Garam masala is a mixture of aromatic spices and is used to give a little panache to curried dishes. There is no standard recipe but it should include cardamom, cinnamon, black cumin seeds, cloves, black peppercorns and nutmeg. I buy it ready-made, storing it in small, air-tight containers. Use garam masala sparingly, adding it to a dish as a final seasoning, just before serving.

SERVES 4
75 ml (3 fl oz) sunflower oil
1 large onion, chopped
4–5 tomatoes, chopped
1 green chilli, finely chopped
1 level tsp red chilli powder
2 tsp turmeric
seasoning
2 aubergines, chopped
3 potatoes, scrubbed and chopped
1–2 tsp garam masala

Heat the oil in a large pan, add the onion and sauté until soft and golden. Add the tomatoes, chilli, red chilli powder, turmeric and seasoning. Fry for a few minutes more, stirring well. Add the aubergines and potatoes and mix, coating well with spices and oil. Barely cover with water. Cover and simmer until the vegetables are tender. Add more water, a little at a time, if the mixture becomes too dry. Stir in the garam masala before serving.

VEGETABLE BIRYANI

3 tbsp groundnut oil
3 onions, finely chopped
2.5 cm (1 in) fresh root ginger, peeled and
grated
3 cloves garlic, peeled and crushed
3 tomatoes, chopped
$\frac{1}{2}$ tsp turmeric
1 tsp ground cumin
1 tsp ground coriander
2 green chillies, finely chopped
2 large potatoes, scrubbed and diced
4 carrots, diced
100 g (4 oz) green peas
225 g (8 oz) long grain brown rice, cooked
50 g (2 oz) raisins, soaked in hot water
for 30 minutes
50 g (2 oz) blanched almonds, finely chopped
75–125 ml (3–4 fl oz) natural yoghurt
fresh coriander leaves
1 tsp garam masala

Heat the oil in a large pan, add the onions and
sauté until soft and golden. Add the ginger,
garlic and tomatoes and cook for a further 4–5
minutes. Stir in the spices, chillies, potatoes,
carrots and peas. Pour over a little water, to a
depth of 1.25 cm ($\frac{1}{2}$ in), cover and cook gently
until the vegetables are tender.

Place a third of the cooked rice in the bottom
of another pan or ovenproof dish and spoon
over half the curried vegetables. Scatter half
the drained raisins and the almonds on the top
before dribbling over half of the yoghurt.
Sprinkle with some finely chopped coriander
and a little garam masala. Repeat the layers
finishing with a layer of rice.

Reheat by placing the pan over a gentle heat
for 10–15 minutes or bake in a preheated oven,
gas mark 5 (190° C/375° F).

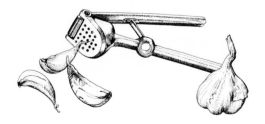

MIXED VEGETABLE CURRY

2 tbsp sunflower oil
1 onion, finely chopped
5 cm (2 in) fresh root ginger, peeled and grated
1 clove garlic, peeled and crushed
1 green chilli, finely chopped
1 tsp black mustard seeds
1 tsp turmeric
1 tbsp ground coriander
675 g (1$\frac{1}{2}$ lb) mixed vegetables, sliced
(carrots, beans, cauliflower, aubergines etc)
25 g (1 oz) creamed coconut
175 ml (6 fl oz) water
2 tbsp fresh coriander, finely chopped

Heat the oil in a large heavy pan, add the onion
and sauté until soft. Add the ginger, garlic,
chilli and mustard seeds and fry for a minute or
two more, stirring frequently. Stir in the
turmeric and coriander and cook for one
minute. Add the vegetables and coat with the
spices. Add the creamed coconut and water
and bring to the boil. Cover and simmer for 25–
30 minutes until the vegetables are tender.
Sprinkle with fresh coriander before serving.

VEGETABLES COOKED IN SPICY YOGHURT SAUCE

1 tbsp sunflower oil
1 onion, finely chopped
2.5 cm (1 in) fresh root ginger, peeled and
grated
4 ripe tomatoes, chopped
1 green chilli, finely chopped
1 tsp turmeric
1 tbsp ground coriander
425 ml (15 fl oz) natural yoghurt
225 g (8 oz) new potatoes, cooked and diced
3 carrots, cooked and diced
$\frac{1}{2}$ small cauliflower,
cooked and broken into florets
100 g (4 oz) French beans, trimmed and
cooked

Heat the oil in a heavy frying pan, add the
onion and ginger and sauté until soft and
golden. Add the tomatoes, chilli, turmeric and
coriander. Cook for a further 2–3 minutes,
stirring frequently. Pour in the yoghurt and
bring to the boil. Simmer gently, uncovered,

for 15–20 minutes until the sauce begins to thicken. Add the cooked vegetables and stir gently. Heat through before serving.

CUCUMBER RAITA

An Indian side salad.

$\frac{1}{4}$ cucumber, finely chopped
1 clove garlic, peeled and crushed
1 tsp dried mint
1 tsp garam masala
150 ml (5 fl oz) natural yoghurt
1 tsp lemon juice
seasoning

Mix all the ingredients together in a bowl.

SPICY TOMATO SALAD

225 g (8 oz) tomatoes, sliced
$\frac{1}{2}$–1 tsp garam masala
$\frac{1}{2}$ onion, finely chopped
1 tbsp fresh coriander, finely chopped

Arrange the tomatoes on a large serving dish. Sprinkle with garam masala and the onion. Garnish with coriander before serving.

SAFFRON RICE

1 tbsp sunflower oil
2 tsp cardamom seeds
2–3 small pieces of cinnamon
3–4 whole cloves
350 g (12 oz) long grain brown rice
a good pinch of saffron strands
a scant 850 ml (1$\frac{1}{2}$ pints) chicken stock
or water

Heat the oil in a pan, add the spices and stir-fry for 1–2 minutes. Stir in the rice and add the saffron. Pour over the stock or water and bring to the boil. Cover and simmer for 35–40 minutes until the rice is dry and tender.

CURRIED BLACKEYE BEANS WITH MUSHROOMS AND CORIANDER

50 g (2 oz) blackeye beans, cooked
3 tbsp sunflower oil
2 onions, chopped
1 aubergine, chopped
225 g (8 oz) flat mushrooms, chopped
4–5 tomatoes, chopped
1 green chilli, finely chopped
2 tsp turmeric
$\frac{1}{2}$ tsp red chilli powder
fresh coriander

To cook the beans place in a pan with 575 ml (1 pint) of water. Cover, bring to the boil and simmer for 45–55 minutes until the beans are tender. Check the pan occasionally and add more water if necessary. If using a pressure cooker cook for 12 minutes. Blackeye beans do not need to be soaked. Drain, reserving the stock.

Heat the oil in a large pan, add the onions and sauté until soft and golden. Add the aubergine and continue to fry for a further 5 minutes. Add the mushrooms, tomatoes, chilli and spices and cook, stirring well, for a minute or two more. Stir in the cooked beans. Pour in a tablespoon or two of bean stock if the curry looks dry. Cover and cook until the vegetables are soft. Finely chop the coriander and sprinkle over the curry before serving.

COOKING WITH A WOK

COOKING WITH A WOK

Interest in Oriental cooking has been growing steadily over the last 20 years and there can be few people who have not eaten in a Chinese restaurant or from a Chinese take-away. The popularity of dishes such as egg fu yung, chow mein and chop suey has resulted in a demand for Chinese cookery books, genuine Chinese ingredients and authentic cookery equipment.

One of the secrets of Chinese food is that it is traditionally prepared in a wok. This is an all-purpose, dished pan used by the Chinese for stir-frying, steaming, braising and deep frying foods. I have even heard of one cook who uses a wok to prepare moules marinière. My old and battered wok, blackened with age and countless stir-fries looks rather out of place among the other bright enamel and steel pans, but its appearance is a measure of its true value for it is the most frequently used and versatile pan in my collection.

There are many different types of wok on the market. Some are sturdy, almost hemispherical steel pans with one wooden handle. Others are electrically operated. By far the best, and fortunately the most common, is the light-weight, two handled type which comes complete with lid, spatula, strainer and chopsticks. Iron and steel woks need to be lightly seasoned with oil before being used. This keeps rust at bay and stops food sticking to the surface during cooking. To treat the metal, brush with a little oil and heat until smoking point is reached. Reduce the heat and keep the wok over a low flame for 20–30 minutes, occasionally brushing the sides with hot oil. The wok is now ready for use. A seasoned wok should not be washed with detergent or a scouring pad. After use simply wipe clean with a paper towel, run under hot water and dry thoroughly.

The wok is ideal for anyone living on their own or cooking for two. I have given up trying to prepare 'wok meals' for more than four people because all the dishes must be served the moment they are cooked and I never have enough woks or hands to co-ordinate the operation.

The technique of stir-frying is particularly valuable for preparing vegetables because the fast cooking helps to retain their flavour, colour, texture and nutrients. An endless variety of dishes can be made simply by using different vegetables, and adding some beansprouts, a few cashew nuts, some slivers of chicken, a handful of prawns or an omelette cut into strips. Eaten with a bowl of brown rice, buckwheat spaghetti or crusty garlic bread a healthy and satisfying meal can be provided fairly quickly.

Little if any planning is required as the basic ingredients (vegetables, oil and soya sauce) are to be found in almost every food cupboard, fridge or freezer. There is also a surprising number of Chinese supermarkets where authentic ingredients can be purchased, but unless you are familiar with them and know what you want they can be rather daunting. Good greengrocers', wholefood shops and supermarkets stock a range of useful ingredients which can be combined to make excellent dishes. These include fresh root ginger, naturally fermented soya sauce (shoyu and tamari), sesame seeds and sesame salt (gomasio). I use cold pressed sesame oil for stir-frying but other light oils such as peanut (groundnut), sunflower and soya oil are just as good. It is essential, however, to use vegetables that are at the peak of freshness. Colour, flavour and texture play an important part in Chinese cooking and must always be considered when planning a meal.

The following recipes have been chosen to make full use of the wok and readily available ingredients. They can be eaten as part of a Chinese meal or with more traditional English dishes.

STIR-FRIED VEGETABLES WITH BEANSPROUTS

3.75 cm (1½ in) fresh root ginger
1 onion
1 large carrot
1 red pepper
50 g (2 oz) button mushrooms
1 tbsp groundnut oil
3 tbsp dry white wine
2 tsp soya sauce
175 g (6 oz) beansprouts
1 bunch of watercress, trimmed
1 tbsp sesame seeds

Peel and grate the ginger. Slice the onion and cut the carrot into thin julienne strips (shaped like matchsticks). Slice the pepper into rings and remove the seeds. Wipe the mushrooms clean.

Heat the oil in a wok, add the onion and stir-fry for 2 minutes. Add the ginger and carrot and cook for a further 2 minutes. Add the red pepper and mushrooms and fry for another minute. Pour over the wine and soya sauce. Lay the beansprouts and watercress on top of the vegetables and cover with a lid. Bring to the boil and cook until the watercress has begun to wilt. Meanwhile, put the sesame seeds in an old pan and dry fry, shaking the pan frequently until the seeds begin to smell deliciously nutty and to pop. Turn out of the pan immediately and sprinkle over the stir-fried vegetables. Serve immediately.

STIR-FRIED CHICKEN WITH MANGETOUT PEAS

4 chicken pieces, cooked
1 tbsp sesame oil
5 cm (2 in) fresh root ginger,
peeled and grated
1 yellow pepper, deseeded and sliced
100 g (4 oz) mangetout peas, trimmed
100 g (4 oz) French beans, sliced
juice of 1 lemon
seasoning

Remove the meat from the chicken bones and cut into bite-sized pieces. Heat the oil in a wok and add the ginger, pepper, mangetouts, beans and chicken. Stir-fry for 5–7 minutes. Pour over the lemon juice and season to taste.

GINGERED VEGETABLES WITH ORANGE AND SESAME SAUCE

sesame oil
1 clove garlic, peeled and crushed
2.5 cm (1 in) fresh root ginger,
peeled and grated
1 large onion, thinly sliced
2 large carrots, cut into julienne strips
2 red peppers, deseeded and thinly sliced
2 leeks, thinly sliced
¼ small red cabbage, finely shredded
juice and grated rind of 2 oranges
2 tbsp tahini
4 tsp soya sauce

Heat 1 tablespoon of oil in a wok, add the vegetables and stir-fry for 5–6 minutes. Mix the juice and grated rind of the oranges, the tahini and the soya sauce together until smooth and creamy. Pour over the vegetables and toss lightly. Heat through for a minute or two before serving.

SUMMER STIR-FRY

olive oil
1 onion, finely chopped
2.5 cm (1 in) fresh root ginger,
peeled and grated
1 red pepper, deseeded and
cut into thin rings
2 carrots, cut into julienne strips
2 courgettes, thinly sliced
100 g (4 oz) mangetout peas
1 crispy lettuce, shredded
50 g (2 oz) blanched almonds, split in half
juice of 1 lemon
seasoning

Heat 1 tablespoon of oil in a wok, add the onion and ginger and stir-fry for several minutes. Add the red pepper and carrots and cook for 2–3 minutes more. Stir in the remaining vegetables and fry until the courgettes become slightly translucent and the lettuce wilts and softens. Add the almonds and lemon juice and toss well. Season to taste.

ONION AND WALNUT WHIRLS

These savoury pastries are an excellent accompaniment or starter to a stir-fried meal. For more information on arame, see page 176.

FOR THE PASTRY:
200 g (7 oz) strong wholewheat flour
$\frac{1}{4}$ tsp cream of tartar
150 g (5 oz) butter
6–7 tbsp cold water

FOR THE FILLING:
7 g ($\frac{1}{4}$ oz) arame
3 medium onions, finely chopped
sesame oil
50 g (2 oz) walnuts, finely chopped
1 tbsp soya sauce

Mix the flour and cream of tartar together in a bowl. Add 25 g (1 oz) butter and rub in using the fingertips until the mixture resembles breadcrumbs. Add the water and, with a fork, mix to form a soft dough. Turn onto a floured board and knead lightly until smooth and pliant. Wrap in polythene and put in a cool place to rest for 30 minutes.

Meanwhile, sprinkle the remainder of the butter with a little flour, and with a rolling pin beat out to form a neat oblong about 1.25 cm ($\frac{1}{2}$ in) thick. Roll out the rested dough to an oblong a little larger than the butter shape and long enough for the two ends to fold over the butter. Place the butter in the centre and fold the pastry over to cover it completely. Press the edges together to seal. Give the dough a half turn to bring the open ends to the top and bottom. With the rolling pin press the dough gently, from the centre to the top and bottom, and then quickly and lightly roll out the dough to an oblong three times as long as it is wide. (Don't roll out too thinly or the layers of dough and butter will merge.) Mark the pastry into thirds, without cutting through the dough, and fold the bottom third over the centre and the top third down over both. Seal the edges and give the pastry a half turn. Repeat the rolling, folding and turning once more. Wrap in polythene and chill for 30 minutes.

After two further rolls, folds and turns the pastry must rest again. Roll, fold and turn twice more. The pastry is now ready for use.

To make the filling soak the arame in boiling water for 15 minutes. Drain well.

Heat 1–2 tablespoons of oil in a wok, add the onions and sauté until soft and golden coloured. Stir in the walnuts, arame and soya sauce. Leave to cool.

Roll out the pastry to form a large rectangle 45 x 30 cm (18 x 12 in). Spread the filling over the top, leaving a 2.5 cm (1 in) margin along one of the long sides. Roll up like a swiss roll until only the uncovered pastry margin remains. Moisten this edge and complete the rolling. With a sharp knife trim the ends. Cut the roll into 12 even-sized pieces. Place on a baking tray. Bake in a preheated oven, gas mark 8 (230° C/450° F) for 20–25 minutes.

STIR-FRIED ARAME WITH WALNUTS

Interest in seaweeds has been growing and in an effort to make this cheap and highly nutritious food more popular some people have begun to refer to them as sea vegetables. I am not sure whether the change in name will have the desired effect but certainly there are one or two seaweeds which deserve more attention.

Arame, originating from the Far East, is my own favourite. It has a delicate flavour and I have served this dish with equal success to the converted and the unsuspecting. It is sold as a tangled mass of thin, crisp strands which weigh next to nothing. Do not be confused into buying or using more than you need for arame, like all seaweeds, swells to three times its original volume when soaked.

15 g ($\frac{1}{2}$ oz) arame
1 tbsp sesame oil
$\frac{1}{4}$ white cabbage, finely shredded
100 g (4 oz) button mushrooms,
halved if necessary
50 g (2 oz) walnuts, chopped
2–3 tsp soya sauce

Put the arame in a small bowl and cover with boiling water. Leave for 15 minutes and then drain well.

Heat the oil in a wok and add the white cabbage. Stir-fry for 8–10 minutes until it begins to soften. Add the mushrooms and arame and cook for a further 5 minutes. Stir in the walnuts and soya sauce. Serve.

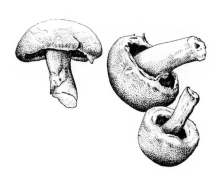

MISO AND ALMONDS

2 tbsp sesame oil
4 tbsp flaked almonds
1 clove garlic, peeled and crushed
6 large spring onions, finely chopped
2 eggs
225 g (8 oz) long grain brown rice, cooked
1 tbsp mugi miso
2 tsp cold water

Heat 1 tablespoon of oil in a wok, add 3 tablespoons of the almonds, the garlic and spring onions and sauté until the almonds become golden brown. Remove from the wok with a slotted spoon and set aside. Beat the eggs and add to the remaining oil in the pan. Lightly scramble them, stirring well. Add the rice and cook for a further 3–4 minutes. Mix the miso with the water and stir into the mixture. Add the sautéed spring onions and almonds to the rice mixture. Adjust the seasoning to taste. Heat through.

Place in a serving dish. Toss the remaining almonds in the wok (there is no need to add more oil; if it is very dirty simply wipe clean) until they become lightly browned. Sprinkle over the top of the rice. Serve hot or cold.

MANGETOUT PEAS WITH FRENCH BEANS AND PARMESAN

1 tbsp olive oil
1 red pepper, deseeded and thinly sliced
1 small onion, thinly sliced
225 g (8 oz) mangetout peas, trimmed
225 g (8 oz) French beans, sliced
1 tbsp fresh basil, finely chopped
4 tbsp Parmesan cheese, grated

Heat the oil in a wok, add the red pepper and onion and stir-fry until both begin to soften. Add the mangetouts, French beans and basil. Pour over a little water, to a depth of 1.25 cm ($\frac{1}{2}$ in) and cover the pan. Bring to the boil and cook until the vegetables soften (they should still have some resistance to the bite). There should be no more than 1–2 tablespoons of juice remaining in the pan. Boil fast to reduce if necessary. Remove from the heat.

Carefully stir in the cheese and cover. Leave to stand for a minute or two before serving.

BROCCOLI WITH THAI SAUCE

450 g (1 lb) broccoli
150 ml (5 fl oz) water
75 g (3 oz) creamed coconut, grated
$\frac{1}{2}$ tsp turmeric
$\frac{1}{2}$ tsp cardamom seeds
1 bay leaf
1–2 tsp lemon juice
a pinch of chilli powder
seasoning

Wash, trim and steam the broccoli until tender. Meanwhile, place all the remaining ingredients in a small pan and bring to the boil. Cook gently for a few minutes and then pour through a fine sieve. Place the broccoli on a serving dish and pour over the sauce. Serve immediately.

STIR-FRIED VEGETABLE MEDLEY

100 g (4 oz) French beans, sliced
1–2 tbsp olive oil
100 g (4 oz) courgettes, sliced
50 g (2 oz) button mushrooms, halved
1 tbsp fresh rosemary, finely chopped
1 tbsp lemon juice
seasoning

Place the beans in a pan of water and boil briskly for 2 minutes. Drain.

Heat the oil in a wok, add the beans and courgettes and stir-fry for 3–4 minutes. Add the mushrooms and cook for a further minute or two. Sprinkle with rosemary and lemon juice and season to taste.

STIR-FRIED VEGETABLES WITH PASTA

175 g (6 oz) wholewheat macaroni
1–2 tbsp olive oil
450 g (1 lb) runner beans, sliced
1 onion, chopped
1 clove garlic, peeled and crushed
1 yellow pepper, deseeded and sliced
50 g (2 oz) pine kernels
seasoning

Cook the macaroni, uncovered, in a large pan of boiling water to which you have added a tablespoon of the olive oil. When al dente drain well.

Steam the beans until barely tender.

Heat the remaining oil in a wok, add the onion and garlic and stir-fry for 5 minutes. Add the yellow pepper and continue to cook until it just begins to soften. Toss in the pine kernels and the cooked macaroni and beans. Season to taste.

CARROTS WITH SESAME SEEDS

2–3 tbsp sesame oil
350 g (12 oz) carrots, grated
2–3 tbsp sesame seeds

Heat the oil in a wok, add the carrots and stir-fry for 4–5 minutes. Sprinkle with sesame seeds and cook for several minutes more. Serve hot.

CHINESE FRIED RICE WITH FOO YUNG

225 g (8 oz) long grain brown rice
a scant 575 ml (1 pint) water
2 tbsp groundnut oil
1 onion, finely chopped
100 g (4 oz) mushrooms, sliced
100 g (4 oz) cooked garden peas
100 g (4 oz) prawns, peeled
seasoning
2 large eggs
1–2 tsp soya sauce
15 g ($\frac{1}{2}$ oz) butter

Put the rice in a heavy pan and pour over the water. Cover and bring to the boil. Simmer, without stirring, for 35–40 minutes until the rice is tender and dry. Remove from the heat but keep covered until needed.

Heat the oil in a wok. When it is hot add the onion and stir-fry for several minutes until soft and golden. Then add the mushrooms, peas and prawns and cook for another minute. Stir in the rice and stir-fry for 2–3 minutes until heated through. Season to taste. Remove from the heat and keep warm while you make the foo yung.

Beat the eggs and soya sauce together in a bowl. Melt the butter in an omelette pan and when foaming pour in the egg mixture. Cook until the underneath is firm and brown and then flip over and cook the other side. Cut into strips and carefully stir into the mixture. Some strips of omelette can be used to decorate the top of the rice.

MALAYSIAN FRIED VEGETABLES WITH PRAWNS

2 tbsp groundnut oil
1 onion, chopped
1 clove garlic, peeled and crushed
1 green chilli, finely chopped
2.5 cm (1 in) fresh root ginger,
peeled and grated
225 g (8 oz) French beans, sliced
1 red pepper, deseeded and sliced
4 courgettes, sliced
2 tbsp ground almonds
1 tbsp soya sauce
225 g (8 oz) prawns, peeled

Heat the oil in a wok. Add the onion, garlic, chilli and ginger and stir-fry for several minutes. Meanwhile, blanch the French beans for 2–3 minutes in a pan and then drain. Add them to the wok with the red pepper and courgettes. Stir-fry for several minutes before adding the ground almonds and soya sauce. Carefully mix in the prawns and continue to cook, stirring occasionally, until the vegetables are just tender and the prawns are heated through.

SUGAR-FREE COOKING

SUGAR-FREE COOKING

Man was quick to discover that sweetness could enhance the flavour and taste of foods, making them more palatable. Traditionally honey, fruit and syrups were used for this purpose but they were never produced on a large scale and consequently were used in small quantities. Refined sugars have been in general use only since the middle of the nineteenth century, but since that time they have gained the dubious distinction of being considered the sweetening agent par excellence. Their appearance, texture, taste and versatility have played an important part in their popularity for they can be used to flavour and enhance almost every conceivable type of food.

From the vast quantity of refined sugar apparently needed to make our modern diet palatable, one might conclude that the quality of food has deteriorated to a huge extent over the last 200 years. While there may be an element of truth in this, sugar is usually added not for obvious reasons of lack of quality, freshness or variety but to satisfy an apparently insatiable desire for sweet-tasting foods. Our consumption of refined sugar has increased to such an extent that some doctors believe that the majority of people living in rich industrialised nations are actually addicted to this apparently innocuous substance. We eat, on average 100 lb a year, the equivalent of 3–4 oz each day. Half this amount is used to sweeten tea, coffee, breakfast cereals, jams, cakes, biscuits etc while the other half is concealed in such savoury foods as peanut butter, tomato ketchup and toothpaste.

In recent years evidence has come to light showing that refined sugar is not quite as innocuous as was first thought. It is believed to be a contributory factor in the incidence of dental caries, obesity, diabetes and other serious illnesses. The problem is that sugar is a highly refined and concentrated product (one teaspoon of refined sugar is equivalent to two and a half feet of unrefined sugar cane) and our bodies simply cannot cope with the unnaturally large amounts we consume daily.

Unfortunately it is widely assumed that refined sugar is an important nutrient essential for energy but in fact our bodies have no physiological need for it and it contains no nutrients of any value. This applies to brown as well as white sugars. Some brown sugars are simply coloured white sugar and even genuine raw cane sugar which contains fibre as well as some vitamins and minerals does not deserve to be called 'natural', 'full of goodness' or 'healthier'. Any benefit such nutrients may provide is far outweighed by the potential health risks attributed to eating refined sugars.

Cutting down on sweets, cakes and sugary foods is easier said than done. After all it is nice to hand round a tin of biscuits with the coffee, to eat a home-made pudding after dinner and to celebrate Christmas and birthdays with a special cake. In fact it really is not difficult to sweeten foods and carry out all types of home baking without using sugar. The secret is to use unrefined foods such as fresh fruit and berries, dried fruits, sweet spices, coconut, fruit juices, honey and malt extract, all of which are naturally sweet tasting.

Be wary about using dried fruits, honey, molasses and other natural syrups for although they will satisfy most people's sweet tooth they contain little water and (with the exception of dried fruits) are also low in fibre. While it is much better to eat them in preference to refined sugars try to use them in moderation and in recipes containing high fibre ingredients such as wholewheat flour. This adds valuable bulk which acts as a safeguard against the common problems associated with eating concentrated and refined foods, notably overconsumption and obesity.

PLUM CRUMBLE

Crumbles are much easier to make than pastry and in the case of this particular recipe contain little saturated fat. By all means omit the coconut if you don't like its flavour or texture. It seems to be one of those ingredients which you either love or hate. You could use sesame seeds instead.

900 g (2 lb) ripe plums
3–4 tbsp concentrated apple juice

FOR THE TOPPING:
100 g (4 oz) porridge oats
75 g (3 oz) wholewheat flour
25 g (1 oz) desiccated coconut
5–6 tbsp sunflower oil
1 tbsp concentrated apple juice
a few drops of vanilla essence

Halve the plums and remove the stones. Place in the bottom of a pie dish. Dribble the concentrated apple juice over the top.

To make the topping mix the oats, flour and coconut together in a bowl. Rub in the oil and concentrated apple juice, using your fingertips, and flavour with vanilla essence. Sprinkle over the fruit and press down lightly with the fingertips. Bake in a preheated oven, gas mark 5 (190° C/375° F) for 25 minutes.

BLACKBERRY AND APPLE FOAM

450 g (1 lb) blackberries
450 g (1 lb) eating apples,
peeled, cored and sliced
150 ml (5 fl oz) natural yoghurt
2 tbsp honey
2 egg whites

Put the blackberries in a pan with the apples. Heat gently until the juices begin to run. Continue to cook until the fruit is soft. Rub through a sieve and discard the seeds. Leave to cool. Stir in the yoghurt and sweeten to taste with the honey. Beat the egg whites until stiff and peaked. Fold into the mixture. Chill for 30 minutes before serving.

BLACKBERRY AND APPLE PIE

This is very much a country dish and tastes as good made from windfalls and hedgerow brambles as it does from first-class, shop-bought fruits. The apples are not essential but they do give body and flavour to the dish.

FOR THE FILLING:
350 g (12 oz) eating apples, peeled, cored and sliced
350 g (12 oz) blackberries
2–3 tbsp concentrated apple juice

FOR THE PASTRY:
200 g (7 oz) wholewheat flour
25 g (1 oz) soya flour
100 gr (4 oz) butter, diced
8 tsps cold water

FOR THE GLAZE:
1 beaten egg

Put the apples in a pan, cover with the minimum of water (barely cover the bottom of the pan) and cook until they begin to soften. Stir the blackberries into the apples. Spoon the mixture into a pie dish. Dribble the concentrated apple juice over the top.

Soya flour makes a delicious light and sweet-tasting pastry. It does, however, tend to crumble so don't roll the dough out too thinly. Mix the wholewheat and soya flours together in a bowl and then rub in the butter. When the mixture resembles breadcrumbs add sufficient water to form a pastry dough. Turn onto a lightly floured surface and roll out the pastry to a circle large enough to cover the pie. Dampen the pie dish rim and cover with the pastry top. Press round the edges to seal. Brush with beaten egg and bake in a preheated oven, gas mark 6 (200° C/400° F) for 25–30 minutes.

BILBERRY TART

FOR THE FILLING:
350 g (12 oz) bilberries
3–4 tbsp concentrated apple juice

FOR THE PASTRY:
175 g (6 oz) wholewheat flour
75 g (3 oz) butter, diced
6 tsp cold water

FOR THE GLAZE:
1 egg, beaten

Put the bilberries into a pie dish and dribble over the concentrated apple juice.

To make the pastry put the flour in a bowl and, using your fingertips, rub in the butter until it resembles breadcrumbs. Add the water and mix to form a soft dough. Turn onto a lightly-floured surface, and roll out the pastry to a circle large enough to cover the pie and about 0.75 cm ($\frac{1}{4}$ in) in thickness. Dampen the pie dish rim and cover with the pastry top. Trim the edges and brush with beaten egg. Bake in a preheated oven, gas mark 6 (200° C/400° F) for 25–30 minutes.

APRICOT SLICE

FOR THE FILLING:
225 g (8 oz) dried apricots
425 ml (15 fl oz) water
a good pinch of ground cinnamon
1 tbsp honey
1 tbsp lemon juice

FOR THE PASTRY:
100 g (4 oz) wholewheat flour
100 g (4 oz) fine wholewheat semolina
125 g ($4\frac{1}{2}$ oz) butter, diced
6 tsp cold water

FOR THE GLAZING:
1 egg, beaten

To make the filling soak the apricots overnight in the water. Next day chop them and put them into a pan with their juice, the cinnamon, honey and lemon juice. Simmer gently until they soften. It may be necessary to add more water but don't add too much at any one time. The mixture should be moist but not wet.

To make the pastry mix the flour and semolina together in a bowl. Rub in the butter, using your fingertips, and stir in the water. Mix to form a dough and then turn onto a lightly floured board. Roll out and cut the pastry into two matching squares and place one piece on an oiled baking tray. Cover with the apricot mixture, leaving a narrow margin around the edge. Lay the remaining pastry on the top, moisten the edges with water and pinch together to seal. Trim away any surplus pastry and brush with beaten egg. Bake in a preheated oven, gas mark 6 (200° C/400° F) for 25 minutes. Leave to cool in the tin before cutting into squares.

APRICOT AND BANANA WHIP

350 g (12 oz) dried apricots, soaked overnight
in plenty of water
2 large ripe bananas, chopped
4–5 tbsp natural yoghurt
a few drops of vanilla essence
1 orange
1–2 tsp honey

Cook the apricots in water until they are soft and then drain. Put them in a blender or food processor with the bananas and yoghurt and process until smooth and creamy. Flavour to taste with vanilla essence. Leave in a cool place for 1–2 hours during which time the whip will thicken. Then spoon into individual glass dishes.

Carefully peel the orange and remove as much of the white pith as possible from the peel. Cut the peel into delicate shreds and then toss into a small pan of water. Add the honey and boil for 3–4 minutes. Drain and cool. Sprinkle over the top of the fruit whip and serve.

MOULDED CHEESE CAKE WITH RASPBERRY PURÉE

225 g (8 oz) natural cottage cheese
1 tbsp natural yoghurt
grated rind of 1 orange
2–3 tsp clear honey
225 g (8 oz) raspberries

Drain the cottage cheese and rub it through a sieve into a bowl. Stir in the yoghurt and orange rind. Sweeten to taste with honey. Mix together well.

Line a coeur de crème mould or similar container with fine muslin. (The container must have some means of drainage; you could use a sieve or colander.) Spoon in the mixture and stand on a plate or baking tray. Leave to drain overnight in a cool place. Pass the raspberries through a sieve, and discard the seeds. Leave the purée to stand overnight to thicken.

Just before serving carefully remove the mould and butter muslin and place the moulded cheese cake on a serving dish. Serve with the purée.

RASPBERRY SNOW

The idea of flavouring raspberries with rose-water dates back to the eighteenth century. Rosewater can be bought at most chemists and it is very reasonably priced. Use with discretion, adding a little at a time, gradually building up the flavour to the desired level. I also like to add a dash to fresh and dried fruit salads.

450 g (1 lb) raspberries
$\frac{1}{2}$ tsp rosewater
3 egg whites

Rub the raspberries through a sieve and discard the seeds. Flavour with rosewater. Beat the egg whites until stiff and peaked and fold into the fruit purée. Spoon into individual glass dishes and serve.

SPICY APPLE SPONGE

FOR THE FILLING:
900 g (2 lb) eating apples,
peeled, cored and sliced
4 tbsp natural unsweetened apple juice
50 g (2 oz) sultanas
$\frac{1}{2}$ tsp ground cinnamon

FOR THE TOPPING:
75 g (3 oz) butter
3 tbsp clear honey
2 eggs
150 g (5 oz) wholewheat self-raising flour
a pinch of baking powder
2–3 tbsp milk

Put the apples in a pan with the apple juice and sultanas. Cook gently until they begin to fall away. The mixture should be fairly dry, boil briskly to drive off surplus moisture if necessary. Stir in the cinnamon. Leave to cool.

Put the butter, honey and eggs into a food processor or blender and process until smooth and creamy. Pour into a large bowl. Mix the flour and baking powder together and fold into the creamed ingredients. Add sufficient milk to form a dropping consistency. Put the apple mixture into the bottom of an ovenproof dish and pour over the sponge topping. Bake in a preheated oven, gas mark 5 (190° C/375° F) for 20–25 minutes until firm to the touch and golden brown. Serve with yoghurt or custard.

KHOSHAF

100 g (4 oz) dried select apricots
100 g (4 oz) seedless raisins
100 g (4 oz) dried figs, halved and
stalks removed
575 ml (1 pint) water
1 tbsp rosewater
50 g (2 oz) split pistachio nuts

Put the dried fruit in a mixing bowl. Pour over the water and rosewater. Leave the fruit to soak for 2–3 days, turning it occasionally to ensure that it softens evenly. The water will become thick and syrupy. Spoon into individual glass dishes and sprinkle with pistachios before serving.

BLACKCURRANT CREAM

50 g (2 oz) blackcurrants
1–2 tbsp concentrated apple juice
225 g (8 oz) curd or cottage cheese
150 ml (5 fl oz) natural yoghurt
2 egg whites

Top and tail the blackcurrants. Put the blackcurrants in a small pan with the concentrated apple juice. Cook gently until reduced to a thick sweet purée. Leave to cool.

Drain the cheese if necessary before rubbing through a sieve into a small bowl. Mix in the yoghurt and fruit purée. Beat the egg whites until stiff and peaked and fold into the mixture.

Line a coeur de crème dish or sieve with muslin and spoon in the mixture. Stand on a tray or plate and leave overnight in a cool place. Just before serving carefully turn out of the mould and remove the muslin. Serve with fresh fruit, a fruit purée or simply with cream.

APRICOT SORBET

100 g (4 oz) dried apricots, chopped
275 ml (10 fl oz) fresh orange juice
275 ml (10 fl oz) orange and apricot juice
2 egg whites

Soak the apricots overnight in the fresh orange juice.

Next day add the remaining juice and put into a blender or food processor. Process until smooth and creamy. Spoon into a large plastic container and cover with a tight-fitting lid. Freeze until semi-solid, stirring every now and then to ensure that the mixture freezes evenly. Beat the egg whites until stiff and peaked. Whisk the semi-frozen apricot slush and then fold in the egg whites. Replace the lid and return to the freezer.

Transfer the sorbet, in its container, to the refrigerator 30–45 minutes before serving.

BLACKCURRANT ICE CREAM

225 g (8 oz) blackcurrants
3–4 tbsp concentrated apple juice
225 g (8 oz) curd cheese
150 ml (5 fl oz) natural yoghurt
3 egg whites

Rub the blackcurrants through a sieve and discard the skins. Mix the concentrated apple juice, curd cheese and yoghurt into the purée and process in a blender or food processor until smooth. Beat the egg whites until stiff and peaked and fold into the fruit mixture. Spoon into a large plastic container and cover with a tight-fitting lid. Freeze.

Transfer the ice cream, in its container, to the refrigerator 30–45 minutes before serving.

SUGAR-FREE JAMS

There is something very satisfying about making jam. The pleasure to be gained from rows of sparkling, brightly-coloured jars, neatly labelled and sealed, is almost sufficient reward in itself but one's efforts are fully appreciated in the dark depths of winter when the fresh fruity taste of home-made preserves brings back memories of warm, balmy summer days.

The price of soft fruit being what it is I never made more than a few pounds of damson or strawberry jam each year but even this stopped when I became concerned about eating white sugar and tried to restrict my consumption. From then on I hung up the jam pan and treated myself to the occasional jar of commercial sugar-free jam to eat with my toast. This year, however, faced with the imminent arrival of pounds and pounds of fruit from the allotment, the time seemed right to tackle the problem of making sugar-free jams. It was really a case of 'if they (the manufacturers) can do it so can I'.

In the event making sugar-free jam proved to be remarkably easy, the only problem being that it doesn't have such good keeping qualities as commercial high sugar varieties. Sugar-free jams are not new, Tom Stobart in his book *The Cook's Encyclopaedia* describes how thick purées of fruit sweetened with honey and natural fruit sugar were eaten all over the world, long before refined sugar was manufactured. Modern jam making is no doubt more scientific but the principles underlying its production have remained the same.

Making jams and preserves at home is fairly straightforward and surprisingly quick. No special equipment is needed. Any large aluminium, stainless steel or copper pan can be used but if you make jam or marmalade regularly, and in any quantity, it is worth while investing in a proper jam pan. Jam pans are specifically designed for the job in hand, and have a heavy base to prevent burning, a wide brim to facilitate maximum evaporation and are sufficiently deep to hold reasonable amounts of fruit. They should, however, never be more than half filled as boiling fruit increases in volume and spits fiercely.

Tracking down supplies of reasonably priced, sound fruit can present problems and it is my guess that most home jam makers rely on produce from their own gardens or local pick-your-own centres. Always select dry, firm fruit which is just ripe and try to use it the same day, preferably the day that it is picked. The pectin content of fruit decreases steadily after being picked and as it ripens. Frozen fruit, of good quality, can be used but it too will have lost pectin and it may be necessary to use 10 per cent more fruit than stipulated in the recipe. (Pectin is a substance present in certain fruits which together, and in balance, with fruit acids and sugars ensures a good set.)

Basic Method
Stage one
Pick over the fruit and discard any that is decayed, damaged or overripe. Remove stalks, leaves and stones where appropriate and if necessary rinse quickly under cold running water. The fruit is now ready to be gently cooked until soft. Depending on the type of fruit this may take from 10–45 minutes. The purpose of this is to reduce the fruit to a virtual purée (assistance from a potato masher may be necessary in some cases) and to release the pectin and fruit acids. When making sugar-free jams the fruit is cooked with concentrated apple juice which not only sweetens the jam but also helps it to set.

To avoid disappointment, it is wise for the novice to check at this stage whether the cooked fruit has sufficient pectin of its own to form a good set. The standard test is to take 1 teaspoon of juice from the pan and put it in a glass to cool. Add 3 teaspoons of methylated spirit and shake the mixture well. After one minute pour it into another glass. If the juice has formed a large, single clot it contains a high level of pectin; a few smaller clots indicate sufficient pectin while a large number of small clots show that there is an insufficient amount and more must be added if the jam is to set.

With a little experience one soon learns which fruits are good setters and which are not, and appropriate steps can be taken to alleviate disaster before cooking the fruit.

I don't bother testing the set of my jams and luckily I haven't had a failure yet; even the sugar-free strawberry jam sets well. The pectin in the apple juice obviously helps but when dealing with low pectin fruits I take the precaution of adding the juice of another high pectin fruit, either 30 ml (2 tbsp) of lemon or lime juice, or 150 ml (5 fl oz) redcurrant juice to 2 kg (4 lb) of fruit.

High Pectin Fruits

some apples	limes
cranberries	some plums
damsons	quince
gooseberries	redcurrants
lemons	Seville oranges

Medium Pectin Fruits

fresh apricots	peaches
early blackberries	raspberries
greengages	sweet oranges
loganberries	

Low Pectin Fruits

late blackberries	medlars
cherries	pears
elderberries	strawberries
marrows	

Stage two

Having decided that the cooked fruit purée contains sufficient pectin for setting it is now time to bring the contents of the jam pan to a brisk boil and to reduce the purée until setting point is reached. The best test for this type of jam is to dip in a wooden spoon and hold it horizontally above the pan to cool for a moment or two. Then turn the spoon vertically and if the purée has a heavy dropping consistency (that is if it lingers on the spoon before falling off in a single dollop), the jam will set. If uncertain leave to cool overnight by which time it should have set. Failure to set necessitates further boiling.

Stage three

Pot the jam as usual, either when very hot or quite cold. Unfortunately the sugar content of these jams is generally below the 50–60 per cent needed to stop the growth of bacteria and even when stored in cool, dark, dry conditions they keep for between four and eight weeks only.

There are two ways round the problem of storing sugar-free jams. They can either be frozen or sterilised. Having a freezer I always opt for the former method, freezing them in yoghurt cartons and spooning the jam into decorative jam pots when it has thawed. Sterilisation is recommended as a way of preserving low sugar jams and I can see no reason why it should not be used, with equal success, for sugar-free varieties. Pour the hot jam into warm, clean kilner jars and seal at once using lids and gaskets, dipped in boiling water immediately beforehand. Stand them in a large pan in which a false bottom has been made with a wire grill or thickly folded newspaper. Pack further layers of newspaper or cloth between the bottles to prevent them banging together. Pour in hot water and bring to the boil. Hold for 5 minutes. Remove the jars and tighten the screw tops. When cold check the seal by removing the screwband and picking each jar up by the lid. If the seal is airtight the vacuum inside the bottle will hold the lid secure.

PEACH CONSERVE

An excellent way of using bruised or grade 2 fruits.

YIELDS 5 JARS
a tray of peaches (approx. 35)
575 ml (1 pint) concentrated apple juice
the juice of 2 oranges

Skin the fruit by dipping each peach into boiling water for $\frac{1}{2}$ minute and then peel off the skin with a blunt knife. Cut the fruit in half and remove the stones and any damaged flesh. Chop and place in a large pan with the apple juice. Simmer gently for 45 minutes or so until the fruit softens. Mash coarsely with a fork or potato masher. Add the orange juice and continue to cook until the mixture thickens, stirring frequently. Spoon into warmed jars and cover as usual. Keeps 4–6 weeks.

GOOSEBERRY AND ELDERFLOWER JAM

The sweet fragrance of elderflowers complements the slightly sharp flavour of the gooseberries perfectly. However, it can be rather overpowering and should be used with discretion.

YIELDS 2 JARS
$1\frac{1}{2}$ kg (3 lb) gooseberries, topped and tailed
575 ml (1 pint) concentrated apple juice
(more to taste if the fruit is sharp)
4–5 sprigs of elderflowers, tied up in muslin

Place all the ingredients in a large pan and slowly bring to the boil. Simmer gently for 1–2 minutes and then remove the elderflowers. Continue to cook for 15–20 minutes, stirring frequently. As the fruit reduces to a thick purée test for setting. Pour into warm jars and seal. Keeps 4–6 weeks.

STRAWBERRY JAM

YIELDS 2 JARS
$1\frac{1}{2}$ kg (3 lb) strawberries, hulled
575 ml (1 pint) concentrated apple juice
juice of 1 lemon

Chop the strawberries and place in a large pan with the apple juice. Slowly bring to the boil and cook for 5–10 minutes, stirring frequently. As the fruit begins to soften lightly crush with a potato masher or fork to form a fairly thick purée. Add the lemon juice and bring to the boil again. Cook for a further 10 minutes until the mixture thickens. Pour into warm jars and seal. Keeps 4–6 weeks.

BLACKCURRANT JAM

YIELDS 3 JARS
$1\frac{1}{2}$ kg (3 lb) ripe blackcurrants
425 ml (15 fl oz) concentrated apple juice
(add more if the fruit is tart)

Top and tail the blackcurrants and remove any that are damaged. Put the blackcurrants in a large pan with the apple juice and bring to the boil. Reduce the heat and cook for 10–15 minutes until the mixture thickens. Ladle into warmed jars and seal. Keeps 4–6 weeks.

APRICOT AND ORANGE JAM

YIELDS 2 JARS
$1\frac{1}{2}$ kg (3 lb) ripe apricots
275 ml (10 fl oz) concentrated apple juice
juice of 2 oranges

Chop and stone the fruit. Place in a large pan with the apple juice. Slowly bring to the boil and cook for 10–15 minutes. Pulp the softened fruit with a fork or potato masher to form a fairly thick purée. Add the orange juice and bring to the boil again. Boil briskly for a further 10 minutes until the mixture thickens. Pour into warm jars and seal. Keeps 4–6 weeks.

INDEX